American / Korean Contrasts

AMERICAN / KOREAN CONTRASTS

Patterns and Expectations in the U. S. and Korea

Susan Oak · Virginia Martin

HOLLYM

Elizabeth, NJ · Seoul

First published in 2000
Second printing, 2001
by Hollym International Corp.
18 Donald Place Elizabeth, New Jersey 07208, USA.
Phone: (908)353-1655   Fax: (908)353-0255
http://www.hollym.com

Published simultaneously in Korea
by Hollym Corporation; Publishers
Core Bldg., 13-13 Kwanchol-dong, Chongno-gu
Seoul 110-111, Korea
Phone: (02)735-7551~4   Fax: (02)730-5149, 8192
http://www.hollym.co.kr

Hardcover edition ISBN: 1-56591-073-7
Paperback edition ISBN: 1-56591-152-0
Library of Congress Catalog Card Number: 98-72259

Illustrations by Hana Lee

Printed in Korea

Acknowledgments

We want to thank all of our Korean students past and present, our Korean colleagues, and numerous Korean friends who have always been willing to speak openly and objectively of the differences between American and Korean culture and society. The idea of the importance of the Bill of Rights to understanding American attitudes and customs comes from Richard Bier, and we thank him.

We would also like to especially thank the many people who have read either all or part of the manuscript in its various stages and provided valuable commentary: Nick Mele, Mary Helene Mele, Jisu Han Lee, Woo-Hae Lim, Rodney Tyson, Joe Weigman, John Holstein, Soon-Bok Ahn, and Bill Burns. We especially thank Jai-Hee Cho, who generously read through the manuscript several times for accuracy and veracity. We also want to thank the many graduate assistants who pursued facts and details at our request: Beth Su, Lucinda Hunter, Kimberly Spallinger, Amy Shin, and Sunny Park. Their considerable assistance helped to make this a better book. Finally, we want to thank Ms. Julie Han and Mr. Kiman Ham of Hollym who have been patient, helpful, and supportive in bringing this book to completion.

Preface

We designed this book for anyone who interacts with Americans or Koreans and wishes to know more about the differences and similarities between American and Korean culture and society. We have written it in a simple and direct style, with emphasis on the more practical aspects of human social interactions and customs. We divide the information into seven chapters, which we then divide into several subheadings that provide details and examples of specific topics covered in each chapter.

The content of each chapter details not only general behavior in each of the two cultures but also emphasizes the attitudes, expectations, and cultural traits that shape that behavior. Thus, this book not only describes what Americans and Koreans generally do, it also describes why they behave as they do. In this respect, the book could also be subtitled "Understanding Two Distinct Cultures" because that is our purpose and intent. There is also a glossary at the end of every chapter.

We want to emphasize that in writing this book we could not avoid generalizations. Our intention is to introduce you, the reader, to American and Korean customs and culture. We also want you to reflect on your own customs and culture as you read about the other. Culture is deep and complex; it extends beyond mere activities. We believe that by reflecting on your own culture, you will see that customs may vary according to individuals. They also may vary according to personal and regional influence. Location — rural or urban; small town or a large city; north or south — has an undeniable influence on the development of customs and on the interpretation of general cultural norms. So does one's family or ethnic background.

In discussing the customs of these two cultures, it is an impossible task to detail every difference. We illustrate the ideal cultural and social norms according to the majority influence in each country.

Thus, the cultural and social norms we indicate reflect those of the middle-class in the U.S. — and of the middle class in Korea. Where possible, we detail regional differences. However, we do not include ethnic differences — which are significant in the U.S. — although we mention them where it is possible to do so. We also are not able to include all the individual, regional, and ethnic differences in either the U.S. or Korea. This book simply would be too long if we had done so.

As you read this book, please keep in mind that the information we provide introduces you to ideal general cultural and social norms. It introduces you to the traditional and ideal patterns of behaviors and general expectations of Americans and Koreans. The patterns we describe will likely not apply to all situations or locations — the United States is a large country with a diverse, heterogenous population and culture, and Korea has many regional cultural differences as well. So, not every American or Korean lives up to these ideals, but they still may measure their behavior against them. We encourage you to consider your own ideal patterns and expectations as you read as well.

Contents

Chapter 6: Food and Drink · *209*

CHAPTER 1

UNDERSTANDING INFLUENCES ON AMERICAN AND KOREAN SOCIETY

UNDERSTANDING INFLUENCES ON AMERICAN AND KOREAN SOCIETY

Introduction

This is a book for Koreans who want to know more about patterns and expectations of behavior in the U.S., and for Americans who want to know more about patterns and expectations of behavior in Korea. When both of us first arrived in Korea, many people gave us advice on how to live with, work with and understand Koreans. One of the most humorous pieces of advice was this: Always expect the Korean to do the opposite of what we would expect an American to do. But when Koreans come to the U.S. for more than a short visit, what advice is given to them to help them understand the cultural norms of the U.S.? Is it the same advice — always expect the opposite? There are many books for Americans on understanding Korea, or for Koreans trying to understand the U.S., but this is the first book to attempt to reach both audiences. We have combined it to show how important it is to think about one's own culture when trying to understand another's. We focus on similarities as well as differences, and sometimes the differences are not obvious ones.

We highlight in this book how average Americans and Koreans generally behave and what they expect in similar circumstances — American ways and Korean ways. We detail their patterns of behavior. Part of understanding another's behavior is knowing the thinking or reasoning of that person in any given situation. What does that person expect of him/herself or of others in this situation or circumstance? And so, we have focused on what the cultural and social norms are in terms of what is ideally expected in various situations. These expectations are not universal — they do not apply to everyone — but we focus on those that can be generalized enough to help the average American or Korean understand the other's ways.

We have each lived and worked with Koreans for nearly twenty years. In that time, we have learned that it is important to understand the concepts and expectations that influence the thinking and behavior of each culture and its customs. It is only by understanding our differences and similarities that we can understand the contrasting ways in which Americans and Koreans live their daily lives. We want to answer the question, "Why do they do that?" For the Korean reader, we explain American patterns and expectations; for the American reader, we explain Korean patterns and expectations. However, we encourage you to read about your own country's customs as well. It is by knowing more about your own expectations that you can come to understand those of others.

We begin by briefly contrasting the philosophical influences on American and Korean expectations. It is often generally accepted that the two primary influences on the development of American ways — social norms and expectations — have been the Judeo-Christian religious tradition and the Bill of Rights. And perhaps one of the primary influences on the development of Korean ways has been **Confucianism**.

What has shaped how Americans think and act?

American Ways

Judeo-Christian Tradition

One of the most important influences on the thinking of Americans is the Judeo-Christian tradition. Americans share this tradition with Western Europe and other countries established by Western Europeans. This sharing has produced similar expectations based on either the Jewish or Christian religious traditions. These two religious traditions are moral foundations which have strongly influenced much of the customs and acceptable behavior of many Western cultures. They are ideals and concepts, not laws. Although not all people follow these guiding ideals and concepts, their behavior may be measured against them.

The first important set of guiding ideals is the **Ten**

Commandments,[1] which is in the Old Testament of the Bible.[2] The second important concept is often referred to as "**The Golden Rule**," which is found in the New Testament of the Bible.

The Ten Commandments

The Ten Commandments dictate the boundaries of Western morality. That is, these rules of behavior apply regardless of the situation or of the personal need of the individual. (A list of the commandments can be found at the end of this chapter.)

The first and second commandments say that

1) there is only one God;
2) God is not to be worshiped as an image.

These two rules influence American culture in that ancestor worship or animist religion is unconventional. That is, to worship the spirit of a dead relative or of the mountains is not common among Americans.

The third commandment states that

3) a person should not use God's name in vain.

This rule influences the speech of Americans. American English contains many **expletives**, or "curse words."[3] According to the third commandment, any word that contains "God," and is spoken in frustration or anger is considered an immoral use of the language and may be insulting to others. (This is also true of the word "God" by itself when it is used outside of prayer.) Thus, one of the worst curse words in English is "Goddamn." Although you may hear this word in movies, on television, from a colleague, or read it in a book, it is still considered a curse word and should not be used.

The fourth commandment states that

4) the Sabbath must be observed as a day of rest.

In Judaism, the Sabbath is Saturday; in Christianity, it is Sunday. Since Judaism is a minority religion in the U.S., the majority of Americans consider Sunday the Sabbath. This is true even though these Americans may not be practicing Christians.

According to the Christian ideal, Sunday should be a day of leisure and rest. The Christian influence in the U.S. is evident in some state laws. For example, in many states, small shops are closed on Sunday, alcohol is not sold on that day, and cars are not sold. These regulations (or **"blue laws"**) are all related to observing Sunday, the Sabbath, as a holy day and reflect the strong influence of the Judeo-Christian tradition in American culture and customs. Nevertheless, many young Americans may not know why these "blue laws" exist because the laws were created many years ago when there was a stronger Christian influence on state governments and on American society as a whole.

The remaining commandments are the basis of the ideals of American family life and of concepts of personal and public morality and honor:

5) **honor your mother and father**
6) **do not commit murder**
7) **do not commit adultery**
8) **do not steal**
9) **do not lie**
10) **do not envy another's property.**

These commandments are the ideals by which most Americans try to live. Unfortunately, of course, not all Americans can or do live by them. For example, the United States has a high crime rate (including robbery and murder), a high divorce rate, and many children have broken relationships with their parents.

Nevertheless, we can see how some of these commandments affect American life and expectations. For example, Americans have holidays to celebrate each parent (Mother's Day in May, and Father's Day in June), but none to celebrate the children. The ninth commandment is also significant: A lie is considered a personal shame and a wrongdoing. Thus, Americans generally expect honesty and forthrightness, regardless of the circumstances.

It is also a great insult to call someone "a liar." If someone is found to have lied — especially to have misled or manipulated another person — that person is considered untrustworthy. Depending on the type of lie, the person may be considered immoral or lacking in

integrity. Finally, the tenth commandment influences American culture in that it encourages happiness for others. The wealth or good fortune of others is encouraged to be a source of happiness, not of envy or hard feelings.

The Golden Rule

In the Christian Bible, the book of Matthew, Chapter 7, verse 12 (Matthew 7:12) states : "Treat others the way you would have them treat you." This is called "The Golden Rule." There are two other similar passages: Matthew 22:39 ("You shall love your neighbor as yourself.") and Luke 6:31 ("Do to others what you would have them do to you.") which reflect the same message.[4] The Golden Rule — treat others as you want them to treat you — has influenced American society's concepts of equality and integrity. Ideally, according to the Golden Rule, every individual should respect others and every individual is worthy of respect. Of course, common practice may not show this to be the common belief. Nevertheless, the Golden Rule still influences how Americans are expected to relate to one another and, most importantly, how they expect to be related to.

In addition to Judeo-Christian influence, the U.S. Constitution is another strong influence on the patterns and expectations of American behavior.

The Bill of Rights

The laws of the United States are based on the Constitution. The first ten amendments of the United States Constitution are commonly referred to as the **Bill of Rights** (1791).[5] The basic premises of the Constitution are that all people are created equal and that they have certain God-given rights which include life, liberty, and the pursuit of happiness. All of these amendments have a strong influence on how Americans think and act, even though many Americans may not be aware of their source or influence.

In general, the Bill of Rights assures freedom from government control or interference. It also reflects a balance between individuality, freedom, and responsibility. Americans in general are skeptical of national government interference in, or control over, personal affairs or state affairs.

Modern Americans often focus on their rights — and these are often rights ensured by the Constitution. Sometimes they are the individual's own interpretation of his/her "rights as an American." You can also expect the average American to criticize elitism in any form, especially in a social hierarchy.

What are the rights of Americans as assured by the U.S. Constitution? How do they influence American ways and expectations?

The first right of Americans is

1. freedom of religion, speech, press, assembly, and grievances to the government.

Therefore, Americans react strongly against any government control over, or intervention in, religion. For example, until about twenty-five years ago, prayer was common in the public schools. But some Americans complained against this practice. They said it interfered with their freedom of religion. As a result of a Supreme Court ruling, now prayer in the public schools is uncommon. In terms of personal relationships, this amendment affects the American's sense of privacy: Religion is considered a personal issue (and thus a personal question if you ask about it). As a Korean, you might ask about an American's religion as a way of finding common interests. But, the American — if you do not know each other well — may refuse to answer the question or at least wonder why you are asking for such information.

Americans also have the right to write or say their opinion without fear of being imprisoned. Therefore, Americans feel free to discuss politics and even the personal lives of their government officials and other leaders. They discuss the problems in the government or publicly criticize leaders without expecting to change the government. Furthermore, there is an attitude among most Americans that even though they may disagree with what someone says, they will defend that person's right to say it.

Finally, the first amendment gives Americans the right to have public meetings. These meetings can be on a small scale, as in a gathering at a restaurant or a specified meeting place, or on a large scale, such as rallies or protest marches (although most states require groups to apply for permission for large gatherings). Americans also have the right to take legal action against the government.

The second right of Americans is

2. to own guns.

The United States is one of the few countries in the world that constitutionally gives its citizens the right to own firearms. This is because the army of the country was mainly a volunteer army at the time the country was established, and therefore citizens needed to own guns to defend themselves and their country. The tradition of owning guns is an established one, and even in the 1990s, many Americans believe that the right to own a gun is essential to their own sense of personal security.

The third right of Americans is

3. freedom from control by the military.

Unless there is a war on American soil, the military cannot acquire a citizen's home and force the citizen to feed or house them. This is another example of the protection of individual rights that Americans so strongly protect.

Americans also have several rights that protect them from being wrongly imprisoned. These rights include:

4. the police must have permission to enter a citizen's home; and the police must have reason for arresting a citizen;

5. a person can be defended against any charge and cannot be tried twice for the same crime;

6. a person should have a speedy trial, can have a lawyer, can choose to have a trial by jury, can know the charges and evidence against him/her, and can confront witnesses;

7. a person can have a jury in a civil suit;

8. **a person's punishment must not be cruel or unusual — i.e. the punishment generally fits the crime.**

In general, the Bill of Rights says that the courts cannot be used as a powerful weapon against the freedom of the individual people of the country. This produces a uniquely American balance of maintaining law and order while simultaneously respecting the individual rights of citizens. It also ensures stability of laws and legal practice. This means that even though there may be new leaders in the government, there are not new laws created solely for that new leader.

The ninth right of Americans is

9. **the enumeration of rights in the Constitution cannot deny or disparage others retained by the people.**

That is, the Constitution cannot be changed to take away rights that the Americans already have. In this way, the Constitution cannot be used by the central government to limit the rights of the people.

Finally, the tenth right of Americans is

10. **the separation of state and national authority.**

That is, individual states can have their own set of laws and regulations separate from the federal laws and regulations of the United States as a whole nation as long as the state laws do not conflict with federal laws. This means that the American government is **decentralized**. The independence of states from the central government is important to Americans and represents their general attitude toward being governed. That is, Americans are generally hesitant to let one governing office become too powerful. They are afraid that when that happens, the rights of individual Americans will be taken away, too. So, we can say that Americans are **skeptical** of government control in any form.

Furthermore, just as Americans prefer decentralized governing, so do they prefer decentralization in other organizations as well. That is, on the personal, professional, and social level most Americans are generally very individualistic and untrusting of collectivism and group-oriented thinking.

To summarize, the influence of the Judeo-Christian tradition raises the expectation that Americans respect each other as people; the democratic tradition raises the expectation that Americans care about society as a whole as a way of protecting their individual rights. It is an odd balance of caring for the whole as a way of caring for the individual, and of caring for the individual as a way of caring for the whole.

The United States is a strongly individualistic, **pluralistic**, heterogenous society. It is also a nation of great cultural and ethnic diversity. This diversity can be regional: Large cities or specific regions may have more cultural and ethnic diversity than do small towns in the Midwest. Even though many modern Americans may not live in culturally or ethnically diverse areas, they are still accustomed to diversity.

So, you as a visitor may find yourself in an area that has never seen a Korean — except on television. Or you may find yourself in an area with many Koreans or people of other ethnic origins. The Americans you meet may be friendly and curious, or they may have no interest in you at all. The people you meet may know a lot about Korea, or may be ignorant of Korea. It will depend on the area you are in and the people you meet. Your interactions with Americans will depend on the individual and on you. Although you may be very conscious of the fact that you are a Korean, most Americans will expect you to simply blend in.

As we have said, the patterns and expectations of the U.S. have been strongly influenced by Judeo-Christian traditions and the U.S. Constitution, particularly the Bill of Rights. What are the influences on Korean patterns and expectations?

What has shaped how Koreans think and act?

Korean Ways

Korea is usually described as a collective, group-oriented, homogenous society.[6] Although there are some ethnic minorities, such as Chinese, and distinct regional differences and rivalries, Korea has one language — Korean — and one culture, the Korean culture. Traditional values still play an important role in the patterns and expectations of modern Koreans. And so, we look at modern Korea from the perspective of its traditional influences.

Confucian Influence

The primary influences on traditional Korean social patterns and expectations of behavior have been Confucianism and Buddhism.[7] **Confucian** thought is deeply ingrained in Korean society and affects all aspects of Korean business and life. Confucianism is primarily a philosophy, rather than a religion,[8] which provides moral and social principles of behavior. Confucius lived from 551-479 B.C., a time of chaos and turmoil in ancient China. He developed his teachings as a way to bring order and caring to society by emphasizing personal duty.[9] Two primary philosophical tenets of Confucianism are:

1) the duty of rulers to be benevolent and just;
2) the duty of the followers to obey and be loyal.

In accordance with these duties, Confucius divided society into levels. To bring harmony and balance to society, each level had its own code of conduct. Confucian philosophy also emphasizes the development of understanding of the self, as well as service to society. It was through personal harmony that a person could serve society, family, and community. While his philosophy emphasizes just and fair treatment in exchange for loyalty and faithfulness, how Confucian philosophy has been interpreted over the generations has been dependent on the interpreters.

Confucian philosophy originally focused on bringing order to a chaotic society by emphasizing internal harmony. This internal harmony would then guide individuals in harmonious relationships with others in their daily lives. In Korea and elsewhere, these ideas of maintaining harmony with others have often been generalized to focus on maintaining the hierarchical nature of society.

Confucian thought was spread to Korea during the Unified Silla Dynasty (668-935 A.D.) through an alliance with China.[10] By this time, popularized Confucianism had already evolved in China as a way of maintaining power and authority over others, and this interpretation of Confucian teachings was brought to Korea as well. Therefore, by the time Confucianism determined the formal social structure of the **Yi Dynasty** (1392 to 1910), Korea was already a **stratified**, strictly hierarchical society, and this influence exists even today. The Korean hierarchy of today regulates behavior according to the relationship one has with another. That is, you can expect Koreans to treat you differently depending on your gender, station in life, age, or existing personal relationship, and according to the situation. This hierarchy is also evident in their language: Koreans use different vocabulary or word endings to distinguish their social position and the position of others. So, specific words or word endings are used with one's parents, boss, or teacher, depending on the speaker's and the receiver's status and relationship. Similarly, a person in a high position in the hierarchy uses terms or word endings as a way to distinguish his/her position.

AMERICAN / KOREAN CONTRAST

Judeo-Christian teachings emphasize respecting others based on the value of every human being. On the other hand, although Confucianism also emphasizes human value, in Korea it also emphasizes a hierarchy of human relationships as a way of maintaining order in society. Thus, American ways can be described as egalitarian and somewhat constant, while Korean ways can be described as stratified, authoritarian, and somewhat shifting depending on the situation. Americans usually define the relationship according to the behavior of the individuals, while Koreans usually establish the relationship as a way to determine behavior. For this reason, Koreans will ask many personal questions of someone they have just met (such as age, marital status, etc.) as a way of establishing the relationship. This will determine Koreans' behavior as well as the language that they use.

Finally, Americans tend to focus on the principle or ideal that may remain constant, regardless of the situation. On the other hand, Koreans tend to focus on the situation, and shift the principle or ideal accordingly.

Based on Confucianism, Koreans determine appropriate behavior according to five relationships, which are the five basic roles in society. It is a very complex system that requires knowledge both of the basic Confucian hierarchy of relationships and of the importance of *ch'emyŏn* [체면], ('face') and collectivism in Korean society. These two cultural concepts dictate the personal interactions and strongly influence all Korean ways. Therefore, the next two sections will discuss the Confucian hierarchy of relationships and the cultural expectations of behavior unique to Korea.

Hierarchy of Relationships

According to Confucianism, there are five primary relationships which dictate how individuals relate to each other and which distinguish and create distinct, individual roles in society:[11]

1) the relationship between king and subject;
2) the relationship between father and son;
3) the relationship between husband and wife;
4) the relationship between elder brother and younger brother;
5) the relationship between friends.

Each of these relationships has its own set of protocol and its own set of behavioral expectations, and yet the relationships are not always clearly distinguishable. The importance of these relationships, their complexity, and their accompanying requirements, expectations, and obligations cannot be underestimated. You will find that they overlap or vary according to the situation — as do most relationships in any society. We include below a simplified chart of each relationship and its behavioral expectations:[12]

Relationship	Behavioral Expectations
king-subject	justice/loyalty
father-son	love/filiality
husband-wife	initiative/obedience
elder brother-younger brother	brotherly love/respect
friends	mutual faith

As we described earlier, a king's duty is to be just and benevolent, and in return the subject is to be loyal. This relationship between king and subject generally applies in most relationships of authority. (For example, our students used to always tell us that the professor is king.) It is a trusting relationship, and the emphasis on loyalty based on trust extends to most Korean personal relationships as well. Koreans will expect those in authority to be just in dealing with them, and in return they will be loyal. But, justice may be relative to the individual relationship or to the situation.

The concept of justice, as we said, can be relative. Justice exists, but it may be variable according to the situation. To contrast these expectations with American expectations, Americans think in terms of the application of abstract laws, which include thinking in terms of American justice (which emphasizes "the letter of the law" and fairness to all), but the Korean may be thinking of personal attention to individual situations and to personal favors. An example of this kind of relationship and interaction might be between an American teacher and a Korean student. The student may want to establish a favorable relationship with a teacher and then later rely on that relationship when asking to be excused from a class requirement because of extenuating personal circumstances. The American teacher may think in terms of fairness to all and deny the personal request "on principle." The American teacher will be afraid of showing favoritism, whereas the Korean student may be depending on it. Thus, the Korean student may lose faith in the teacher and break communication with the teacher. To re-establish communication and trust in that relationship, the teacher may need to apologize and excuse the student from the requirement.

The second major relationship is between father and son, or parent and child. In this relationship, the parent is expected to love and take care of the child. In return, the child is expected to have what is called *hyo* [효], ('**filial piety**'). That is, the child is expected to obey the parents and show respect through this obedience. This is an authoritarian relationship — with the father at the head. It also extends beyond the blood-relation: A friend's parents may establish a parental relationship with the friends of their children, as occurs in the U.S. as well.

The third relationship is between husband and wife. In this authoritarian relationship, the behavioral expectations are that the couple fulfill their respective duties: The wife provides children, especially a son, and takes care of the home; the husband makes decisions and provides financial security. The husband is seen as active and dominant, and the wife as passive and submissive. That is, the husband provides initiative and the wife obeys. In Korea today, the conflict between the expectations and customs of these traditional patterns and the changes brought about by Westernization is a growing source of tension between men and women.

The fourth level of relationship is between the elder brother and the younger brother. In this case, the elder brother is responsible to and for his younger brother and shows brotherly love through financial generosity and by being interested and helpful in the younger brother's life. In return, the younger brother respects the older — through loyalty and obedience. This hierarchy between older and younger applies to older sisters as well as extending beyond blood relationships. Thus, most relationships between co-workers, schoolmates, and friends are formed around the idea of an elder/younger hierarchy. This hierarchy decides the boundaries and responsibilities within a relationship.

The fifth and final type of relationship is the relationship between friends. The trust and loyalty established in the other four relationships are especially evident in this relationship: Between friends there is mutual faith, i.e., trust and reliance. You must show yourself to be dependable and trustworthy in Korean society, often by not refusing a friend's request (or *putak* [부탁], ('favor')). For example, you may meet a Korean business colleague with whom you wish to establish a good business relationship and who wishes to establish a good relationship with you. As a way of determining the direction of your business relationship, the Korean may ask you to spend social time with him. He may also ask for a favor, such as some information or an indulgence from your company. He may ask you to sign a contract without filling in the details, or to form an agreement without a contract at all. According to the Korean's perspective, how you respond to these various requests will determine the degree of mutual faith possible in the relationship.

We have briefly described the polite behavior and social interactions of Koreans that have been formed over fourteen hundred years of applying Confucian ideals to Korean reality. The result of Confucian influence on Korean society is a focus on meeting duties and obligations and on a hierarchy of male-dominated relationships that are mostly based on one group's authority over another. The second tier of understanding Korean ways is to know the patterns and expectations of individual personal interactions. We discuss these in the next section.

Patterns of Personal Interaction

In Korean personal interactions, there are seven basic concepts that determine expectations of one's own behavior and the behavior of others. They determine concepts of common courtesy and how Koreans interact with one another according to their various relationships.[13] These seven patterns/notions include a sense of **collectivism** and a group of concepts not easily translatable: *ch'emyŏn* [체면], *nunch'i* [눈치], *kibun* [기분], *chŏng* [정], *bunuiki* [분위기], and *han* [한]. The first three — *ch'emyŏn*, *nunch'i*, and *kibun* — are closely linked to how people speak with one another. The last three — *bunuiki*, *chŏng*, and *han* — are emotional concepts that are closely linked to behavior. These concepts are perpetually intertwined in affecting Korean behavior. That is, a Korean may use *nunch'i* to determine if *ch'emyŏn* has been affected. If it has been, that may affect the *kibun* of either or both individuals, which will then affect the *bunuiki* of a situation, etc.

Furthermore, for the average Korean, the development of personal relationships has priority over the following of abstract laws and regulations. Personal context and situation help determine behavior, and for this reason we can call Koreans "situation dependent."[14]

An example of "situation dependence" is in how Koreans respect form and protocol — expected behavior in specific situations — but may not always follow specific rules outside of a relationship. For example, a Korean student may be told that he must attend classes in the United States in order to meet immigration requirements. He/she may acknowledge this requirement out of politeness. Two months later, the foreign student advisor may discover that the student has not been attending classes and calls the student into the office. In their exchange, the student cites personal difficulties and asks for understanding of his/her situation. The student may be deferential, put him/herself at the mercy of the advisor, and promise to attend classes. The advisor helps and then discovers two months later that the student is still not attending classes. What happened? The student did not relate the rule to him/herself personally. The rule is abstract, but the relationship with the advisor is concrete. For this reason, the student was respectful of the relationship (one of authority), and humbled him/herself. Accordingly, the student also wanted to maintain harmony. He/she will be loyal to the advisor but not necessarily to the rule, which has little meaning outside of the immediate, personal relationship.

To return to the seven patterns/notions that dictate Korean patterns of behavior and their expectations of others, the first is collectivism. You will find that Koreans are group-oriented, that Korea is a collective society, and that harmony within those groups is of premier importance. Koreans see themselves in relationship to others — as part of a larger group first and as individuals second. Thus, the needs of the group, e.g. family or company, are primary over the needs of the individual. How Koreans interact is a reflection of this collectivism. For the Korean, relationships must be established so that appropriate behavior can be determined and harmony maintained. Thus, a Korean will seek to establish a framework for a relationship first — based on the Confucian hierarchy — and the relationship, in turn, directs the Korean's behavior.

AMERICAN / KOREAN CONTRAST

Americans see themselves as individuals first, and as members of a group second. Koreans, on the other hand, see themselves as a member of a group first, and as individuals second. Thus, an American might define a group as made up of individuals, but a Korean would define individuals as people belonging to specific groups.

There are six notions indigenous to Koreans that guide how they interact with one another and which reflect the fact that they see themselves in relation to others. The first of these notions is *ch'emyŏn*. As with most terms closely related to cultural norms and attitudes, it is not easily translatable. But, roughly, *ch'emyŏn* can be translated as 'social face' or 'outside show.'[15] We can also describe *ch'emyŏn* as the prestige, pride, dignity, honor, and reputation related to one's position. It is living up to the expectations of others according to your — and your family's — position and situation in society — and sometimes in spite of it. For example, a family may spend more money than they can afford on a meal to treat others. To treat based on their meager resources would be a loss of pride, or *ch'emyŏn*. Yet a reverse of pride — what Americans might even call "false humility" — is also related to *ch'emyŏn*. A noteworthy illustration of this is an expression commonly used at meals. The cook may have prepared a very grand meal, but will say, *ch'arin gŏn ŏbjiman manhi tŭsseyo* [차린 건 없지만 많이 드세요.], which translates literally to 'there's nothing delicious to eat, but please eat a lot.' This false modesty is a reflection of Confucian concepts of modesty and humility, which can dictate social face or *ch'emyŏn*.

On the other hand, *ch'emyŏn* is also related to how others behave toward you according to your expectations based on your own position and situation. In the above situation, those who are eating the meal must contradict the cook with exclamations of how much food there is and how delicious it looks. In that way, both they and the cook or host will maintain *ch'emyŏn*: The cook or host has been modest, and the guest has been gracious or appreciative. However, polite guests should not be overly eager to begin eating, even if they are starved. The polite guest waits to be encouraged to eat — usually three times. And the good host encourages the person to eat. The relationship of this custom to *ch'emyŏn* can be traced back to its reputed origin: Peasants, even though starving, would wait to eat their meal rather than show their degree of need.[16] However, because status and expectations vary according to the situation, *ch'emyŏn* is dependent both on the situation and on the relationships of the people involved. In every interaction, both parties are responsible for helping the other maintain *ch'emyŏn*.

Americans tend to have a vague sense of face, equating it with either "Keeping up with the Joneses" or momentary embarrassment. But the Korean sense of face is much more pervasive and subtle. Koreans tend to focus their daily lives, actions, and social interactions around maintaining — and not losing *ch'emyŏn*. For Americans, face depends on the individual; for Koreans it is both the individual and the group or family the person belongs to. For example, if a Korean high school graduate cannot get admission to a prestigious university, then not only will that student have lost face, but his/her entire family will have also. To regain *ch'emyŏn*, the student may postpone attending university in order to retake college entrance examinations and perhaps score high enough to gain entrance to a prestigious university. In recent years, some such students opt to study abroad rather than attend a less prestigious Korean university. Thus, the family will regain some face by their efforts to still provide a good education for the child, but the child may feel like a failure for having to go abroad to study. Studying abroad is still prestigious, but more so for graduate students than for undergraduates.

As you can see, the concept of *ch'emyŏn* is similar to shame and is thus much stronger than mere embarrassment. Shame — which is directly related to *ch'emyŏn* — is a basis for Korean discourse and behavior, much like guilt has been in the West. Koreans look for harmony in relationships, and their behavioral norms (based on Confucian principles) help maintain that harmony. When *ch'emyŏn* has been affected, and the relationship put out of balance, there are ways to restore that balance. Koreans will be more interested in restoring that balance than they will be interested in fairness or equal treatment. To restore *ch'emyŏn* and thus harmony in the relationship, sometimes an apology by one party can both re-establish that person's own face and re-establish the face of the other. (As in the previous example of an American teacher and a Korean student). Because of the Korean focus on status, hierarchical relationships, and preset notions of appropriate behavior, *ch'emyŏn* is a strong, controlling force in society.

In addition to the example of not gaining admission to a prestigious university, another example of the effect of *ch'emyŏn* is an occurrence during the 1988 Seoul Olympics. During one of the middle-weight boxing matches, the favored Korean boxer lost a close match. Instead of shaking hands with the winner and departing, he refused to leave the ring. Not only did he refuse to leave, but he stayed there for several hours. He had lost face, and his refusal to leave the ring was his way of restoring it. Only after much coaxing did he begrudgingly leave. The coaxing helped to restore his feeling of *ch'emyŏn* and provided him a forum to appear gracious when he did finally leave and allow the games to continue.

As you can see, the Korean concept of *ch'emyŏn* (and shame) differs from the American concept of face. In the previous example, an American boxer would be labeled a "sore loser" and lose face for unsportsmanlike conduct for not leaving the ring. It would be his shame that he could not have put his feelings and pride aside. However, the Korean boxer needed to restore the *ch'emyŏn* which had been taken from him by what he considered an unfair call. Americans usually measure face according to general social norms, which may make the person embarrassed regardless of a situation — for example, being caught in a lie, or having your boss yell at you in front of your family. But for Koreans, the degree of *ch'emyŏn* related to any behavior depends on the larger focus and on the relationship one has with the individuals involved.

To use another example, we have both had students beg us for grades or favors. Americans generally consider begging undignified and would consider it a loss of face. Koreans would, too, in certain situations. But when a Korean student begs an American professor, the student is not concerned with losing face with us. First, as university professors we have more authority and status than a student does. Second, and most importantly, we are not part of that student's peer group or family, i.e. we do not have a relationship upon which to base *ch'emyŏn*. That is, at that moment in that relationship we are non-persons. Thus, the act of begging on the part of the student is no loss of face. The student may be more concerned with the face that would be lost in front of peers or family if he/she failed the course. Thus, a Korean may beg — or do other things that do not correspond to an American's concept of pride or face — as part of the larger focus of protecting *ch'emyŏn*.

We have spent considerable time explaining the concept of *ch'emyŏn* because an understanding of it is essential to understanding Korean behavior. It is the primary concept and sense of self that affects and relates to the other notions which influence Korean daily life. Related to *ch'emyŏn*, then, is the second notion, *nunch'i*, which is often used to help protect *ch'emyŏn*. *Nunch'i* can be defined as "reading the situation" or inferring meaning without overtly stating it. That is, a person reads the situation and acts accordingly in a way that does not endanger *ch'emyŏn* for either person. *Nunch'i* may also lead a Korean to speak words which differ from the meaning the Korean wishes to convey. In that case, the Korean is relying on the *nunch'i* of the other to interpret the desired meaning.[17] For example, after being invited to join some Koreans for a meal, you may say that you are not hungry. But the Koreans would read into your reply that you are being polite or do not want to intrude and may continue to encourage you to join them. On the other hand, if the situation were such that it would be inappropriate for you to join a group for a meal, the Koreans may appreciate your sense of tact and propriety. In either case, they have used *nunch'i* to appreciate your motives and intentions, and you have maintained *ch'emyŏn*. By being sensitive to you, they have maintained *ch'emyŏn* as well.

As you can see, English speakers might describe using *nunch'i* as being tactful, but it is much more complex than mere tact. *Nunch'i* is also situational. In some situations, it can require a dependence on inferencing to convey meaning. For example, if a teacher asks a Korean student a question, and the student hesitates or otherwise avoids a response, then the student expects the teacher to infer that the student is uncomfortable or does not know the answer. Understanding that not knowing the answer would embarrass the student and may cause a loss of face, the teacher is expected to avert the question to another student (unless the teacher wishes to assert his/her authority or shame the student). In this way, the teacher would use *nunch'i* to preserve the *ch'emyŏn* of the student, and by extension his own *ch'emyŏn*. According to Confucian thought, the teacher would be benevolent and just in his/her authoritarian role and in turn earn the loyalty of the student/subject. The teacher would also be showing sensitivity toward the class as a whole and understanding of the student's role within the group. Thus in this example, collectivism and the two notions of **ch'emyŏn** and *nunch'i* are played out in accordance with Confucian roles and expectations. They are concepts familiar to Americans but have more depth, importance, and intensity than Americans are accustomed to.

The third indigenous cultural notion, *kibun*, is often translated as 'mood,' but it is much stronger than mood. We have heard it translated as 'aura,' 'vitality' or 'life force.'[18] What affects the emotions can indeed affect one's life force. (The Korean word *maŭm* [마음], or its Chinese equivalent *sim* [心], is translated as both 'heart' and 'mind,' i.e. emotions and thoughts are inseparable.) In the previous example of the teacher and the unresponsive student, the teacher preserved the student's (and the class') *kibun* by using *nunch'i* to respect *ch'emyŏn*. If a person's lost *ch'emyŏn*, then the person's *kibun* will be greatly affected. Most importantly, the relationship will be affected, and trust may be broken. Sometimes, the way to re-establish the relationship will be to do something to re-establish the *ch'emyŏn* of the individual or group concerned, such as praising the student or the class. While the motive may not be overtly stated, it may be understood through inferencing, i.e. using *nunch'i* to interpret and respond to the situation.

For example, you may have occasion to go out drinking with a Korean colleague. The Korean may be quite insistent that you drink, even though you do not normally drink alcohol. If you refuse to let him pour you a drink, you may cause him embarrassment, which would affect his *ch'emyŏn*. He has been trying to establish a convivial atmosphere through which your relationship can become closer, and so your refusal may be interpreted as an unwillingness to establish that relationship. At the least, it is insensitive to the present situation. And so, the *kibun* of conviviality and togetherness has been broken. However, you have another option that will maintain *ch'emyŏn* and *kibun*. You can allow the colleague to pour you a drink, you can have a sip, but then let the drink sit. After a while, the gracious host will use *nunch'i* to see that you do not want to drink and order some soft drink for you. You will be respected because you did not want to confront or embarrass the host by refusing the alcohol, and because you wanted to share in the conviviality of the evening. In another scenario, the colleague may insist you share at least one glass. If you do so, you would be showing your colleague the importance of your relationship, your awareness of the colleague's feelings, and your willingness to cooperate. In both cases, *kibun* can be maintained. If your colleague's *kibun* has been hurt, then it can be restored through your willingness to pour your host a drink, or by a well-timed joke or gesture. What is most important in this situation is that you demonstrate a concern for your colleague's feelings and for the feelings of the group as a whole, as opposed to indulging in your own individual wishes.

Ch'emyŏn, *nunch'i*, and *kibun* all affect how Koreans interact with one another. There are three somewhat more nebulous notions as well that also affect personal interactions and expectations: *bunuiki*, *chŏng*, and *han*. A notion closely related to *kibun* is *bunuiki*, which can be loosely translated as 'atmosphere' or 'mood'. It is associated with collectivism, in that Koreans will exert great effort to create the appropriate *bunuiki* for a situation. This atmosphere is usually a convivial one in which everyone's *ch'emyŏn* can be preserved and no one's *kibun* will be adversely affected. Therefore, there may not be very much surprise — in the form of variation or spontaneity — in gatherings or activities. There may also be very little individuality except in how it relates back to the group. That is, parties usually include everyone and follow an inflexible, traditional pattern that ensures the emotional comfort of all involved. This distinguishes itself strongly from the American emphasis on spontaneity, individuality, and originality. For example, at an American party, the guests are usually expected to find different people to talk to and entertain themselves through small group conversation. A good American host will walk around periodically to make sure that all guests are enjoying themselves. On the other hand, at a Korean party, most guests are expected to sit together in one large group, with everyone participating in organized activity or play. A good Korean host will try to keep everyone a part of that group.

Next, *chŏng*, one of two basic concepts of emotion for Koreans, can be loosely translated as 'affection,' 'fondness,' or 'attachment.' *Chŏng*, thus, affects the *kibun* and *ch'emyŏn* of the individual.[19] This affection, *chŏng*, refers to emotional attachment not just for people one likes or loves, but also for those one may not like, but knows well such as a colleague. When *chŏng* exists, you might be invited to a Korean's home to meet his/her family. You may be expected to spend more time together or to be able to rely more on that person's understanding of you.

Finally, the other basic concept of emotions for Koreans, *han*, might best be described as a collection of tension and feelings that come from one's daily existence and position in life. It can also be associated with feelings of being victimized or aggrieved. In general, a person, a group, or a nation's behavior can be excused or explained based on the person's level of *han*. *Han* can have both a positive and a negative effect on an individual, depending on the degree to which the person is able to release it.

In the example of the aggrieved Olympic boxer, he had a lot of *han* because of his lost *ch'emyŏn*. He was able to regain some of his *ch'emyŏn* by refusing to leave the ring. But he has retained in his heart the *han* from the experience. He will then train very hard for the next match. If he wins the next match, he can say that he has released his *han*. And it is important to find a release for the *han*.

Han is a deeply suppressed emotion that can explode or cause emotional damage when not released in a constructive fashion. A common example of this could be the traditional relationship between mother-in-law and daughter-in-law. Within the hierarchical structure of the Korean family, the daughter-in-law must obey the mother-in-law and is often at her mercy. If the mother-in-law is jealous of the daughter-in-law or particularly unkind — such as encouraging the husband/son to divorce — the daughter-in-law may have no real outlet for her *han*. She will not have a voice in the courts or in society. She will keep her *han* from the betrayal of both her husband and her mother-in-law bottled up inside of her. Unless she can find a positive way to release her *han*, the aggrieved daughter-in-law may become not only bitter but mentally ill.

Another example involves Korean students. As mentioned earlier an undergraduate male student may be disappointed to be coming to the U.S. to study — he may not have gotten admission to one of the major Korean universities and so see his sojourn in the U.S. as a kind of failure. Perhaps it was his parents' choice or a self-imposed exile. In that case, this young man would have a lot of *han*, which he might use destructively by drinking excessively, refusing to go to classes, etc. He could also use it constructively by studying very hard and being a conscientious student.

AMERICAN / KOREAN CONTRAST

How do the differences in American and Korean ways affect communication? How do their patterns and expectations differ? Let us look at the example again involving social drinking.

A Korean has gone out for the evening with a group of Americans. The Americans expect him to pay for his own drinks and do not offer to buy him even one. When he leaves the group, no one encourages him to stay. The Korean may leave feeling that Americans are unfriendly and uncaring because a group atmosphere was not established. He may have been uncertain about who was in charge and what his relationship to others is. The Americans may see themselves as having been friendly by inviting him along. By not persuading him to stay longer, they have respected his busy schedule and individuality. They have not bought his drinks because they do not want him to feel obligated.

In another scenario, an American has gone out with a group of Koreans, and the host has ordered beer for everyone. The Korean's concern is to establish a convivial mood and satisfy the group's thirst. By such actions, the Korean may be fulfilling many roles, one of which would be that of a generous host. The American, on the other hand, may not have been asked whether he/she would like a beer and wish to exercise his/her individual rights and make an individual choice. The American would use polite language and say, "No, thank you," feeling he/she had the right to refuse the drink. The Korean might then think that his/her hospitality, which may be connected to his/her position and relationship to the whole group as well as to the American, was not being respected. To an American, refusing a drink may be a simple act of choice, but to the Korean this refusal is ungracious. The refusal would affect the *bunuiki* between the two (or of the group) because it has affected the *ch'emyŏn* and *kibun* of the host. The American did not see his or her relationship as part of the group, did not use *nunch'i* to evaluate the relationship, and did not see accepting the drink would show consideration for the friend's feelings. It never entered the American's mind.

In the next six chapters we explain contrasts in American and Korean ways — their patterns and expectations — as they relate to common courtesy [Chapter 2]; greetings and farewells [Chapter 3]; family life and expectations [Chapter 4]; celebrating family rituals [Chapter 5]; food and drink [Chapter 6]; and money, employment and business [Chapter 7]. As you read through these chapters, we want you to keep in mind your own cultural influences.

As we have said, Americans are influenced by concepts of equal rights and opportunity, as well as of treating all people fairly. Americans are individualistic and ideally base their behavior on abstract concepts of morality and law that are separate from personal relationships and feelings. American ways are not situational, yet place importance on respect for individual rights. Koreans, on the other hand, are influenced by ideals of harmony established through appropriate behavior according to a social hierarchy. They base their behavior on relationships and personal feelings. Korean ways are relative to the situation and value the group over the individual.

assembly Gathering together in a public place.

bear arms To own weapons such as guns.

Bill of Rights The first ten amendments to the U.S. Constitution.

blue laws Laws that control which products can be bought or sold on Sundays.

capital offense A major crime such as murder or kidnapping.

decentralization of government States have as much or more power than the national government. That is, the President does not have all the power in the country.

due process of law According to the rules of the legal system.

expletives Words and expressions that have a negative meaning and are not socially acceptable; curse words.

the Golden Rule A term given to the passage from Matthew 22:39: "You shall love your neighbor as yourself."

indictment When the court accuses someone of a crime.

integrity The ability to represent yourself honestly to others. Personal integrity includes being trustworthy and without pretense.

the military A general term for the Army, Air Force, Marines, and Navy, which are the four branches of the U.S. armed forces.

pluralistic Describes a society made up of many social levels and many ethnic groups.

press The news media.

sanctity Something is deeply respected and honored.

skeptical Do not trust or believe.

stratified Different levels which do not overlap.

the Ten Commandments The commandments that the Hebrew God gave to Moses in the Old Testament of the Christian Bible in the book of Genesis. These

Commandments describe the moral rules the ancient Hebrews were to follow.

Glossary of Korean Terms

bunuiki [분위기] A general atmosphere at a meeting, in a classroom, at a party, etc.

ch'emyŏn [체면] A concept of "face" particular to Koreans.

chŏng [정] A feeling of affection and connection to another.

collectivism Making decisions and performing based on one's role in a larger group and the effect of those actions on the group.

Confucianism A philosophy based on the teachings of Confucius (547-479 B.C.).

filial piety The honor and loyalty of a child toward a parent. This extends itself beyond the boundaries of blood relations.

han [한] The long-held, pent up emotions and frustrations of an individual

kibun [기분] An individual's personal feelings and mood.

nunch'i [눈치] The ability to infer meaning from unspoken messages.

Yi **Dynasty** 1392 to 1910.

Notes

[1] *The Bible* is the compilation of Christian religious readings from before the time of Jesus (the Old Testament) and during and after the time of Jesus (the New Testament).

[2] There are many versions of *The Bible;* each version depends on who has translated it. According to *The New American Bible* (translated by the members of the Catholic Biblical Association of America, New York: Thomas Nelson Publishers, 1983), the Ten Commandments are as follows:

> 1. **I, the Lord, am your God....You shall not have other gods besides me.**

2. You shall not carve idols for yourselves in the shape of anything in the sky above or on the earth below or in the waters beneath the earth; you shall not bow down before them or worship them.
3. You shall not take the name of the Lord, your God, in vain.
4. Remember to keep holy the Sabbath day.
5. Honor your father and your mother.
6. You shall not kill.
7. You shall not commit adultery.
8. You shall not steal.
9. You shall not bear false witness against your neighbor.
10. You shall not covet your neighbor's house. You shall not covet your neighbor's wife, nor his male or female slave, nor his ox or ass, nor anything else that belongs to him.

[3] For a full discussion of curse words in American English, we recommend *Dangerous English* by Elizabeth Claire (Rachelle Park, N.J.: Eardley Publications, 1983). While you may hear cursing or other vulgar expressions, especially in films, they are still not commonly accepted in polite society.

[4] These passages are according to the translation in *The New American Bible* (New York: Thomas Nelson Publishers, 1983), pp. 1055; 1074; 1115.

[5] The following is a summary of the Bill of Rights:
Amendment 1: assures freedom of religion, speech, press, assembly, and grievances to the government.
Amendment 2: assures the right of Americans to bear arms.
Amendment 3: assures that civilians are not required to house soldiers in a time of peace.
Amendment 4: assures that the sanctity of the home will be protected against search or seizure by the police.
Amendment 5: assures the due process of law. It also protects citizens from giving witness against themselves in a court of law, or from standing trial twice for the same offense. Finally, it states that a Grand Jury must pass an indictment for a capital offense.
Amendment 6: assures a speedy trial, the option of trial by jury,

the right to a defense counsel, the right to know the charges against him or her, the right to examine evidence, and the right to confront witnesses.

Amendment 7: assures the right to trial by jury in cases of civil suits.

Amendment 8: assures that citizens will not face cruel and unusual punishment or excessively high bail or fines.

Amendment 9: assures that the Constitution will not be applied to deny rights to certain segments of society.

Amendment 10: assures the separation of the national government and state governments in terms of establishing laws.

[6] See three articles on Korean collectivism in *Individualism and Collectivism: Theory, Method, and Applications* (Thousand Oaks, CA: Sage Publications, 1994): Cha, Jae-Ho, "Aspects of Individualism and Collectivism in Korea" (157-174); Han, Gyuseog and Choe Sug-Man, "Effects of Family, Region, and School Network Ties on Interpersonal Intentions and the Analysis of Network Activities in Korea" (213-224); and Kim, Uimyong M., "Significance of Paternalism and Communalism in the Occupational Welfare System of Korean Firms: A National Survey."

[7] For a fuller discussion, see *The Asian Mind Game* by Chin-ning Chu (New York: Rawson Associates, 1991), pp. 179-184; 229; and *The Sacred Books of Confucius*, Chai, Chu'u and Chai, Winberg (editors and translators), (New Hyde Park, New York: University Books, 1965).

[8] Confucianism is primarily a philosophy. It is not an organized religion that focuses on a deity even though Confucianism does focus on spiritual and personal development. However, there are some Confucian scholars who do consider Confucianism a religion and worship Confucius.

[9] See *The Asian Mind Game* by Chin-ning Chu (New York: Rawson Associates, 1991), pp. 179-184; 229; and Chai Ch'u and Chai Winberg (editors and translators), *The Sacred Books of Confucius* (New Hyde Park, New York: University Books, 1965).

[10] For a fuller discussion, see *The Koreans* by Russell Warren Howe (New York: Harcourt Brace Jovanovich, 1988), pp. 41-49.

[11] This chart is adapted from *Korean Ideas and Views* by Michael Kalton (Elkins Park, PA: The Philip Jaisohn Memorial Foundation, Inc., 1979).

[12] Ibid.

[13] There are a variety of books and articles that touch on the topic of communication styles and cultural notions among Koreans. We have used Choi, Sang-Chin and Choi, Soo-Hyang, *We-ness: A Korean Discourse of Collectivism* (Unpublished), Howe Russell Warren, *The Koreans* (New York: Harcourt Brace Jovanovich, 1988), pp. 1-32; Park, Myung-Seok, *Communication Styles in Two Different Cultures: Korean and American* (Seoul: Han Shin Publishing Co., 1979), Robinson, James and Patrick J. Dunham, "Confucian Orthodoxy Meets ESL: Teaching across Academic Cultures" (MinneTESOL Journal, Vol. 11, 1993), pp.21-37; Robinson, James, "The Importance of a Good *Kibun* in the ESL Classroom" (MinneTESOL Journal, Vol. 10, 1992), pp. 87-99.

[14] We want to thank John Holstein of Sungkyunkwan University for his comments. Park, Myung-Seok in *Communication Styles in Two Different Cultures: Korean and American* (Seoul: Han Shin Publishing Co., 1979, p. 91) uses the term "situation-dependent" to describe the various ways Korean customs and speech vary according to the situation and the individual's status within situations. Park states that according to the Korean, "it is better to be harmonious than right or sincere."

[15] See *Communication Styles in Two Different Cultures: Korean and American* by Myung-Seok Park, (Seoul: Han Shin Publishing Co., 1979, pp. 75-83); Robinson, James, "*Ch'emyŏn* in the EFL Classroom" (unpublished paper), Robinson, James, "*Ch'emyŏn* in the EFL Classroom" (unpublished paper), Robinson, James and Karen Becker, "Playing Things by Eye with Korean Students" (Paper presented at the 46th NAFSA Annual Conference, Miami Beach, FLA, May, 1994)

[16] Thanks to Jai-Hee Cho for providing this example in conversation.

[17] See *Communication Styles in Two Different Cultures: Korean and American*

by Myung-Seok Park, (Seoul: Han Shin Publishing Co., 1979), pp. 76; 85; 92-96.

[18] See *Communication Styles in Two Different Cultures: Korean and American* by Myung-Seok Park, (Seoul: Han Shin Publishing Co., 1979), pp. 89-92; thanks also to Jai-Hee Cho for his elaboration of the term ……

[19] See *The Long Season of Rain* by Helen Kim (New York: Henry Holt and Company, 1996), p. 62.

CHAPTER 2

COMMON
COURTESY

COMMON COURTESY

Introduction

Every culture has a concept of courtesy. Courtesy is often also called "politeness" or "good manners." What is polite behavior? What is its opposite, rude behavior? These are difficult questions to answer because concepts of politeness — or courtesy — vary within cultures and across cultures. The polite behavior patterns — or common courtesy — of Americans may seem strange to Koreans, and the common courtesy of Koreans may seem strange to Americans. The differences in concepts of common courtesy are often sources of unhappiness, misunderstanding, frustration, and conflict. Indeed, it is often much easier to learn to use a language than it is to learn and adhere to the behavioral norms of another culture.

In this chapter, we discuss "common courtesy." Common courtesy is expected polite behavior on a daily basis and within relationships. We focus on those behaviors which would make someone "rude" if the behaviors are not followed. In general, politeness is related to one's concept of himself or herself in relation to other people.

The expectations may differ according to the formality of the situation, but politeness — common courtesy — exists and is expected regardless of whether the situation is formal or informal. It has sometimes been suggested that the U.S. is an "informal" society, and Korea is a "formal society." People have made these distinctions based on the number and type of rules that restrict individual behavior in each society. Regardless of whether the society can be called informal or formal, both cultures have common expectations of common courtesy. So, in this chapter, we introduce you to American and Korean concepts of courtesy. We then discuss how polite behavior (courtesy) differs in the United States and Korea among family and friends, among strangers and in business. Because how one dresses can be related to appropriateness in social situations — or etiquette — we have included a section on clothing at the end of the chapter.

We think you will find that Americans and Koreans are both concerned about being courteous and polite, but how each culture practices courtesy is what makes the difference. It is also true that not every American or every Korean will practice these courtesies. That is why we also discuss rude behavior.

What is common courtesy?

American Ways

To be polite is important in every culture, but what does it mean to be polite? For the American, politeness — common courtesy — is related to several concepts that we discussed in Chapter 1. The two strongest influences governing polite behavior in the U.S. are "The Golden Rule" and The Bill of Rights.

"The Golden Rule" states "Do unto others as you would have them do unto you." That is, treat others as you want them to treat you. This "Golden Rule" is related to The Bill of Rights and the concepts related to it, namely equality and individual rights and responsibilities. We list some basic American concepts of common courtesy below, which we further explain in the following pages.[1]

1) **wait one's turn**
2) **give right of way on the street**
3) **keep promises**
4) **be punctual (on time)**
5) **respect another person's privacy**
6) **use words such as "please" or "thank you" when appropriate**
7) **show appreciation to others**
8) **generally do not interrupt people who are talking**
9) **allow someone to make a decision without undue pressure**
10) **help others that need help**
11) **do not laugh at others or point at them**

When Americans teach their children how to be polite in society, they often tell them to recognize that others have needs, too. That is, Americans ideally teach their children to consider others as they consider themselves (The Golden Rule). The list we provide above reflects that attitude.

Americans are taught **1) to wait one's turn**. That is, Americans are taught to wait in line at bus stops, to wait for food at the table, to wait at meetings until questions are raised, to wait at stop signs when driving, etc.. To wait one's turn is related to the concept of "first come, first served."

A good example of **waiting one's turn** is when Americans are getting on a subway. Americans would most likely politely wait their turn in line and expect others to do the same. That is, Americans would treat people they know or those they do not know in the same manner (not show favoritism) when trying to get on a crowded subway. Of course, not every American behaves in this manner, but if they do not, they are criticized by others.

Item **2), to give the right of way on the street**, is also related to waiting one's turn. Americans are expected to take turns in driving as they do in speaking. They also must consider the other driver. Although not all drivers do this, the ones who do not are considered rude drivers. Giving the right of way also applies to walking on the streets.

Next, Americans are taught **3) to keep promises**. Keeping promises includes personal promises and appointments. If someone cannot keep a personal promise, the person is generally expected to tell the other person that the promise cannot be met. If someone cannot keep an appointment, he or she is expected to notify the other person in advance. Notifying individuals when a promise cannot be kept is considered polite behavior and common courtesy. Americans often say, "If you can't keep a promise, don't make it." Keeping promises also extends to completing deadlines and honoring contracts.

Americans generally consider **4) punctuality**, or being on time, as a form of politeness. They believe that being on time shows respect for the other person. If a person is **tardy**, then the person usually apologizes for being late. The tardy person also thanks the person/people for waiting, and may give an explanation. If the person is late for a meeting or other gathering, he or she tries to enter quietly and not disturb the other people who were on time.

As we have just discussed, some ways Americans show respect for the rights of individuals are to be on time, give right of way, etc. Another way they show respect for individuals is **5) to respect privacy**. Privacy is a culture-specific term, and so means different things according to the culture. In general, however, one way Americans respect privacy is by not asking personal questions. They also respect privacy by respecting each person's right to make decisions or solve problems for him or herself.

Americans often use language to show politeness. They **6) use expressions such as "please" or "thank you" when appropriate** and they avoid using **vulgar language**. Some of the most common polite expressions are:

*please: This is used when making a request. For example, "Please hand me the bread."

*excuse me: This is used when walking in front of someone, bumping into someone, when not understanding what someone has said, and before asking a question of a stranger. For example, "Excuse me, but do you know what time it is?" Americans also say "excuse me" after doing something considered rude such as burping while talking to someone.

*I'm sorry: This is used both as an apology and to mean the same as "excuse me." For example, "I'm sorry, I am late." and "I'm sorry, but could you repeat what you said?"

*thank you: This is said in response to every kindness, large or small, and regardless of the individual's status. For example, Americans say "thank you" to cashiers, to children, to waitresses, to teachers, and to students.

Saying "thank you" to someone is one way **7) to show appreciation to others**. Americans generally show appreciation after a gift has been received or after a **favor** has been granted. When Americans receive a gift or have visited someone's home, they often write a thank you note. They also try to invite the other person in return, or reciprocate the kindness.

AMERICAN / KOREAN CONTRAST

Americans often send written invitations for birthday parties, special dinners, or other events. These invitations are extended well in advance to allow others to plan their schedules. Usually, the person inviting expects the recipients of the invitation to respond — will they or will they not attend. In Korea, invitations are often extended only a few days in advance (sometimes only a few hours). With the exception of wedding invitations, written invitations are rarely given, but that custom is slowly changing.

Another sign of general respect for others is **8) not to interrupt people who are talking**. When an American must interrupt someone, he/she normally says something like "Excuse me" or "I'm sorry to interrupt, but..." before the interruption. This rule may not apply among close friends and family, but it is still a common expectation.

Americans are taught to respect the rights of other individuals, and so they are taught **9) to allow someone to make a decision without undue pressure**. A person who continues to try to persuade someone who has already said "no" several times is considered rude, inconsiderate, or "**pushy**."

Another part of general respect for others is **10) to help others that need help** regardless of whether you know them or of their general status. This kind of help includes holding doors open for others. Some of the situations when someone holds a door open for someone else include:

*for women in general (by men)
*for pregnant women and the elderly
*for someone who is carrying packages
*for someone who is in a wheelchair
*for someone who arrived at the door at the same time as you
*for someone who is following directly behind you

In addition, it is also considered polite to allow women or others to enter a door before you. Some of these rules have changed since the 1980s, especially rules related to deference to women. Often, to show equality, some women — especially women of the younger generation — may hold a door open for a man, or even refuse to have the door held open for them. Still, holding doors open for others is generally considered polite behavior despite these occasional individual differences.

A final courtesy is **11) not to point and laugh at strangers**. It is generally considered rude to point at someone who looks different, to stare at them, or to laugh. If a situation is odd or embarrassing, most Americans prefer to look away. If it is a situation where help is needed, Americans may help.

Korean Ways

For the Korean, politeness and manners (*yechŏl* or *yeŭi* [예절/예의]) — common courtesy — are related to a strong Confucian influence as well as to the situation and the nature of the relationship. In Korea, a stratified society, polite behavior may be more situation-dependent than in American society. That is, the formal rules and expectations for polite behavior may vary depending on the situation.

In Korean culture, when there is no established relationship with another person, the need for politeness does not exist. Crane[2], in *Korean Patterns*, calls the stranger an "unperson" because he is outside the group of interwoven relationships that gives each person in that group an identity. So, if the person is not personally known to a Korean, then appropriate rules of courtesy cannot be followed since the parameters and boundaries of behavior which the information about a person creates are absent. In these cases, however, the speaker usually does use general honorifics to speak to the "outsider."

Confucian principles mandate harmonious relationships, including treating others well and with generosity. They also dictate hierarchical relationships. The collective nature of Korean society dictates the exclusive and situation-dependent nature of politeness. Politeness, manners, and courtesy are also affected by personal interpretations of the concepts of *ch'emyŏn* [체면] ('personal face') and *bunuiki* [분위기] ('group atmosphere'). These concepts make politeness, manners, and courtesy more situation dependent than they are in American society. Respecting the hierarchy and fulfilling one's expected role are two of the foundations of politeness and expected behavior in Korean society.

AMERICAN / KOREAN CONTRAST

Ideally, American manners/courtesy are a set of rules that affect all people regardless of their relationship, and so will not vary from relationship to relationship. Korean manners/courtesy, on the other hand, often vary according to the nature of the relationships of the individuals involved.

Basic Korean concepts of common courtesy can be summarized as the following:

1) **help and show respect to the elderly**
2) **show respect for superiors**
3) **avoid confrontation or embarrassment for yourself and others**
4) **refuse a gift upon the first offering; do not be overzealous or overeager**
5) **respect a person's privacy**
6) **use polite forms of language when making a request**
7) **show appreciation for others**
8) **give a gift before a request**
9) **show generosity**
10) **pay for a meal if you have suggested it**

When Koreans teach their children how to be polite in society, they first teach them to **1) help and show respect to those older than themselves, especially the elderly**. Many polite behaviors are related to this respect, including:

*do not smoke in front of someone older
*do not drink in front of someone older without permission
*do not cross your legs in front of someone older
*do not begin eating before the older person has
*give up your seat to the elderly
*do not turn your back on someone older when leaving a room

Since it is important to know a person's age in order to decide what will be polite behavior, Koreans usually ask a person's age after meeting them if the person's age is not evident by appearance or has not been given in another way.

Because the elderly or someone older is one's superior, many of the polite behaviors associated with the elderly or someone older are also the behaviors of a Korean who **2) shows respect for superiors.** Superiors include those older than you in family and friendship hierarchies, as well as those senior in status on the job. Superiors can include professors, office personnel (including government bureaucrats), and others in authority. A Korean would always bow rather than wave at a superior. A Korean would also stand up when the superior entered the room. Finally, a Korean is likely to back out of a room when leaving it, rather than turn his or her back on the superior.

Face, or *ch'emyŏn*, is integral to a Korean's sense of identity, and the awareness of another's *ch'emyŏn*, or the need to maintain one's own *ch'emyŏn* will often dictate the politeness of another. To protect their own *ch'emyŏn* or that of another, Koreans **3) avoid confrontation or embarrassment in any situation.** (Therefore, politeness would be situation dependent.) A Korean will avoid embarrassment or confrontation in many ways, some of which are:

*finding a way to indirectly say "no"
*attempting to resolve a conflict between others
*giving someone extra attention according to his/her status
*agreeing to an appointment, promise, etc., but later changing the conditions of the appointment or promise
*ordering food for someone else without consulting him/her
*being indirect in making a request

Modesty is prized in Korean society, and so polite behavior for a Korean also includes **4) not being overzealous or overeager** in receiving gifts or compliments. Therefore, a Korean will usually refuse a gift the first and second time it is offered. It also means a Korean might force a gift on someone else because the Korean assumes that person is being modest in refusing it. Another way Koreans show modesty is in saying negative things about themselves or denying a compliment. It is quite common for a father to say his son is stupid (when his son has a scholarship to Seoul National University) or for a husband to say his wife is not a good cook (when she is a superb cook). Sometimes, Westerners see Korean modesty as "fishing for compliments."

Privacy is an issue in every culture. Koreans, who are sensitive to avoiding embarrassment in themselves or others, are careful to **5) respect a person's privacy.** For a Korean, privacy is also situation dependent. In general, however, privacy includes one's inner feelings and thoughts, but not necessarily the details of one's life. For example, privacy would not include respecting a person's ability to make individual choices or to solve problems individually, as an American might understand privacy. Rather, for a Korean, privacy might be exhibited in an unwillingness to give one's true opinion in a confrontation or express one's true feelings in words.

In Korea, the complex social hierarchy is reflected in how language is used. Thus, more so than Americans do, Koreans 6) **use polite forms of language when making requests**, but who they use that language with depends on the relationship between the individuals. Thus, Koreans will not use such polite expressions as "excuse me" or "thank you" in every situation. Rather, they use such expressions with people they know, or in a situation where it is necessary in order get people to move out of the way. Some of the most common polite forms of language are:

jom [좀]+ **verb + imperative/question form** ('please'): This word is used when making a request. The level of politeness is determined by the verb ending and sometimes by the verb choice. For example,

maekju jom juseyo [맥주 좀 주세요]
('Please give me a/the beer.')

sillye hamnida [haessǔmnida; hagessǔmnida] [실례합니다(했습니다/하겠습니다)] ('excuse me'): Koreans use three different verb tenses with this expression: the present *hamnida* [합니다], the past *haessǔmnida* [했습니다], and the future *hagessǔmnida* [하겠습니다]. This fact underscores the importance and common usage of such an expression. It is usually used when bumping into someone, or to excuse some other physical intrusion. It is also used politely before asking a question of a stranger, or in asking a question that might be personal. Finally it is also used when not understanding what someone has said. For example:

sillye hajiman, myǒtsimnikka? [실례하지만, 몇십니까?]
('Excuse me, but what time is it?')
sillye hajiman, tasi hanbǒn malssǔmhae jusigessǒyo?
[실례하지만, 다시 한번 말씀해 주시겠어요?]
('Excuse me, but will you please repeat what you just said?')

Koreans do not normally use this expression after burping or some other such action, but otherwise this equivalent to "excuse me" is quite comparable to use in the U.S., with the exception that it is used most frequently with people one knows.

choesonghamnida/mianhamnida [죄송합니다/미안합니다] ('I'm sorry.'): This is used primarily as an apology. For example:
choesonghajiman, tasi hanbŏn malssŭmhae jusigessŏyo?
[죄송하지만, 다시 한번 말씀해 주시겠어요?]
('I'm sorry, but could you please repeat what you said?')
aigu! choesonghamnida! [아이구! 죄송합니다!]
('Oh, my! I'm sorry!')

kamsahamnida/komapsŭmnida [감사합니다/고맙습니다] ('Thank you'): Koreans use this expression quite often, but not necessarily to service personnel or waiters, etc. They also usually do not use it with each other when the action is a daily occurrence.

oraekanmaniyeyo [오래간만이예요] ('It's been a long time since I've seen you.'): This is a very polite expression to use when seeing a family member, friend, or acquaintance after several months of separation.

NOTE: Koreans usually do not say "thank you" after being treated to a meal. Instead, they say "*chalmŏkŏssŭmnida*" [잘 먹었습니다] ('I ate very well').

Korean society is a generous one. It is often based on doing favors for one another, so it is important in Korea 7) **to show appreciation for others**, especially through verbal praise or by giving a gift. Americans generally show appreciation after a gift has been received or after a favor has been granted. Koreans show appreciation by 8) **giving a gift before asking for the favor**. This gift can be seen as a form of apology for asking the favor. It can also be a way to establish a friendly association between the two parties. Americans might give a gift to a friend after a relationship has been long established. A Korean might give the gift at the first meeting to show good intentions and hope in the relationship. Koreans do not have the custom of writing thank you notes, but they do expect and appreciate a reciprocation of a kindness.

As we said, Koreans value generosity in themselves and in others. Koreans **9) show generosity** in their material gifts, and also in their willingness to help and assist a friend. A person who does not show generosity may lose face — and thus be deemed impolite. This can be tricky, however, to an American interacting with a Korean. A Korean may place the American in a position to spend money or to help someone. By requiring the American to show generosity, the Korean wants reassurance in the friendship or to see how much the American values the relationship. The American might interpret this as manipulation, feel trapped, and either not respond generously or cut off the relationship.

Whereas Americans are taught to allow someone to make up his mind without undue pressure, Koreans are taught not to respond too eagerly. Thus, a Korean might continue to pressure someone to accept an invitation or gift that a person has refused in order to show his/her own generosity. Although this is changing in modern society, the old rule of thumb for a Korean is to say "no" twice and then accept on the third offer. The Korean will continue to persuade because it is polite to show one's willingness to be generous and provide the gift. If a person wishes to politely refuse a gift, he/she must do so without directly saying "no." The best way to politely say "no" to a Korean is to be silent or to postpone the decision. Koreans also show generosity of spirit by accepting a gift or by helping another person avoid embarrassment.

Another aspect of Korean generosity is to **10) pay for a meal if you have suggested it**. This is done even among close friends.

None of these polite behaviors apply to all people at all times in either society. Yet, they are often the rules for expected behavior by which politeness or rudeness is judged. There are also many similar behaviors between the two cultures, but the major difference between Americans and Koreans is that the behavior may be expected of all Americans, but only according to the situation for Koreans.

Here is a list of some common behaviors that are considered acceptable in one culture, but rude in the other:

AMERICAN / KOREAN CONTRAST

U.S.	Korea
acceptable	rude

*crook the index finger, with the palm up to indicate "come here"
*point with the index finger
*gesture with a knife, fork, or chop sticks
*discipline children in public
*drink or smoke in front of a superior/elder
*cross one's arms while talking
*give or accept something with just one hand

U.S.	Korea
rude	acceptable

*tell another person about his/her own culture
*pull on someone's clothes to get his/her attention
*use the middle finger to point
*avoid eye contact when talking to someone
*not control children in public
*bump into others in a crowd (and not apologize)
*not hold the door open for the person behind you
*for the host to order food for others without asking what they want
*ask "personal" questions of someone you have just met

U.S.	Korea
acceptable but different	acceptable

*suck air between one's teeth
*cover one's mouth when smiling
*sniffle instead of blowing your nose
*clean ears or nails in public
*pick one's teeth in public
*sit with long periods of silence in the conversation

U.S.	Korea
acceptable	acceptable but different

*for women to shake hands, especially with men
*make "small talk" with strangers
*avoid long periods of silence in the conversation

We have looked at common courtesy or politeness in a general sense. Sometimes families or other social groups have their own, distinct patterns of courtesy as well. The next section discusses the concept of privacy. Finally, three short sections deal with expectations of common courtesy among family, friends, and in business.

What is privacy?

American Ways

AMERICAN / KOREAN CONTRAST

Americans may often want to be alone and value that opportunity for privacy and relaxation. On the other hand, Koreans often equate "alone" with lonely, and indeed have an expression that means both 'bored' and 'lonely:' *simsimhada.* [심심하다]

Americans value and respect privacy. To an American, privacy includes both personal space and personal information. A person who does not respect this privacy is called "rude," "nosy," or "inconsiderate." Americans expect others to respect their privacy both in the family and outside of the family. Inside of the family, privacy can include allowing others to make their own decisions. It can include children having individual bedrooms, respecting the property of others, and knocking on doors before entering. Therefore, the family can be together for dinner or activities, yet still respect the privacy of the individual family members.

In terms of personal information, Americans generally do not give personal details about themselves to strangers or casual acquaintances. Sometimes even family members do not ask about personal information. Some common topics one should be careful in

asking about are:
* *age
* *finances
* *religion
* *health (in terms of details)

Other topics that are considered personal are why a couple does not have any children and why someone is not married. In addition, money in general is a sensitive topic. Americans do not ask others how much they earn or how much something cost, often even among family members. In general, Americans do not push an opinion or advice on another or ask for too many details. Questions of this nature are considered **invading the privacy** of another.

> **NOTE:** For Americans, privacy can extend to personal space when standing close to someone. In general, Americans are uncomfortable when someone stands "too close" because Americans usually stand about 20-36 inches apart.[3] When they stand more closely together, it takes on a meaning of intimacy. Americans may also talk about a person wanting to be "too close." This can refer to a person's physical distance or to someone asking too many personal questions. Touching an American's hair is also considered an invasion of privacy.

AMERICAN / KOREAN CONTRAST

Personal information (such as address and phone number) can be considered private. It can be illegal for a public office to give that kind of information out to the public. There is a law that restricts who can give out that kind of information and who they can give it to. The 1974 Family Educational Rights and Privacy Act stipulates that all educational records are protected under the Constitutional right to privacy. So, schools are not allowed to disclose a student's educational or disciplinary records to anyone. If the school does, it can lose federal funding for education. In Korea, there are no such rules or laws. Therefore, it can be easy to find out personal information without "invading privacy" or breaking the law.

Korean Ways

Koreans, too, protect information from the scrutiny of others, including family members. However, because Koreans see themselves as family members first and individuals second (as compared to Americans who see themselves as individuals first and family members second), most information and decision making is viewed as open knowledge for all.

Because of the nature of the Korean language, which has different forms dependent on the status and relationship of the individuals, certain personal information such as age and marital status are necessary in order to maintain a polite level of discourse. In addition to linguistic constraints determining personal information, Koreans generally may give personal details about themselves to strangers or casual acquaintances as a way of becoming more intimate (whereas Americans usually require intimacy before providing such information). Topics such as why a couple does not have any children or why someone is not married are considered communal since marriage and children affect society as a whole. Other questions, such as how much money one earns, are personal questions because they protect the individual from the expectations of others or protect *ch'emyŏn*. In Korea privacy generally does not include allowing others to make their own decisions. A good example of this is in choosing one's husband or wife. Even in modern Korea, young people usually still need permission from their parents to get married and their approval of the prospective bride or bridegroom. A person who does not respect this privacy is called "*yeŭi ŏbnŭn saram*" [예의없는 사람] ('a person without manners').

NOTE: For Koreans, personal space when standing close to someone is a little closer than that of an American — about 12-20 inches.

AMERICAN / KOREAN CONTRAST

There is a difference between what an American considers a personal question and what a Korean considers a personal question.

To an American questions about age, money, marital status, and religion are considered personal and private. To a Korean, these are necessary questions that will enable the Korean to decide the appropriate language and behavior to use in this relationship.

A NOTE ON SMALL TALK: In the U.S. when people meet for the first time, they often introduce themselves. Following the introduction, they usually talk about topics of general interest, such as the weather, work, school, or local events. This is called "small talk", and strangers use it on a bus, at the airport, at the supermarket, or in a doctor's office. Small talk is a way to meet someone or to start a conversation. It is considered polite and important even in a marriage. But "small talk" is usually used with only a number of polite safe topics. Koreans generally do not engage in "small talk" with strangers, but they do value it and much social interaction depends on it. However, there is also a respect for quiet and listening, which is a mainstay of Korean personal interactions and communication. So, where an American might engage in small talk to avoid silences in a conversation, Koreans will expect and appreciate silences in a conversation.

What is common courtesy among family members?

American Ways

In most cultures, there is a difference between behavior among family members and among strangers or colleagues. That difference usually revolves around a person's ability to relax at home. Nevertheless, there are still expectations of courtesy and politeness among family members. In this section, we discuss the expectations of common courtesy between parents and children, among the **extended family**, and between husband and wife.

NOTE: Because of the high divorce rate in the U.S., the term "parents" can be extended to include **stepmothers and stepfathers.**

Parents and Children: Much of the common courtesy between immediate family members is based on the belief that each individual is more important than the family as a whole, rather than the family being more important than the individual.[4] Some of the common courtesy of <u>parents to their children</u> can be described as:

*Not forcing the child to attend college, take jobs, etc.
*respecting the privacy of the child
*knocking on the door of the child's bedroom before entering
*respecting the physical privacy of a child after puberty

Some of the common courtesy of <u>children to their parents</u> can be described as:

*using polite language with parents
*becoming independent
*knocking on the door of the parent's bedroom before entering

Extended Family: It is currently uncommon for parents to live with their married children. These rules often apply to the relationship of parents and their adult children:

*parents and their children visit one another's homes
*parents and their children keep in touch by phone
*grandparents love and care about their grandchildren but they usually do not play a major role in their upbringing
*extended family members usually call before visiting
*extended family members usually help with chores and sometimes bring gifts when coming for a visit, although gifts are not required or expected
*extended family members do not tell other family members what to do

Husband and Wife: The relationship of the husband and wife is based on affection, equality and togetherness. The common courtesy that a married couple usually expects of each other includes:

*greeting each other with a kiss
*respecting the privacy of the other
*saying nice things about each other in public
*using all the polite forms of language
*asking the partner before accepting invitations
*asking the partner before inviting someone to the home
*keeping the other informed of their schedule, location, etc.
*respecting the property of the other

AMERICAN / KOREAN CONTRAST

The role of women has been changing in both the U.S. and in Korea. In the U.S., polite behavior toward women by men has changed as well. Traditionally, common courtesy toward women included:
*opening doors for women
*allowing a woman to enter the door first
*walking on the left side of women when on the street
*lifting one's hat toward a woman
*not using vulgar language in front of a woman
*giving one's seat to a woman on the subway or bus or in a meeting (especially pregnant women)
*helping women with packages
*asking for permission to smoke in the front of a woman
*helping a woman put on her coat
*standing up when a woman enters a room

Since the advent of the women's equality movement in the 1960's, many of these courtesies have changed. Many women do not want such courtesies because they believe it shows women as less than the man's equal. Nevertheless, many of these traditional polite behaviors and expectations still exist. What has changed is that often women offer these same courtesies to men. Men rarely wear hats nowadays, and so the courtesy of a man lifting his hat is now considered very **old-fashioned**.

In Korea, many of these courtesies have not traditionally been a part of daily life. One reason for this has been the division between men and women in society. Thus Korean men in general do not have the attitude of:

*opening doors for women
*allowing a woman to enter the door first
*walking on the left side of women when on the street
*lifting one's hat toward a woman
*giving one's seat to a woman on the subway or bus or in a meeting
(even pregnant women), unless she is elderly
*helping women with packages
*asking for permission to smoke
*helping a woman put on her coat

Korean men and women are still expected to extend these courtesies to the elderly, but otherwise many of these are courtesies Korean men expect to receive from the woman because of the man's superior social status.

Korean Ways

Korean family life has depended on the extended family. While this is changing, the family is still the basis for society and continues to thrive on love, loyalty, and honor, but the nuclear family system has become commonplace in the cities and suburbs.

Parents and Children: Much of the common courtesy between immediate family members reflects the fact that the needs of the family are more important than the needs of the individual. Some of the common courtesy of parents to their children can be described as:

*encouraging and determining a child's future
*not boasting about the child in front of others
*encouraging the child with gifts

Some of the common courtesy of children to their parents can be described[5] as:

*not speaking unless spoken to
*not talking excessively in front of an older person

*not smoking or drinking in front of elders
*not crossing one's legs while sitting in a chair before an elder
*not wearing sunglasses while speaking to an elder
*not sitting down and eating before the eldest person has begun eating
*not initiating physical contact as an adult

AMERICAN / KOREAN CONTRAST

Americans do not touch or otherwise discuss the genitals of children. They also generally do not pat the backside of children not their own. However, in Korea, a boy baby is treasured above a girl baby. One way that Koreans show their pleasure at this gender difference is by asking little boys to show their penises. This is shocking behavior to Americans. If a Korean were to do this to a boy in the U.S., the family might accuse the Korean of child molesting.

Another way Koreans show their pleasure at having a boy is to take studio pictures of the child naked which show the child's genitals. Americans would not do this but might take pictures of the naked child from behind at home.

Extended Family: While family life in modern Korea is changing, it is still common for parents to live with their married children, especially with the eldest son. Most rules for common courtesy among extended family members resemble those of parents and children.

*parents and their children visit one another's homes
*parents and their children keep in touch by phone
*grandparents love and take care of their grandchildren
*extended family members usually visit without calling in advance
*extended family members usually help with chores and bring gifts when coming for a visit
*parents or grandparents can advise and be a part of the larger family unit

Husband and Wife: The relationship of the husband and wife is often based on affection in modern Korean society, but it also is based on following distinct gender-based roles. The wife still maintains the role of homemaker, and the husband works outside of the home. This distinction is reflected in the language: the wife is called *jibsaram* [집사람] ('house person'), and the husband is called *jibjuin* [집주인] ('house master'). The common courtesy that a Korean married couple usually expects of each other includes:

*using all the polite forms of language, especially the wife to the husband
*the wife preparing meals and serving her husband and his guests
*the husband and wife leading lives individual of each other
*the wife deferring to the husband in public
*the husband and wife being self-effacing in public regarding their relationship (As a result, they may not compliment each other or may even speak disparagingly of each other)

AMERICAN / KOREAN CONTRAST

In the U.S., the husband and wife are seen ideally as a team or partnership. They value time together and develop intimacy and sharing on all matters involving themselves as well as involving the family as a whole. In Korea, the husband and wife are also seen as a team, but with distinctly separate lives brought together through the family.

What is common courtesy among friends?

American Ways

A friend to an American may include someone a person knows very well and cares about, but the word "friend" may also be used to refer to someone one knows only casually. The general rules of common courtesy apply to friends as well, but there are also some other general restrictions among friends. Some of these restrictions include:

*not borrowing money
*respecting privacy
*not putting another under obligation

Korean Ways

In Korean society, relationships to and with others are valued highly. Thus the word "friend" is not used superficially in Korea. A friend (*ch'ingu* [친구]) to a Korean is a close friend, not an acquaintance. Close friends often become like family members, and so many of the courtesies expected of family members also apply to friends. The friendship may be tested and proven through a friend's willingness to extend such courtesies as those listed below to another:

*not refusing a request
*becoming involved in the individual's life
*being willing to be placed under obligation

Although we have discussed general concepts of common courtesy in the first sections of this chapter, we would like to address it a little further in order to draw a contrast between American and Korean courtesy in public or among strangers.

What is common courtesy among strangers?

As mentioned, concepts of politeness in the U.S. are based on concepts of mutual respect and human dignity. That is, American customs are based on a general concept of the inherent human dignity of each individual.[6] Even if this concept is not practiced consciously on a daily basis, it is the foundation of the courtesies Americans expect. American democracy is also based on the belief that God created each of us alike without regard to intelligence, physical condition or economic status. In other words, humans have all been created equal and have the inherent right to be treated with politeness and respect. This concept of human dignity within each individual is at the foundation of how Americans relate to strangers.

Thus, a general courtesy — or common courtesy as we have called it in this text — is expected toward all people, including strangers. Common courtesy is shown among strangers by:

*waiting in line
*respecting and helping those with less power, such as the elderly, the handicapped, or pregnant women
*acknowledging another's presence on the street or in some other public place by smiling or saying "Hi" or "How are you?"

Korean Ways

Buddhist principles regarding respect for other human beings and all living creatures have affected Korean society. However, Confucian principles dictate a social hierarchy and stratification. Thus, while Koreans are taught to be kind and considerate and maintain harmony, they are also taught that society as a whole is more important than the individual, and that there are levels of superiority among groups. Thus, Koreans may have many of the behaviors of Americans in relation to those they do not know, but for different reasons. In general, common courtesy towards strangers can be summarized as:

*respecting the elderly
*respecting foreigners

NOTE: Korean society has been influenced by the West in a growing tendency to wait in line, but it still is quite uncommon.

AMERICAN / KOREAN CONTRAST

As mentioned at the beginning of this chapter, in the U.S. the Golden Rule applies, and strangers are treated as equals. This contrasts with Korean common courtesy toward a stranger, which an American might consider no etiquette at all. That is, in Korea a person with whom one has not been introduced or has had no previous relationship is not recognized or treated as well as a person one knows. It is as if that person does not have an identity, is an "unperson." Since Korean society is hierarchical, the moral foundation for behavior and treatment toward others is based on personal relationships: if the person is unknown to you, then there are no rules to follow. Some people claim that this indifference toward strangers comes from the village family clan system where everyone knew and had some relationship with everyone else. Others have said that the Confucian system had specific instructions for how to behave inside a group, but little to say of how to behave outside of one. This behavior toward strangers is in contrast with the impressive Korean reputation regarding their hospitality. Koreans are indeed very hospitable. But this hospitality does not extend to all people. For example, Koreans generally do not begin a conversation with someone with whom they have not been introduced unless it is a foreigner. Thus, the concept of polite small talk or friendly greeting as cultivated in the U.S. is not part of Korean common courtesy toward strangers.

What is common courtesy in doing business?

American Ways

By Korean standards, the U.S. can be a very informal society. Indeed to outsiders Americans may even appear to be disrespectful of people in authority. This may be especially true when doing business. However, there are boundaries to this informality, and nowhere is this more evident than in the business world. Some American attitudes toward doing business that affect courtesy and politeness are:

*Americans generally are very aggressive in their business approach.
*Americans separate business from the personal.[7]
*Americans value equal opportunity.

*Americans value competition in business.

*Americans view competition in business as an open and fair race where success goes to the most talented person irrespective of his or her personal connections, background, gender, race, or age.[8]

*Americans value brevity and speed in business negotiations.

*Americans want to "get to the point" and not "waste time" in business.

*Americans deal with business quickly, with very little small talk.

*Americans view time as money, and thus expect American businessmen to be prompt with appointments, orders, and contracts.

*Americans expect all phone calls to be returned.

*Americans may treat superiors equally, i.e. on the same basis as they themselves expect to be treated.

*Americans often do not use titles (e.g. Dr.) in doing business except with those in the medical profession or sometimes at the university.

*Americans may introduce themselves to prospective clients.

*Americans may call an associate by his or her first name in an effort to be friendly. They would normally ask permission to call their superiors by their first names.

American aggressiveness in doing business can be seen in the focus on business issues during business interactions. This aggressiveness is also related to their emphasis on competition, which is seen as an open and fair race where success goes to the most talented person irrespective of his personal connections, background, gender, race, or age. Thus, there is an emphasis on equal opportunity. If Americans speak negatively of these ideals, it is out of cynicism, not because these ideals do not exist. Common courtesy in doing business, then, involves fair competition.

Americans are well known for their step-by-step approach in business. Americans generally value knowledge and talent, and efficiency is valued over personal interaction. Americans would like to think that these three qualities can lead to success as much as personal ties do. A common expression in the U.S. has been "It's not

<u>who</u> you know, but <u>what</u> you know." This expression emphasizes the American businessman's attitude that an employee's knowledge and **expertise** enhances the company's **competitive edge**. To be sure, in the fast-paced world of American business, managers with knowledge and talent are often singled out for rewards, praise, and promotions.[9] However, another common expression, "It's not <u>what</u> you know, but <u>who</u> you know," also reflects the attitudes and experiences of some Americans. The difference between these two expressions, which are opposites, is that the first ("It's not who you know, but what you know") is what Americans would like to think is true. It reflects the American ideal of equal opportunity, that anyone can succeed if he or she works or tries hard enough. The second expression ("It's not what you know, but who you know"), however, reflects the cynical reality of many people in modern times.

Another common courtesy involves separating business from the personal. A common expression in American business is "it's just business." This expression means that business is something objective that involves rules to be followed. This expression is often used to express dissatisfaction with impersonal business practices. To separate the business from the personal does not mean that there is no personal interaction. Indeed, although Americans stress efficiency and brevity in doing business, business associates still socialize with (or "**wine and dine**") their prospective clients before or while the business deal is being negotiated. At these business lunches or dinners, the business associates usually talk about business. In addition, Americans view time as money, and thus expect American businessmen to be prompt with appointments, orders, and contracts. A contract is more valued than a personal promise. Courtesy in doing business also puts an emphasis on not "wasting the time" of the other person by being brief, fast, efficient, and by keeping promises. Keeping promises and respecting the time of others includes returning phone calls.

Separating the business from the personal also allows Americans to introduce themselves to prospective clients. Although it is also common to be introduced by a third party, it is equally as common — and often expected — to introduce oneself directly. Introducing oneself directly avoids obligation and saves everyone time. Thus, the American would believe that he/she is being considerate of all involved.

Courtesy in personal interactions within a company can vary from company to company. In general, Americans may treat their superiors or colleagues equally, i.e. on the same basis as they themselves expect to be treated. They usually do not use titles (such as Dr.) outside of the medical and education professions, and will likely call an associate by his or her first name in an effort to be friendly. However, to show respect and social distance, Americans would normally ask permission to call their superiors by their first names.

> **NOTE:** American informality can confuse non-Americans into misinterpreting it to mean no formality — or rules of courtesy — at all. They may not understand where the informality ends. A boss, though friendly in the work place, evaluates each employees' performance carefully. In the business world, employers may call employees by their first names. However, the employee will not automatically address their superiors by first names unless they have been given permission. They will address their employer as "Mr. Davis" or "Mrs. Diaz", for example.[10] This would be especially true if the employer is the chairman or president of a company. American businessmen may stand up when colleagues come into a room, especially top executives in a company. When the chairman, president, or top executive vice presidents enter a middle manager's or a supervisor's office, the manager, etc. will stand up. However, when an immediate supervisor enters the office of his/her section, the employees will greet him/her politely, but will likely not stand up.

Korean Ways

By American standards, Korea can be a very formal society. However, there are boundaries to this formality which are quite evident in the business world. To outsiders, Korean formality may seem impersonal, but personal interactions and relationships play an important role in how Koreans conduct business. Actually, the formality can be hidden by friendliness, camaraderie, and personal attention in all social and business interactions. However, the attention to social activity is in itself a formality designed to study and test individuals to get a measure of their character and trustworthiness. Some Korean attitudes toward doing business that effect courtesy and politeness are:

*Koreans generally are very aggressive in their business approach.
*Koreans integrate business with the personal.[11]
*Koreans value competition in business.
*Koreans view competition in business as secondary to personal loyalties.
*Koreans value process over completion.
*Koreans value conversation and deal with business only at the end of a meeting.
*Koreans view personal situations and the understanding of others as more important than promptness with appointments, orders, and contracts, etc.
*Koreans treat superiors formally and never on the same basis as they themselves expect to be treated.
*Koreans value titles (e.g. Dr.) in personal interactions, and especially in doing business where terms such as 'chairman,' 'section chief,' 'supervisor,' etc. are expected to be used.
*Koreans may introduce themselves to prospective clients.
*Koreans rarely call an associate by his or her first name.
*Koreans avoid embarrassment, and so may not return all phone calls .

Korea's development of its national economy over the last 30 years has depended highly on its success in the business world. This success has been the result of Korean tenacity, hard work and aggressiveness in doing business. However, this aggressiveness does not always translate to aggressiveness on a personal level. While Koreans value competition, this competition can be restricted to rival companies or used as a motivation for individual employees. Korean competition varies from American competition in that it is not based on a concept of openness and fairness. Rather personal connections, background, gender, race, or age all play a role in hiring and promotion. Common courtesy in doing business in Korea, then, involves developing personal connections. For a Korean, that means avoiding conflict and maintaining *ch'emyŏn* ('face') and *kibun* ('mood'), both of which are situation dependent. It also involves establishing a reputation for dependability and loyalty.

Korean businessmen and women are well known for their hospitality and graciousness. To Americans, the Korean may seem indefinite and slow to make decisions, while suddenly expecting a lot of work done at the last minute. Actually, Korean businessmen may seem slow because they value process over completion — although completion is important, too. They also value *kibun*, and so do business only at the end of a meeting in order to establish a good atmosphere and state of mind for conducting the business. For example, if during a social evening the Korean businessman senses that his colleague is not in a mood for discussion, then the business may not be addressed at all. Instead, it may be postponed until the next meeting. The American businessman, on the other hand, would more likely place feelings second to the importance of efficiently finishing the business at hand. That is, Koreans view personal situation and understanding as more important than promptness with appointments, orders, and contracts, etc.

AMERICAN / KOREAN CONTRAST

Americans and Koreans have opposite views of what might be considered courtesy within the business relationship. The American places business outside of the personal relationship, and so expects business to be processed quickly. The Korean, on the other hand, values the business process, and takes time to establish the personal connections necessary for a long-term, trusting business relationship. Trust, too, is based on different expectations. For the American, trust is built on the business associate's ability to sign a contract and provide the stipulations of the contract on time. But for the Korean, trust is based on how well the business associate understands the variables affecting the Korean businessman and his company (for example, an inability to sign a contract).

An example of these opposing views in doing business is of a young American business manager who left Korea after only three months because he found the emphasis on relationships in Korean business excessive and slow. He did not like the drinking parties or the seeming indecision of his Korean counterpart. He felt that the manager he was working with did not have the authority to close the business deal, and so he demanded to see the president of the company. The president of the company introduced this manager to another business manager in the company who he hoped would be more to the American manager's liking. This points out the Korean tendency to delegate work to managers and the expectation that work will be done on the appropriate level it has been delegated to.[12]

Koreans generally value knowledge, talent, efficiency, and especially loyalty in doing business, and the competition for jobs in the business world is very keen. Nevertheless, Koreans place greater value on personal connections and loyalty than on such concepts as equal opportunity. Thus, it is often considered more secure and trustworthy to hire someone one knows or knows of, often through the connections one has made in high school and college. It is assumed that these "known" individuals will have the same amount of knowledge, talent, efficiency, and loyalty as the "unknown." Furthermore, in the fast-paced world of Korean business, managers who meet the demands of the company are often singled out for rewards, praise, and promotions.[13]

AMERICAN / KOREAN CONTRAST

Americans dislike working after the normal business hours of 8 to 5 (in most companies). They generally have a strong sense of their own private time, and separate work time and private time. In contrast, a loyal Korean employee commits most of his time to his working day. Although his job may list him as working 8 to 5, he may well be expected to spend his evening hours at the office or with his colleagues. Part of Saturday, too, may be committed to office work.

While it is common courtesy in the U.S. to separate business from the personal (but still extend all other courtesies to an individual), in Korea it is common courtesy to spend time getting to know the individual before doing business. To a Korean, getting to know the person is doing business. However, the personal connection in business exists only while the business relationship exists. To an American, a personal relationship established while doing business may exist long after the business relationship has ended. On the other hand, although Koreans stress socializing in doing business, business associates may not be in any contact with each other after the immediate business relationship has ended. The Korean and American approaches to business differ in another important aspect as well. That is, the Korean may view the American's insistence on contracts and deadlines as insincere. On the other hand, the American may view the Korean's personal style as insincere. The following story highlights this difference in perspective:

A Korean businessman who was sent to negotiate a contract with a U.S. firm in New York was dismayed by the impersonal level of business practices in the U.S. He had expected to remain for a month to negotiate the deal, but the American side had made their presentation and were ready to close the business deal at the end of the first week. In fact, two new associates to whom he had previously been introduced did not even know his name: they called him Mr. Lee instead of Mr. Kim. The Korean businessman felt like a computer. To him, the only thing the Americans were concerned about was the business package and maximizing their profits. From the American perspective, they had been polite and considerate because they had not taken too much of their associate's time and had saved him the expense of staying longer in a foreign country.

Because Koreans value the "known," they would likely not introduce themselves to prospective clients. Rather, they would depend on a third party to introduce them. Introducing oneself directly is more likely considered forward or rude to a Korean, while a third party introduction may meet previous obligations and solidify relationships by establishing new obligations.

Courtesy in personal interactions within a company reflect the hierarchical structure of Korean society. In general, Koreans treat all superiors, and often even associates, formally. They use titles for the various positions, e.g. *wonjangnim* [원장님] ('honorable head of the department'), and call colleagues by titles such as Mr. and Miss. First names are seldom used. If two colleagues become friends, or attended the same school, then they might use the titles they would use for family members or school mates, e.g. *hyŏng* [형] ('older brother') *hubae* [후배] ('lower classman'). Koreans would normally never ask permission to call their superiors by their first names because they would never presume to address them so informally. In contrast to practices in the U.S., intimacy for the Korean businessman is brought about through social activity, not through the titles one uses. One's social position is always respected, and titles serve to remind the Korean of that position.

Here are some similarities and distinctions between courtesy in doing business in the U.S. and Korea:

AMERICAN / KOREAN CONTRAST

U.S.	Korea
common	uncommon

*completing a "deal" in a short amount of time
*discussing business during the meal
*calling superiors by first names
*expecting to confirm a business relationship by signing a contract
*establishing trustworthiness based on meeting the contract's stipulations
*separating business from the personal
*placing emphasis on not wasting time

U.S.	Korea
uncommon	common

*taking a long time to complete a "deal"
*discussing business after the meal
*calling all superiors and often colleague by titles
*placing trust outside of signing a contract
*establishing trustworthiness based on the person's willingness to understand the company's limitations.

What is common courtesy on the telephone?

American Ways

Most telephone courtesy in the U.S. applies to both private homes and businesses. Nevertheless, we divide the two below in order to point out that there may be some distinctions.

Answering the Phone

Private Home: Most Americans answer the telephone by saying "hello." Some Americans choose to identify themselves by name as well, for example:

"Hello. This is the Martin residence."
or
"Hello. Martin's."

Business: Most American businesses answer the telephone by saying "hello" and then identifying the company's name. They then say "May I help you?" or "How can I direct your call?" (Which means "What is the matter you are calling about?" or "To whom would you like to speak?"). A typical polite exchange might be:

"Hello. This is Jones Manufacturing. May I help you?"
or
A: "Hello. Jones Manufacturing. How can I direct your call?"
B: "I'd like to speak to someone in charge of billing, please."
A: "I'll connect your call."

Concluding a Call

Private Home: Most Americans conclude a telephone call by saying "Goodbye" or "I'll talk to you later." Some can be quite abrupt in hanging up the phone, and others may say "Goodbye" several times. If the call is between two people who do not normally talk on the phone, they may say "Thanks for calling."

Business: Most American businesses conclude a telephone call by thanking the caller and telling them to call again. They then say "Goodbye" or something similar. For example:

"Thank you for calling. If there's anything else you need, feel free to call again. Have a nice day. Goodbye."

Wrong Numbers

When an American has dialed a wrong number, the most polite response is to say, "I'm sorry. I must have dialed the wrong number." It is generally impolite to simply hang up the phone.

NOTE: Nowadays, the majority of American homes have answering machines on their telephones. There are a variety of ways to set a message on a machine. Many people choose to include a clever message or music. The majority of messages, however, state a person's phone number and give instructions to the caller. Some people use the machine all the time to screen calls and only answer the phone when they want to speak to the caller.

Many businesses — especially larger companies — have voice mail (a more complex form of answering machine that is connected directly into their telephone service). The message on the voice mail may include a directory and instructions for how to use it. A directory specifies numbers to push to direct the call to the appropriate office.

Korean Ways

Answering the Phone

Private Home: Most Koreans answer the telephone by saying "*yŏboseyo*" [여보세요] ('Hello.') Koreans do not identify their name or residence.

Business: Most Korean businesses answer the telephone by saying "*yŏboseyo*" and sometimes identifying the company's name. They then ask how to direct the call, "*ŏdi jŏnhwa hashŏtsŏyo ?*" [어디 전화 하셨어요?] ('Whom/where are you calling?') or "*ŏdi (or nuku) bakwŏ julkkayo ?*" [어디(누구)바꿔줄까요?] ('Where (who) shall I transfer you to?').

However, they may also ask who is calling: "*shillyejiman, nuku simnikka?*" [실례지만, 누구십니까?] ('Excuse me, but who is calling?')

Concluding a Call

Private Homes and Businesses: Most Koreans — whether at home or at a business — conclude a telephone call by saying "*kkŭnnŏyŏ*" [끊어요] ('I'm cutting the connection.') This is usually repeated several times.

For example:

A: *(kŭrŏm) kkŭnnŏyo.* [(그럼) 끊어요.] ('Well, I'll hang up now.')
B: *ne, ne. kkŭnnŏyo.* [네, 네 끊어요.] ('Yes, yes. I'll hang up.')
A: *ne.* [네] ('Yes.')
B: *ne.* [네] ('Yes.')

Wrong Numbers

When Koreans have dialed a wrong number, they will most likely say:

"*mianhamnida. chalmot jŏnhwa haetssŏyo*" [미안합니다. 잘못전화했어요] ('I'm sorry. I have dialed the wrong number.')

What is common courtesy in a public office?

American Ways

Courtesy in a public office includes all of the courtesies used for the general public. Some special courtesies are:

*greeting the secretary or other person at the front desk

*waiting in line
*asking politely how long one might have to wait

Korean Ways

Courtesy in a public office includes all of the courtesies used for the general public. Some special courtesies are:

*greeting the secretary or other person at the front desk
*asking politely how long one might have to wait

Koreans generally do not wait in line, but rather crowd around a desk or other waiting area and vie for attention. While this is changing, especially in Seoul, it is still the common practice. The effect this custom has on an individual can be seen in the following personal story.

When Virginia returned from living in Seoul, she went to the post office. As she had become accustomed to doing in Korea, she followed the person ahead of her in line up to the desk and stood by the desk while the first customer took care of business. It was only after she left the post office that she realized why the American clerk had given her such a funny look.

What is appropriate dress?

There is not much difference in how Americans and Koreans **dress**. Both societies have concepts of casual, "dressy," and formal wear. And what is appropriate is changing rapidly among the younger generation — especially in Korea. In this section we will briefly touch on what is considered appropriate dress in different situations and environments.

American Ways

NOTE: In the U.S., clothes reveal much about individualism and the diversity of the culture. They often reflect an individual's personality, his/her mood, and the image he/she wants to project to others. Some of the ways Americans of all ages and in all jobs and professions express individuality is by wearing earrings or ponytails [men]; having holes in their clothing; or coloring their hair green or purple, etc.

Casual Wear: Americans wear casual clothing for all forms of recreation, such as sports, sightseeing and casual entertainment. Casual wear includes comfortable clothing such as jeans, a T-shirt and tennis shoes. Americans often dress casually in public, such as when shopping or going to the doctor's office, as well as at home. Casual clothing also reflects one's lifestyle and generation. The older generation may be less likely to wear blue jeans, and 'casual' may mean nice slacks and shirts or blouses. For college students, casual dress may be the norm.

Being casual has many levels of acceptability. Men who are working outside or who are involved in sports such as playing tennis or jogging may remove their shirts when it gets too hot. When it is hot, women may wear halter tops and shorts. It is in this area of casual clothing that Americans make their own individual statements the most. It is where they have the most freedom to experiment and try out new styles. Although all casual dress is appropriate; there are occasions when casual dress may not be appropriate, for example:

*the opera or another type of formal concert
*weddings and funerals
*applying for a job
*at a formal occasion such as giving a speech

Formal Wear: Americans wear a more sophisticated style of clothing for evening entertainment. Many Americans enjoy "dressing up" for the opera, ballet, and symphony concerts (but young people may be seen wearing more casual clothing styles at such events). Dressing up usually means wearing a dress for women and a suit for men. Many American women distinguish between their "everyday" dresses or skirts and the dresses they might wear for an evening out.

There are some occasions, such as weddings or formal parties, when women wear evening gowns (long or short dresses in styles inappropriate for everyday), and men may wear a tuxedo (black tie). However, these occasions are usually only for a small section of the population. (One exception is a tradition in American high schools called "the prom." It is a very formal dance where the young men wear tuxedos, and the young women wear formal gowns.)

Business: In the business world, Americans tend to dress more formally than at other times. In fact, Americans often joke about the business "uniform." Both American men and women tend to wear conservatively tailored dark suits in the winter months and lighter-colored suits in the summer months.

Dark suits represent serious-mindedness. While suits are considered appropriate dress for business, those in the business world and those in other fields still distinguish themselves by the accessories they choose. That is, although suits, dress shirts, and ties are common dress customarily worn by men, individuality is often expressed by wearing bright colored ties or shirts.

However, in the U.S. the type of business one works for often determines what type of clothing one wears. For example, if a person works for an advertising agency, the employees might wear a variety of different types of clothing depending on the type of company they work for. If, on the other hand, they work on Wall Street or for a law firm, they will probably be expected to wear more conservative type clothing, such as a dark suit, fairly dark tie, and a white shirt.

Nevertheless, there have been some changes and relaxing of norms in recent years. For example, Americans — both women and men — frequently wear jogging shoes with their business suits to work. They usually change into dress shoes once they get to their office or place of business, but not always. Some men wear black jogging shoes which look like dress shoes, and women increasingly wear flat sole shoes. The following general rules apply for appropriate business dress:

Appropriate:
Suits and ties for men; suits, dresses, or slacks for women. A woman's make-up and hairstyle is normally conservative. The

type of office one works in determines the degree of how conservatively the employee dresses.

<u>Inappropriate:</u>

Blue jeans, jogging clothes, very revealing clothes.

A NOTE ABOUT UNIVERSITY DRESS: While the staff of a university usually dresses according to business norms, the faculty may dress according to their own individual tastes, which would include shorts in the summer and blue jeans, but can also include sport coats, suits, and dresses.

Korean Ways

NOTE: Koreans normally dress conservatively. However, Japanese and Western influence can increasingly be seen, especially among young people. Koreans are quite fashion conscious, but also tend toward conservative uniformity. Even the poorest of Koreans take great care with their clothes and appearance. So, rather than reflecting an individual's personality, styles of dress in Korea tend to reflect the country's conservative, collective personality and popular trends. While young people are moving away from conservatism in dress, it is still uncommon to see men wearing earrings or ponytails, young people having holes in their clothing, or men or women coloring their hair green or purple, etc. What is valued is modesty and conformity of dress.

Casual Wear: Casual clothing for a Korean includes comfortable clothing such as jeans, a T-shirt and tennis shoes, but it also includes jogging outfits, house dresses and pajamas. When going out in public (except in their neighborhood), Koreans will likely not dress casually, but rather wear some of their nicer clothes. As in the U.S., however, for college students casual dress may be the norm. (But young college women may wear fashionable clothes every day.)

Wearing appropriate clothes for the occasion is important to most Koreans. When one plays golf or goes mountain climbing for example, one should dress the part. It is not unusual to see a group of mountain climbers all **decked out** in their Alpine hats, socks and gear or golfers with their golf type caps and gloves. One would rarely attend one of these group functions dressed differently.

Casual dress for many men includes slacks and a polo shirt, a sweater, or a short-sleeved shirt. Korean men would never take off their shirt in public to play sports or work. Older Koreans may wear traditional Korean clothing as well. Korean businessmen may wear slacks and a dress shirt even on picnics or during other outdoor activities.

> **NOTE:** Korean style of dress usually prohibits revealing bare legs or arms. Although in recent years young women have copied Western styles and have begun to wear sleeveless tops and shorts as well as mini-skirts, the government has appealed in recent years for the fashion to return to a more modest and conservative dress.

Formal Wear: Koreans wear formal clothing, such as suits and dresses, even when engaged in sightseeing and casual entertainment. Evening wear, such as evening gowns and tuxedos, is rare and limited to events attended by a small section of society.

Business: In the business world and in the white-collar workplace in general, Koreans dress more formally than at other times. Koreans, too, often joke about the business "uniform." This "uniform" tends to consist of conservatively tailored dark or gray suits, white shirts, and dark ties in the winter months, and somewhat lighter-colored suits in the summer. The men often wear white cotton socks with their suits. In the summer, they will wear short-sleeved shirts. There is very little variation, and colorful ties or colorful shirts are generally not worn, at least not as a statement of individuality. Women in the workplace usually dress fashionably and well if they are secretaries or receptionists. However, female employees are likely to wear uniforms in companies such as banks, large businesses, and department stores.

> **A NOTE ABOUT UNIVERSITY DRESS:** Korean university faculty and staff usually dress according to business norms with little variation.

A NOTE ABOUT KOREAN TRADITIONAL DRESS: Until the 1960's, Koreans mostly wore a traditional style of clothing called *hanbok* [한복] (literally: 'Korean clothes'), especially in the countryside. A woman's *hanbok* normally consists of a long skirt that wraps around the body and ties above the breasts and a short jacket with billowing sleeves that gather at the wrist. A man's *hanbok* includes loose-fitting pants and a loose-fitting jacket similar to a woman's. Koreans traditionally wore rubber or straw-mat shoes with tight-fitting padded socks that rise up to mid-calf. Except for the elderly, it is rare to see this dress on a daily basis anymore in modern Korea. However, women often choose to wear a *hanbok* to formal occasions, and both men and women choose to wear *hanbok* on special holidays such as Ch'usŏk and New Year's Day.

AMERICAN / KOREAN CONTRAST

Americans normally wear pajamas or other types of "night clothes" to sleep in. While Americans can be casual or informal at home, it would be unusual to wear pajamas or a nightgown when one has guests. Americans also normally wear a bathrobe over their nightclothes. Korean women, on the other hand, often wear loose house dresses which they may also wear to sleep in. Korean men may put on pajamas after coming home. In addition, it is not uncommon for Koreans — especially men — not to wear overcoats in the winter, or gloves, hats, or scarves.

Glossary of English Terms

competitive Competes with others to be the best.

decked out (slang) Dressed in; wearing.

dress As a noun, this means 'clothing;' as a verb, it means 'wear clothes'.

disclose a student's educational or disciplinary records Provide information about a student's grades or behavior.

extended family Grandparents, aunts, uncles, cousins, nieces, nephews.

expertise A person's knowledge and experience.

favor A special request. For example, "Can you do me a favor? Can you watch my apartment while I am away on vacation?"

invade one's privacy Not respect the privacy of another, either physically or by asking personal questions.

old-fashioned Not according to modern ideas and practices.

pushy 'Aggressive.'

stepmothers and stepfathers When the father remarries, his new wife is the children's stepmother. When the mother remarries, the new husband is the children's stepfather.

tardy Be late.

vulgar language Terms that refer to sexual behavior or bodily functions.

wine and dine Literally, this means to treat someone to good meals and good liquor. This expression can be used to refer to special treatment in general, especially when someone wants something, or wishes to please another person.

Glossary of Korean Terms

bunŭiki [분위기] A general atmosphere at a meeting, in a classroom, at a party, etc.

ch'emyŏn [체면] A concept of "face" particular to Koreans.

chŏng [정] A feeling of affection and connection to another.

ch'usŏk [추석] An important Korean family holiday which is celebrated August 15 according to the Lunar Calendar.

hanbok [한복] Korean traditional clothing.

hyŏng [형] The term a younger brother uses for an older brother.

jibjuin [집주인] The term a wife uses to refer to her husband. It translates literally as 'house master.'

jibsaram [집사람] The term a husband uses to refer to his wife. It translates literally as 'house person.'

wonjangnim [원장님] The term given to the manager of an office.

yeŭi ŏbnŭn saram [예의없는 사람] An impolite person.

yechŏl [예절] Manners; etiquette.

yeŭi [예의] Manners; etiquette.

Notes

[1] This list was based on personal observations as well as on the following texts:

Ugly Koreans, Ugly Americans by Byoung-Chul Min (Seoul, Korea: BCM Publishers, Inc., 1995) and *Culture Shock: Korea* by Sonja Vegdahl Hur and Ben Seunghwa Hur (Singapore: Times Books International, 1988).

[2] See *Korean Patterns* by Paul S. Crane (Seoul: Kwangjin Publishing Company, 1978), pp. 29-31.

[3] See *The Silent Language* by Edward T. Hall (New York: Doubleday Anchor Books, 1973), pp.184-185. Hall discusses the American concept of space and presents a chart indicating the personal nature of different distances when speaking to someone.

[4] See *The American Way: An Introduction to American Culture* (Kearny, et al. Prentice Hall, 1984), p.202.

[5] See *Korean Patterns* by Paul S. Crane (Seoul: Kwangjin Publishing Company, 1978), pp. 25-26.

[6] See *Korean Ideas and Views* by Michael Kalton (Elkins Park, PA: The Philip Jaisohn Memorial Foundation, Inc., 1979), p. 4.

[7] The idea of Americans separating business from the personal comes from the concept of equality that is so cherished in American life. This concept serves as a basis for the belief that all people have an equal opportunity to succeed in life. Competition in American business, which is believed to strengthen the ideal of equal opportunity, is seen as an open and fair race where success goes to the most talented person, irrespective of his or her personal connections, background, gender, race, or age. Thus, brevity and speed in business negotiations are preferred. It is considered polite to get to the point and not waste time. Americans have a strong sense of self-importance; they feel that they are "just as good" as everyone else and want to be treated in that way. The informality in American manners and social distinctions can be easily misinterpreted by Koreans as having no standards of distinction at all.

[8] See *The American Way: An Introduction to American Culture* by Kearny, et al. (N.J. Prentice Hall, 1984) p.202.

[9] The U.S. is seen as "the land of opportunity" where hard work and ingenuity pays off. Americans revere the independent man, whose

hard work has allowed him to succeed. They do not have a great deal of respect for those people who have only succeeded because they are born into a rich family or have achieved success through their personal relationships and connections. Obtaining a job because of personal connections, referred to as "nepotism," is especially frowned upon by American society, and can even be considered illegal. The expression "Who you know is not as important as what you know," reflects this important American ideal which has made it possible for Americans to move up the social ladder. Therefore, people who have worked hard and succeeded are given a great deal of respect. Competition in business is seen as a challenge that forces a person to reach his or her full potential.

[10] See *Language and life in the U.S.A.* by Doty, G. & Ross, J. (New York: Harper & Row Publishers, 1981), p.24.

[11] See *The Business of Korean Culture* by Richard Saccone (Seoul: Hollym Corporation; Publishers, 1994), p.27.

[12] See *Korean Etiquette and Ethics in Business* (second edition) by B.L. De Mente, B.L. (Lincolnwood, Illinois: NTC Publishing Group, 1994), pp. 73-74.

[13] Ibid.

CHAPTER 3

GREETINGS AND FAREWELLS

GREETINGS AND FAREWELLS

Introduction

Humans are social beings who find connection to each other in their interactions: How they meet, greet, and separate from family, friends, and others with whom they come in contact. It is a natural part of life. All people want to make a good impression when they meet someone for the first time. They want to convey their feelings when they greet someone after an absence. And they want their farewells to ensure another meeting. The customs and expectations in the U.S. and in Korea determine what people say and do in these various situations. They also determine what Americans and Koreans expect others to do when they **encounter** other people or take leave from them.

In this chapter, you will read about the general customs and expectations of greetings and leavetakings in the U.S. and Korea. It is impossible to account for all of the many personal variations and differences according to situation, the nature of the relationships, and to personal preference. So, we give you details of what you can generally expect in a variety of situations.

When we traveled to Korea for the first time, we were told that Koreans bow and Americans shake hands. We soon learned that this is not true all the time, especially as modern Korea becomes increasingly influenced by the West. But what are the exceptions to this general rule? When is the right time to bow, to shake hands, or to do neither? Does age or **gender** affect these behaviors? How do Koreans and Americans greet each other or **take their leave** of each other? These are some of the questions we answer in this chapter.

How do family members greet and part from one another?

American Ways

The United States is a culturally diverse country. The many ways American family members might greet and part from one another reflect this cultural diversity. That is, family habits are often formed according to each family's **cultural heritage** and family practices. So, some families may be quite formal in their greetings and farewells, and others may be quite informal. Furthermore, each family has its own customs and expectations as a group, but the individual members of a family also have their own customs and habits as well. Customs and expectations can also be situation dependent (as it can be in Korea), so that one person may behave differently with the same group of people according to the situation.

> **NOTE:** Cultural diversity in the U.S. can make Americans accepting of variations in greeting and parting behavior in others. It also means that you cannot observe just one American as a model to generalize how all Americans greet or part from one another.

You may discover that the average American can be quite informal among family members, including parents and grandparents. If you observe American family members (even on television), you will notice that each individual family may have different practices in how to greet and part from one another. This is another example of the American focus on individuality.

You will also observe that despite American cultural diversity and individuality, it is still possible to make some general statements about how Americans greet and part from each other. First, Americans often show affection when they greet or part from someone, especially a family member. Indeed, how Americans behave toward another family member is more an expression of their feelings than a symbol of respect. That is, family relationships are not as restricted or formalized in the U.S. as they are in Korea, and so Americans generally do not follow a specific ritual of behavior that is determined by social or family position. Here are some examples of American customs of greetings and farewells within the framework of general social expectations.

What Americans Say

Among family members, Americans usually greet each other by saying "Hello," "Hi," or "Good morning (afternoon, or evening)." "How are you?" usually follows this initial greeting. "How are you?" is usually responded to with "Fine. How are you?" It does not call for a literal response (for example, "Terrible"), unless there is a special relationship. (If you want to know about health or other concerns, you should ask that question specifically. For example, "How is your health?") Next, Americans often say "It's good to see you." They comment on each other's appearance. They try to be positive and courteous. For example, "You look great!" or "You look very healthy!" They then talk about the travel if someone has arrived from a trip.

When Americans separate, they usually say "Goodbye" or several of its variants, such as "See you" or "Talk to you later." If someone is driving, they will say "Drive safely" or "Take good care of yourself." They may tell either the person staying or the person leaving to enjoy a specific activity they have discussed, such as "Enjoy the party." In addition, family members may regularly say "I love you" upon separating, even if it is only for a few hours. This tendency has increased in recent years.

Here are a few examples of some common interchanges:
Greeting:

Example #1
(Between a mother and an adult child after a short or long separation.)

Child: Hello, Mom. It's great to see you.
Mother: Hello, **sweetie**. I'm so glad to see you. How's my girl?
Child: Fine, just fine.
Mother: Really? How's your health been?

Example #2

(Between a brother and sister after a short or long separation.)

Brother: Hello.

Sister: Hi. How are you?

Brother: I'm doing well. I can't complain. How about you?

Sister: I'm doing well, too.

Brother: Did you have a good trip?

Sister: Yes, it went very smoothly.

Brother: Well, you look great.

Sister: Thanks. So do you.

Parting:

Example #1

(Between a mother and child. The child may only be driving home across town, or to a distant city.)

Child: Well, I've got to go. Goodbye. I'll call you later.

Mother: Goodbye. Take good care of yourself and drive safely. Don't forget to call me. I love you.

Child: I love you too. Bye.

Mother: Bye.

Example #2

(Between a brother and sister when the sister lives either in the same town or a distant town.)

Brother: Are you leaving?

Sister: Yes, I've got to go.

Brother: Well, I'm sorry to see you leave so soon. Be careful driving.

Sister: Thanks, I will. Take care of yourself, and tell the kids "hello" from me.

Brother: I will. Bye.

Sister: Bye. I love you. It was great seeing you.

What Americans Do

Americans often display emotion, affection, and warmth — or even humor — when greeting another family member. You need to remember, though, that each family's approach may differ according to the family's cultural background and customs, the **gender** of the family member, or how emotionally close the family members are. (For example, a woman might hug her brother, but shake hands with or only nod to a cousin she is meeting for the first time or doesn't see very often and isn't emotionally close to.) American family members might:

*hug
*kiss
*shake hands
*shake hands while **slapping the person on the shoulder**
***nod** to each other
*lift up or **wave** a hand
*say "hello" with no physical contact
*stand or sit arm in arm
*stand or sit with one person's arm around the other's waist or shoulder
*hold hands

Hugging, either in a full-arm **embrace** from the front or an arm around one's shoulder from the side, is a common way for many Americans to greet other family members. To **slap someone on the shoulder** instead of or while shaking hands is also another expression of affection, especially among men. The family custom may vary according to each family's tradition, which is sometimes related to their ethnic origin.

NOTE: In general, women most often hug each other and men most often shake hands or slap each other on the shoulder. However, it has become increasingly more common since the 1960s for people of both genders to hug one another. Often, a hug is accompanied by a kiss on the cheek or on the lips, depending on the family. Still, American women are more physically affectionate than American men are when greeting or parting.

The amount and degree of physical contact also depends on the occasion. On a daily basis, couples — both married and unmarried — normally kiss and embrace when greeting. Hugs, kisses, and nods of the head, as well as a general "Good morning," "Good afternoon," "Good evening" or "How are you?" are common greetings for even those family members who see each other daily and have already seen each other during the day. Shaking hands between family members is usually done only when meeting after a long time or when saying good-bye. Family members also hug and embrace each other, as well as hold hands, etc., during times of sadness (such as a funeral) or at other special occasions.

NOTE: Americans often hug or shake hands when congratulating each other.

The type of physical contact adult family members have with one another may also depend on the family relationship, particularly the gender. For example, when greeting his mother a son might hug and kiss her, but when greeting his father, a son might only shake hands. Or a son may hug and kiss both parents. Depending on their cultural heritage, American men in general might be less physically affectionate towards other men, while American women might show physical affection for both men and women. Hugging and kissing may occur at every meeting, and in both greeting and parting. **Siblings** quite often both hug and kiss each other or at least hug. Whether you hug and kiss children depends on family custom. As you can see, there can be a variety of behaviors. We summarize the general social expectations for you below:

Between women: hugging, a kiss on the cheek, shaking hands, no physical contact.

Between men: shaking hands, a slap on the shoulder, sometimes hugging.

Between women and men: a nod, shaking hands, sometimes hugging, sometimes a kiss on the cheek.

In American families, there is a hierarchy of relationships, but it is less strict than the Korean hierarchy. For example, Americans show respect for older relatives in other ways than how they greet them. That is, they ideally hold doors open for senior citizens (over 60 years of age) or use polite terms such as "ma'am" or "sir."

This is also true of showing respect for someone in authority, such as a boss or teacher. In general, Americans show affection first and respect in the relationship second. But greetings are important. A greeting is primarily a way to display affection and to acknowledge the presence of one another in a **courteous** manner. It is impolite not to greet someone — it is known as a "snub" — but it can be common not to announce a departure or say "Good-bye."

Korean Ways

You will find that there is less variety in the ways adult family members greet or part from one another in Korea than in the U.S. In addition, Korea's social stratification, which prescribes specific roles and behaviors, strongly affects the types of behaviors expected from family members when greeting or when interacting with other family members.

Korean family relationships according to the family hierarchy are quite complex, and so describing the various appropriate behaviors is also complex.

NOTE: It is difficult to describe general American behaviors because of the great cultural diversity in the U.S. It is difficult to describe general Korean behaviors because of the complexity of relationships.

There is a formal and ritualistic quality to most Korean greetings and leavetakings. In general, Koreans use greetings not only to acknowledge the presence of others and to acknowledge their relationship with a person, but also to acknowledge their own position in the social hierarchy as well.

This is not to say that Koreans are always formal with other family members in every situation. But it is true that even among family members, Koreans can seem quite formal (to an American observer), and this is because of prescribed behaviors related to age, social position, gender, and many other factors.

AMERICAN / KOREAN CONTRAST

In the U.S., greetings reflect the feelings of the individuals toward each other. While they are vehicles of politeness and good manners, they are also ways of showing affection for others. They do not by themselves represent the person's position in the family hierarchy. This type of respect for family members is displayed in other ways in addition to a greeting. On the other hand, in Korea greetings are essential expressions of politeness and good manners as determined by the person's position in the family and social hierarchy. In fact, there are certain prescribed ways to greet family members — especially those older than you — which are symbols of respect. In these relationships, physical contact such as shaking hands (primarily among men) may exist as well. The greeting and the parting take on a formality and importance that exceed that in the U.S.

What Koreans Say

What Koreans say to each other in greeting depends on the nature of the relationship and how recently they have seen each other. Often, the family member will ask if the other has eaten. This is a polite question comparable to "How are you?" and although it can be answered with "yes" or "no," it should not be interpreted literally. That is, one should not expect a meal or a suggestion of going for food after being asked "Have you eaten?"

AMERICAN / KOREAN CONTRAST

When Americans ask "Have you eaten?", it is generally an invitation to eat or to find out if a meal needs to be cooked. When Koreans ask "Have you eaten?," it is a general polite greeting and not a request for information. It is usually not an invitation to eat.

Among family and friends, Koreans usually say "*orae kanmanieyo*" [오래간만이에요] ('A long time has passed since I've seen you) if weeks or months have passed since last they saw each other. They also comment on appearance, sometimes negatively. For example, Korean family members may tell each other "You are too fat." Korean family members or friends rarely tell each other "I love you" when parting. Instead, they will tell each other to be careful of their health, *momjosim haseyo* [몸조심 하세요] or to work hard, *sugohaseyo* [수고하세요]. Koreans say this good wish in addition to or instead of "good-bye," *annyŏngh'i kaseyo* [안녕히 가세요].

The Korean language reflects the strict hierarchy of Korean relationships. So, the relationship of the individuals determines the way Koreans speak to each other and their choice of words. For example, the Korean language contains an honorific term, *nim* [님], which is attached to a person's title. Furthermore, there is another honorific title, *ssi* [씨], which is attached to a given name or a full name. Specific words which refer to daily items or activities may vary according to the relationship of the individual. Verb endings also reflect this relationship. One example of these variations according to relationships is the following expression for "good-bye" which indicates that the people leaving are going somewhere, but returning:

(chal) kattawa [잘 갔다 와]: literally 'Go and come back well,' but with a plain ending. It is used by very close friends or by the older to the younger, especially to children. Teachers may speak to students using this form, or an office manager to an office worker, an older brother to a younger, a husband to a wife.

(chal) kattaoseyo [(잘) 갔다 오세요]: literally 'Go and come back well,' but with a polite verb ending (*oseyo*). Like *chal kattawa*, it is a familiar term used with someone of similar position or with a close friend who is older and requires respect. It is not as commonly used as *chal kattawa* or *chal tanyŏoseyo*.

(chal) tanyŏoseyo [(잘)다녀오세요] literally 'Go and come back well.' This term is used by children to parents, by a younger brother to an older brother, by students to teachers, or by a wife to a husband.

josimhae tanyŏoseyo [조심해 다녀오세요]: literally 'Go and come back carefully.' This is a familiar, informal term used for close friends and businessmen who know each other well. It is also used by a superior to an underling. When the relationship is more deferential, then the expression *josim haseyo* [조심하세요] literally 'Be careful' is used.

[See the glossary at the end of this section for a list of terms for family members and for honorifics.]

What Koreans Do

In general, when adult Koreans meet another family member after a long separation, they may be very **demonstrative**. Koreans may cry and shout and otherwise display emotion and affection, especially women or mothers and children, and embrace each other. They may rub the other's cheek in affection. Adult Korean family members generally do not kiss one another, but they do kiss children and show much physical affection to them.

NOTE: Korean family members may be very affectionate when greeting each other after a long absence. But Korean married couples may be very reserved in how they greet each other. They may simply nod respectfully to each other and save physical expressions of greetings until they are alone.

Although adult Korean family members can be very demonstrative after a long separation or very demonstrative with children, you probably will not see such signs of affection on a daily basis. Koreans do hold hands with family members or even drape an arm around another family member's shoulders, but there are restrictions to such behaviors according to one's position in a family. For example, a parent may put an arm around the adult child, but the adult child does not initiate this gesture. In everyday greetings, Koreans emphasize showing respect according to one's position in the family. Generally, Koreans show this respect and personal acknowledgment in the form of a bow. This bow can be a deep bow at the waist, or it can be a gentle, quick movement forward of the head and shoulders. The degree of the bow depends on the family relationship and many other factors, such as the occasion.

NOTE: Koreans have specific bows for showing special honor and obedience. The 'large bow' (*k'ŭnchŏl* [큰절]) consists of sitting on the floor with legs crossed, lifting the back of the hands to the forehead, and then bending over to touch the palms of the hands on the floor. This bow is performed by the bride at weddings. At all other times, the woman's *k'ŭnchŏl* consists of kneeling on the right knee, placing the palms of the hands flat on the floor next to the knees. The woman then bows at the waist with eyes downcast and head slightly tilted forward. The *k'ŭnchŏl* performed by men consists of lifting the hands over the head while in the standing position, bringing them down as he comes down in a kneeling position on both knees. The man then places his palms down on the floor above his knees with his hands turned inwards. He bows over and touches his forehead to the back of his hands. This *k'ŭnchŏl* is performed by the groom at his wedding, as well as at funerals, and to parents or someone else of respect after long separations. It is also performed at *chesa* (ancestor worship) and on specific holidays.

In order to show respect to their elders or to someone of higher status, Koreans may bow formally (a deep bow at the waist). They may even sit on the floor and bow. Younger **siblings** may bow formally to older siblings. In Korea, the older person or the one of higher status — whether it be parent, uncle, or older sibling — determines the degree of familiarity in a relationship. The older person also initiates this familiarity. On a daily basis, Koreans do not generally hug, kiss, or shake hands in greeting or in parting from other family members. When someone of lesser status leaves a room in parting from someone of higher status, the person of lesser status backs out of the room. It would be impolite to turn one's back on the one of superior status.

AMERICAN / KOREAN CONTRAST

In the U.S., when someone treats you informally or familiarly, it is a sign that you can treat them the same way. In Korea, the older person or the person of higher status may be at liberty to be familiar and informal, but it would be rude for the younger person or person of lower status to reciprocate. Older persons can be familiar because of the authority of their status; younger persons do not have that authority.

In general, Korean men bow slightly among family; they may shake hands among extended family. (In recent years, some younger Korean men only shake hands.) When shaking hands, the individual often will clasp his left hand onto his right wrist or forearm as he extends it for the shake. Sometimes, a parent or older sibling (male or female) may embrace (hug) the younger, but the elder person always initiates the embrace. Korean women usually bow. They almost never shake hands with men or with other women.

NOTE: Korean family relationships follow a strict hierarchy that is based on Confucian principles, and the terminology to identify different relationships is quite complex. Furthermore, there are expected and appropriate behaviors according to each relationship. The following is a list of some of the terms identifying family relationships. The list is not exhaustive. We provide it to give you an indication of the complexity of relationships.

Terms for Korean Immediate Family Relationships

haraböji [할아버지] Grandfather. This term is also applied to any aged male. It can also be used by friends for each others' grandfathers.

halmŏni [할머니] Grandmother. This term is also applied to any aged female. It can also be used by friends for each others' grandmothers.

aböji [아버지] Father. This term can be applied not only to one's own father, but also to the fathers of close friends.

ŏmŏni [어머니] Mother. This term can be applied not only to one's own mother, but also to the mothers of close friends.

hyŏng [형]: An older brother of a male. This term can be used between close friends as well as to signal that one is older than the other, and thus has the responsibilities inherent in one's position as an older brother. Similarly, the younger friend must follow a certain code of behavior as well.

oppa [오빠]: An older brother of a female. This term can be used between close friends as well as to signal that one is older than the other, and thus has the responsibilities inherent in one's position as an older brother. Similarly, the younger friend must follow a certain code of behavior as well.

nuna [누나] An older sister of a male. This term can be used between close friends as well as to signal that one is older than the other, and thus has the responsibilities inherent in one's position as an older sister. Similarly, the younger friend must follow a certain code of behavior as well.

ŏnni [언니] An older sister of a female. This term can be used between close friends as well as to signal that one is older than the other, and thus has the responsibilities inherent in one's position as an older sister. Similarly, the younger friend must follow a certain code of behavior as well.

tongsaeng [동생] A younger sister or brother of either a male or female. A younger sister is specified by *yŏja tongsaeng* [여자동생] (literally: 'girl younger sibling'); a younger brother with *namja tongsaeng* [남자동생] (literally: 'boy younger sibling').

k'ŭn abŏji [큰아버지] Paternal uncles who are older brothers to the father. When referring to the person, the uncle's family position is marked by adding "first, second, etc." before the title.

jakŭn abŏji [작은아버지]: Married paternal uncles who are younger brothers to the father. When referring to the person, this uncle's family position is marked by adding "first, second, etc." before the title.

samch'on [삼촌] Unmarried paternal uncles who are younger brothers to the father.

woe samch'on [외삼촌] Maternal uncles. Older and younger brothers to the mother.

komo [고모] Father's sister. If there are older sisters, the oldest is called *k'ŭn komo* [큰 고모] ('big aunt'), the second oldest is called *dultchae komo* [둘째 고

모] ('second aunt'), etc. A younger sister is called *jakŭn komo* ('little aunt'). The husband of the father's sister is called *komobu* [고모부]('paternal aunt's husband'(*bu* means 'man' or 'husband')). The wife of the father's older brother is called *k'ŭn ŏmŏni* [큰 어머니] ('big mother'); the wife of the younger brother *jakŭn ŏmŏni* [작은 어머니] ('little mother').

imo [이모]: Mother's sister. The husband of the mother's sister is call *imobu* [이모부] ('maternal aunt's husband'). The wife of the mother's brothers is called *sukmo* [숙모].

sach'on [사촌]: Cousins. Paternal cousins are called *kojong sach'on* [고종 사촌]; maternal cousins *ijong sach'on* [이종사촌].

In-Laws

siabŏji [시아버지] Father-in-law.

siŏmŏni [시어머니] Mother-in-law.

maehyŏng [매형] Older sister's husband.

maeje [매제] Younger sister's husband.

ch'ŏje [처제] Wife's younger sister.

ch'ŏhyŏng [처형] Wife's older sister.

sŏbangnim [서방님] Husband's brother. The older brother is *k'ŭn sŏbangnim* [큰 서방님]; the younger *jakŭn sŏbangnim* [작은 서방님].

hyŏngsunim [형수님] Older brother's wife.

siajubŏnim [시아주버님] Husband's brothers.

jesussi [제수씨] Younger brother's wife.

Other

sŏnsaeng(nim) [선생(님)]: Teacher. This term is a term of respect given not only to teachers, but to anyone in a position that requires honor and respect from another, including family friends. This can be used as a general polite term (attached to the family name if it is known) when addressing someone unfamiliar.

nim [님] An honorific particle which is attached to the end of some titles (such as *hyŏng, nuna,* and *sŏnsaeng*) and which indicates respect.

ssi [씨] A particle attached to the ends of given names which indicates respect. It is normally not used between close friends.

Koreans generally do not call each other by their first names, (but they can be referred to in the third person by the first name, depending on the relationship). Family members usually refer to each other by their family relationship. For example, a Korean man may address his younger sister as *tongsaeng* [동생], and use this term when referring to her to a third person. If there are several younger sisters, the brother may identify each one by her location, such as Seoul *tongsaeng* (the younger sister who lives in Seoul), or some other signification, such as *jakŭn tongsaeng* [작은동생], (the younger of two younger sisters). Another way to refer to younger brothers or sisters is to use their first names plus *a* [아] (literally 'child').

NOTE: In families, married women are usually identified in the third person by being the mother of their oldest child, using a shortened form of the word mother, *ŏmma,* e.g. *Duk-Hee ŏmma* [덕희 엄마]. Neighbors usually will not know a woman neighbor's name unless they ask for it specifically.

How do friends greet and part from one another?

American Ways

As in most cultures, there is a loose hierarchy or classification among adult American friendships: **casual friends, social friends, family friends, close friends,** and **business friends.** Often the type of friendship determines how people greet and part from one another, as does cultural heritage, personal preference, and the situation.

NOTE: Some individuals have developed their own style of greeting, regardless of the person being greeted or the situation.

One popular personal style is to shake hands and kiss both cheeks when greeting a person, regardless of their relationship (for women and women or men and women.).

Both close friends and social friends might hug each other when either greeting or parting. Sometimes women or women and men kiss one another on the cheek as do women and men. Casual friends, social friends, and business friends often shake hands, but this can also be true of family and close friends — it depends on the individual preference of those involved, especially if it is two men. At a large gathering, friends may sometimes wave at each other across a room as a greeting. Casual friends may simply nod toward each other. Sometimes there is no physical gesture that shows acknowledgment at all.

As you can see, there is no specifically prescribed behavior for how friends greet one another, except that they be courteous. Friends may or may not be affectionate to each other both in greeting and leavetaking, depending on the nature of the friendship and of the individual. Furthermore, some friends purposely are not courteous with each other as a joke. Below, we give you a general description of common ways of greeting according to gender:

women and women: acquaintances nod or shake hands; close friends and family friends hug and sometimes kiss each other on the cheek; business friends may shake hands.

men and men: men generally shake hands, or shake hands and slap each other on the back or shoulder. Very close friends may hug each other. Hugging between men has gradually become more common since the 1960s.

women and men: casual, social, and business friends most commonly nod to one another or shake hands. Close friends normally hug one another and may kiss each other on the cheek or beside the mouth.

AMERICAN / KOREAN CONTRAST

The U.S. has a **homophobic** culture, and so there are limitations on physical contact with the same gender. That is, although women may kiss each other on the cheek, men generally do not kiss other men. Friends of the same gender — especially men — generally do not hold hands with one another, drape arms over each other's shoulders, or otherwise hug each other when sitting together. On the other hand, Korea does not have a homophobic culture. Physical affection is regularly shown in public and private between the same gender: women regularly hold hands with other women, and men hold hands with other men. However, women and men do not generally hold hands in public or otherwise show physical affection. While this has changed over the last twenty years, it is still not socially acceptable to publicly demonstrate such affection between the genders.

Casual friends are friends who may meet each other occasionally or participate in social activities together. They generally do not share personal information with each other and do not have a close emotional bond. However, depending on the area of the country and the nature of the gathering, they may hug each other when greeting or when saying goodbye or they may shake hands. Sometimes a hug when saying goodbye is a sign that the friendship may be getting closer.

Social friends are friends who may go to parties together or meet only at parties. They may like and enjoy one another but not have a personal commitment to one another or discuss personal matters. When greeting or saying goodbye, they may hug, shake hands or merely nod at each other.

AMERICAN / KOREAN CONTRAST

In the U.S., Americans consider using first names as a step toward informality, and even intimacy. On the other hand, in Korea using first names may be considered rude unless the individuals have a close personal history, such as being high school classmates. However, Koreans who interact with Westerners or Americans will often adopt the American custom of using first names.

Family friends are friends to an entire family and participate in family activities although they are not related by blood. They may greet and part from the family members as a member of the family would — with hugs, kisses, and handshakes — or they may be more limited in their behavior. The behavior of family friends in these situations depends on the individual.

Close friends are friends who share a personal commitment to one another and share personal information. They may meet the friends' family, and share in family activities. They often show physical affection toward one another in the forms of hugs, hand-holding (for women), or kisses upon greeting and leavetaking. As stated, however, all of the behaviors of friends depends on the gender of the friends, their cultural heritage, and personal preference.

Business friends are people you know through your employment or profession. They can often be social friends, but their greetings and leavetakings are often more formal. They will involve handshakes, but no other physical contact. There is a friendly distance to American business friends although people who meet through business can choose to become friends on a more personal level.

There are other terms used to describe non-family relationships as well, including: **good friend**, **best friend**, and **acquaintance**.

Korean Ways

As in the U.S., there is a hierarchy or classification among adult Korean friendships; for example, acquaintance, friend, close friend, or business friend. However, friendships take on an importance in Korea that they do not have in the U.S. Friendships may develop gradually over time, but often they can be established by simply stating or asking someone to be your friend. Once Koreans become friends, they may have certain expectations of one another that American friends do not: Friendship is one of the five basic Confucian relationships. As one of these valued relationships, the loyalty inherently expected in a Korean friendship may last a lifetime.

AMERICAN / KOREAN CONTRAST

American and Korean expectations of friendship differ. Americans do not expect a lot of commitment from friends. You may find them very friendly, but uncommitted to you as a person. For this reason, you may think they are shallow or insincere. "I'll call you" or "Let's get together" are general statements of friendliness, not promises. Koreans, on the other hand, take friendships very seriously, and may want to meet you regularly and frequently if you are establishing a friendship with them.

How Korean friends greet or part from each other is in accordance with the hierarchic nature of Korean society. The prescribed behaviors, distinctions, and obligations according to status, age, and gender apply to friends as well as to family. Therefore, you may have difficulty becoming friends with someone significantly older than you or with someone of another gender. Futhermore Koreans retain the formalities in language even among close friends, depending on the age and status of the friends (more respect is shown to the older friend, even if the person is older only by a few months), but they also display affection.

Indeed, you will find that sometimes Koreans show more affection to their friends when greeting or leavetaking than they do with family members because the stratification is not as strict among friends as with family. In general, Korean friends do not kiss one another or hug when greeting, but some of these behaviors are becoming more common as a result of Western influence. Normally, men slightly bow at the waist or shoulders and shake hands. Women may take the other's hand. Very often, these are combined: male friends may shake hands while bowing to each other in greeting or in parting.

Male friends may also slap each other on the back, bow and shake hands, or take each other's hand and hold it. They may stand arm in arm or with a hand around the other's waist or shoulder. Female friends, too, may bow, take the other's hand and hold it, or stand arm-in-arm or with a hand around the waist. Male and female friends, however, maintain a formal distance from one another, restricting their physical contact to bowing or shaking hands. Friends of all levels of intensity normally bow or shake hands when leavetaking.

We distinguish behavior among friends according to gender for you below:

women and women: acquaintances, friends, and close friends nod or bow slightly; they might also take the other person's arm or hand in theirs. (If the Korean woman is familiar with Western customs and has developed a friendship with a Westerner, she may hug.) Business friends may shake hands. It is becoming more common in recent years for Korean women to shake hands, but it is still considered unusual.

men and men: acquaintances and friends may bow while shaking hands; close friends bow or shake hands or shake hands and slap each other on the back or shoulder. There is little hugging between Korean men.

women and men: In general, friendships between women and men are not as common in Korea as in the West. Male and female friends will normally nod to one another or bow. The younger generation may shake hands, but the older generation will not. There is no kissing and seldom is there hugging.

In American society, there is little segregation between men and women. Men and women work together and socialize together. Men and women also show affection in public. In Korean society, on the other hand, there is still a great deal of segregation between men and women, especially when it comes to touching. However, Korean society does not have the homophobic tendencies as does American society, and so there is touching among the same gender. It is quite common for friends of the same sex, both men and women, to hold hands, or to drape an arm around the other's shoulder. This is true not just for close friends, but for general friends as well.

The following are the Korean terms for the level of friendships:

anŭn saram [아는 사람] Acquaintance or casual friend.

ch'ingu [친구] Friend, which can be a casual friend, a social friend, or a close friend.

ch'inhan ch'ingu [친한 친구] A close friend.

Family friends and other close friends often use family hierarchical terms to refer to each other, e.g. big brother or sister or little brother or sister. They may also use terms according to their ranking at school or university, such as "elder classman" (*sŏnbae* [선배]) or "younger classman" (*hubae* [후배]).[1]

What are some general leavetaking customs in the U.S and Korea?

In both the U.S. and Korea, when greeting and parting the degree and amount of bowing, handshaking, and formal leavetaking depends on the level of the relationship, and sometimes on the situation. In the U.S., there are also regional variations, especially in the South, which is known for its hospitality and manners. You may find that there are some similarities in expectations between American and Korean customs in our summary:

American Ways

1) Most Americans will "**see you to the door**," but not walk out to the car or street with a guest or even a family member, unless that person is leaving on a long trip. Goodbyes can be casual, such as a wave of the hand when someone is leaving. In the South, people often stand a long time at the door and talk before leaving. They also often walk the person to the car or to the road if the person is walking.

2) "**You can see yourself out**," and "**You know where the door is**" are generally impolite expressions. However, "I'll see myself out," and "You don't have to come out with me" are courteous, and tell the host/hostess to stay seated where he/she is comfortable.

Korean Ways

1) The host in a home usually walks the person to the door, to a car, or out onto the street. He/she stands until the person has driven or walked away. If a guest does not want the host to do that, the guest must tell the host, sometimes repeatedly, not to do it. This allows both people to save face in the situation and still conform to conventions of hospitality.

2) When Koreans separate in a restaurant or coffee shop, if one is remaining that person may get up and walk the departing person to the door or out onto the street. You must tell friends or family members to remain seated if you do not wish them to see you to the door. Ideally, you leave together.

3) When Koreans separate on the street, one will often go to the bus stop with the other and wait before going to his/her own stop. If they separate, they make a point of telling each other where they are going (often repeatedly) and offering and declining to wait with the other person. This interplay is quite important, as it shows respect for the other person.

How do stranges greet and part from one another?

There are two ways to understand the word "stranger." A stranger can be someone unknown to you that you pass on the street or a stranger can be someone you are meeting for the first time. We address both of these situations in this section.

In general, Americans and Koreans have different perspectives on how to treat others they do not have a personal relationship with. That is, they have different concepts of courtesy. In both countries, rules of common courtesy have changed since the 1960s. For this reason, courtesy toward strangers may differ between generations. However, rules for meeting someone for the first time have remained fairly constant. Courtesy toward strangers can also be situation dependent.

American Ways

On the street

You may find that Americans are very friendly. Americans generally smile at or nod to each other when passing on the street. Sometimes, they even say "Hello" or "Good morning," (depending on the time of day) or comment on the weather.

NOTE: Americans in small towns are usually friendlier than those in large cities such as New York, where the people may be more **gruff**. But the United States is a collection of small towns and cities, with only a few large cities in each state (and in the Midwest, West and Southwest the largest cities may have less than 100,000 inhabitants), and so the friendly gestures of smiling, nodding, or a verbal greeting such as "Hi" or "Good morning" are generally common.

You may find that when Americans stand next to each other in a line, they may also engage in small talk, even though they do not know each other. Americans consider such greetings a sign of respect for others, regardless of whether they know them personally. This is a general, courteous friendliness which you may find superficial because it generally is not an invitation to friendship. Small talk also occurs in restaurants or while waiting for a bus. Similarly, Americans generally value helpfulness to strangers as well.

In a room, such as a large meeting room

When Americans enter a room where others are already seated, they usually prefer to be quiet and unobtrusive. When Americans go alone into a meeting or a meeting room, they often look around to see if they know someone. If they do know someone, they might greet that person with a nod of the head or a quiet "Hello." Depending on how well they know that person, they might go and sit with him or her. It is acceptable, however, if one enters and does not look around and merely goes to an available seat. When leaving such a gathering, Americans may simply leave without saying goodbye to anyone, stand and talk about the meeting with someone, or make small talk. Finally, one person may look at his or her watch and say, "Well, I've got to get back. See you around," and leave.

AMERICAN / KOREAN CONTRAST

When Americans arrive late for a meeting, the ideal is to quietly open the door and enter. This avoids disturbing others who have arrived on time. When Koreans arrive late for a meeting, they may either knock on the door or stand outside the door until they are noticed and invited to enter.

When meeting for the first time

At a party or a meeting, it is common for Americans to introduce themselves to each other. To start the introduction, they often say "I don't believe we've met" or "Let me introduce myself." When introduced, Americans usually say "It's nice to meet you," introduce themselves, and then try to find interests, experiences, or people that they have in common.

NOTE: If two strangers have met while waiting in line, they may begin to make small talk, and then find that they like each other. At this point, they may introduce themselves to each other. However, it is also common to have a long discussion with someone without an introduction and then part.

When meeting for the first time, Americans often shake hands after the introduction. While women often shake hands both with other women or with men, women are expected to offer their hand first when meeting a man for the first time. This has been changing, however, and since the 1960s varies from person to person. When two new acquaintances part, they often shake hands again, or nod and say "It was nice to meet you."

Korean Ways

On the street

Koreans do not have the customs or expectations of superficial friendly courtesy that Americans have, and so at first you may think that Koreans are unfriendly. Koreans do not acknowledge strangers on the street at all. That is, they generally do not greet strangers on the street with a smile or nod. Koreans value relationships, and so do not acknowledge you until you have established some sort of relationship with them.

For this reason, many American visitors to Korea often comment on how unfriendly the Koreans are until one gets to know them. This is often because Koreans do not offer the kind of courtesy to strangers on the street that Americans are accustomed to, i.e. they don't smile or nod at strangers or say "excuse me" when bumping into you. You may even be put off by Koreans pointing at you, laughing in your presence, or using English expressions out of context.

NOTE: Koreans may acknowledge foreigners on the street by saying "Hello" or some other phrase they have learned from English class, television, or the movies. This is not a greeting; rather, it is a way to point out that you are a foreigner. In general, Koreans are sometimes hesitant to have a conversation or otherwise speak to foreigners because of the language barrier. On the other hand, ambitious students of English may speak to you because they want to practice language. In these cases, the general rules of etiquette regarding strangers do not apply because you are a foreigner.

In general, Koreans avoid looking at a stranger or drawing attention to themselves in public. Koreans may understand eye contact or a smile on a bus as a challenge. Thus, when Koreans pass a stranger on the street or in a hallway, they generally will not look at each other. One exception to this tendency is the treatment of the elderly, who generally are greeted by a bow. However, respect for the aged has diminished since the 1970s and '80s. (This can be seen by the reduction of such outward signs of respect for senior citizens as automatically giving up one's seat on a bus, etc.)

AMERICAN / KOREAN CONTRAST

Americans often greet strangers that they pass on the street or engage in small talk while waiting in lines, etc. Koreans do not acknowledge those whom they have not met, and so do not greet strangers on the street or engage in small talk while in line. Both Americans and Koreans will avoid eye contact with strangers.

In a room, such as a large meeting room

Koreans often avoid going alone to meetings or to new places, and thus avoid the situation of being alone at such meetings. When Koreans are late, they often wait outside the door until they are noticed and then invited into the room. If they are not noticed, then they knock before entering. When they enter such a room, they may bow to the whole room several times while uttering a modest *mianhamnida* [미안합니다] ('I am sorry') or *sillyehamnida / choesonghamnida* [실례합니다/죄송합니다] ('Excuse me'). The Koreans already present in the room will likely take responsibility for accepting the person into the room and finding him/her a seat, depending on the person's relationship to the others. The Korean entering will in turn not look around the room, but quietly accept a place while still assuming a modest posture.

When meeting for the first time

Koreans do not commonly introduce themselves to strangers; they need a third party introduction.

NOTE: Koreans may introduce themselves to foreigners because many of the social boundaries do not apply to foreigners.

When Koreans are introduced to someone new, they usually bow formally. Men may then shake hands, depending on the age and status of the other person, but women generally do not shake hands. When introduced, Koreans say *ch'ŏŭm boepsŭmnida* [처음 뵙습니다] ('I am meeting you for the first time'), and when they part they say *mannasŏ bangapsŭmnida* [만나서 반갑습니다] ('I am glad because I have met you'). Koreans generally do not engage in small talk before an introduction.

After the introduction, Koreans find out information about each other that will help guide them to know the appropriate behavior for the situation and relationship (such as age, profession, marital status, etc.). Koreans generally call all senior citizens *harabŏji* [할아 버지] ('grandfather') or *halmŏni* [할머니] ('grandmother'). They call people older than themselves, but not past middle age *ajŏssi* [아저 씨] ('uncle') or *ajumŏni* [아주머니] ('aunt') if no other specific relationship has been established. If they are greeting people with known higher status, they may call them *sŏnsaengnim* [선생님] ('teacher'). Young women are called *agassi* [아가씨] ('miss'). Students are called *haksaeng* [학생] ('student') rather than by their first names.

NOTE: Koreans address foreigners with Mr., Miss, Dr., etc. as a sign of respect. However, when Koreans call each other by the titles of Mr., Miss, etc., it is not as an honorific. It is to signify their distinct status. For example, an office manager at a company will call his employees Mr. Kim or Miss Park, etc.

AMERICAN / KOREAN CONTRAST

When Americans first meet someone, they may comment on something the person is wearing as a way to start the conversation. For example, they may say "I like your shoes. Where did you get them?" They, rarely, however, comment on the person's overall appearance. If Americans say such things as "You are an attractive woman" or "You are a handsome man," etc., it is usually a "come-on," that is, a sign of physical attraction. On the other hand, when Koreans meet they may comment on clothing, but only as a means of generous flattery, not as a conversation starter. Koreans may very openly comment on another's appearance even when they are meeting for the first time.

How do customers and shopowners greet and part from one another?

Americans and Koreans both value congeniality and respect in all relationships, including when shopping. They each have different customs and expectations of how to interpret congeniality and respect, however.

American Ways

For Americans, there is an expectation that "the customer is king," i.e. that the shopkeeper should take care of the customer. Americans also have a saying that "The customer is always right." Therefore, American shopkeepers, clerks, or **cashiers** may be very friendly to the customer, and even engage in small talk. This is especially true when the customer is paying for a purchase. For example, customers and clerks may talk about the weather or families, or make general comments about work or prices, etc. This is considered genial, courteous interaction and reflects the **egalitarian** attitude inherent in American culture. Shopkeepers also want to maintain a friendly relationship so that the customer will return.

Because American shopkeepers or clerks value and respect the customer, they do not hover over or pressure the customer. Usually a shopkeeper or clerk may ask "May I help you," and then expect a factual reply. A factual reply might be "No, thank you. I'm just **browsing**," or "Yes, please. I am looking for (something)." If the shop does not have the item, the clerk may offer to order it for you. Sometimes they will direct you to another shop that offers that item.

In the U.S., shopkeepers will not be aggressively helpful. Instead, they offer help and then wait for the customer to reply or seek out help. Shopkeepers and customers are both addressed as **sir** (men), **ma'am** (women), or **miss** (young women). When a customer leaves, a shopkeeper or clerk will often say, "Thank you. Come again." You may see signs saying this on the shop wall or door as well. If the shop is small and the shopowner, clerk, or cashier is present when the customer is leaving, the customer may say "Goodbye," "Thank you," or "Have a nice day" when you leave.

NOTE: Shopkeepers and clerks behave differently according to the size and type of store. The owner or employee of a small store or specialty shop may be more solicitous of customers and generally pay more attention to them than the employees of a large department store might. In recent years, large department stores have reduced the number of clerks who walk around the store to help customers, and so the customer may have to actively seek out a clerk. Furthermore, in the U.S. of the 1990's, many department stores hire young, inexperienced employees who work part-time. These employees often do not know how to deal with the public, and so may not be solicitous or helpful to the customer. They may also not know how to handle difficult situations.

Korean Ways

For Koreans, there is an expectation that "the customer is king," i.e. that the shopkeeper should take care of the customer. Therefore, Korean shopkeepers, clerks, or cashiers may be very friendly to and solicitous of the customer, and even engage in small talk. But, it is important that the customer be courteous to the shopkeeper as well since their status on the social hierarchy may be involved.

You will find many family-owned small shops and specialty stores in Korea, although since the 1970s large department stores have also become more common throughout the country. In small shops, both the owner or clerk and the customer may greet each other with *annyŏnghaseyo*? [안녕하세요] ('Hello'), and say *annyŏnghi kaseyo* [안녕히 가세요] ('Goodbye') or *tto oseyo* [또 오세요] ('Come again') when the customer leaves. Or, very often, the shopkeeper may say nothing. In department stores, there may be greeters who bow to the customers and welcome them to the store. There are also many clerks in the different departments who are there to help the customer. As in the U.S., they most often ask customers if they need assistance and then retreat if the customers say they are just looking.

However, you may discover that Korean shopkeepers can be aggressively helpful, even rude by American expectations. That is, the shopkeeper may constantly stay with you, show you many items from the shop you have not asked to see, or aggressively try to persuade you to buy something. If you are shopping in a location that is not frequented by foreigners, you may receive a lot of special attention. You may find this personal attention very helpful or you may find it oppressive. It will vary from shop to shop.

In general, you can call shopkeepers, clerks, or cashiers *ajŏsi* [아저씨] ('uncle') or *ajumŏni* [아주머니] ('aunt'). A young female clerk may also be called *agassi* [아가씨] ('miss'). You may also be able to engage in friendly conversation (especially if you are a frequent customer), but as a foreigner be prepared to answer a lot of questions about yourself.

NOTE: Koreans generally engage in conversation with shopkeepers as a way to establish a relationship before beginning to bargain. Except in department and grocery stores, you can expect to be able to bargain for a price reduction at most shops and in the market place.

The customer often nods his/her head in greeting upon entering or leaving a shop, but does not bow. The shopkeeper or clerk may bow (especially greeters at department stores) both when a customer enters and leaves, or they may make no gesture at all.

How do business associates greet and part from one another?

American Ways

Americans are individualistic, and so American businesses each have different practices of formality and familiarity in greeting and leavetaking. Each company may have its own particular work atmosphere that it encourages. For this reason, it is difficult for us to describe one specific way in which all American business colleagues greet and part from one another. It is also difficult because the customs and expectations vary according to whether people work closely together or seldom have contact. It also varies according to whether individuals are employed at the same company or work for different companies and are only doing business together. Despite these variables, we believe we can make some generalizations that can guide you in your interactions with American business colleagues.

When greeting or parting, American business associates generally follow the same rules of courtesy as they do with casual friends or with strangers. That is, when meeting, they will likely shake hands and make small talk. When parting, they may say "Well, see you later," say nothing at all, or repeat the details of plans to meet again. If they work closely together, they may talk about the next day's work hours or simply chat as close friends would do. Associates may be very informal and relaxed with one another especially in terms of the language they use. This is true even with **superiors**. Employees and colleagues often call each other by their **first names**. In some circumstances, they call their superiors by their first names as well.

AMERICAN / KOREAN CONTRAST

Americans expect formality to lessen with familiarity and/or affection. For example, bosses may suggest you call them by their first name after you have worked with them for a while. Americans believe this familiarity and informality helps promote a relaxed and comfortable work environment. Koreans, on the other hand, maintain the formality of language and behavior despite familiarity. The formality is determined by your hierarchical status, not by familiarity. To the Korean, a relaxed and comfortable work environment will depend on maintaining *ch'emyŏn*, usually through meeting expectations and fulfilling one's role within the hierarchy.

Americans may have either a formal or informal relationship with superiors, depending on the individuals involved. Often, superiors may tell employees to call them by their first name. This may be in order to establish an informal or more relaxed working atmosphere or to show that a working relationship has become closer and more trusting. Associates may also give each other permission to call each other by their first names if the relationship began as a formal one. Often, an employee or associate may ask for permission to call someone by his/her first name. For example: "May I call you (your name)?" Superiors may also be addressed as "Sir" or "Ma'am." Associates may refer to each other by titles such as "Mr." or "Ms."

AMERICAN / KOREAN CONTRAST

While there are specific approaches to addressing a person that signify respect, the calling of someone by his/her first name is not a sign of disrespect. To an American, respect is built into a position and determined by the person's behavior in a variety of situations. So, superiors and colleagues both must "earn respect." They do this by being informed and fair in their dealings with others and by doing their jobs well. On the other hand, in Korea, using someone's first name would be a great sign of disrespect. Korean businessmen with Western contact may use first names with Western clients, but it is because they are accommodating Western customs and expectations. American businessmen should never call a new Korean associate by his first name as a way of "breaking the ice."

Korean Ways

Koreans value congeniality and respect in all relationships, and especially in business. Within their strict social hierarchy, there are many formal restrictions or expectations of behavior among colleagues or superiors and employees. Colleagues who work at the same institution, may be extremely formal with each other in greeting and in leavetaking in both the degree of bowing they do and in the language they use. They will expect congeniality, but also a display of deference. They will show respect based on social position and age as well as on their working relationship. Below, we distinguish expected behavior in greeting and leavetaking according to two broad divisions in the Korean social hierarchy: with superiors and with colleagues.

NOTE: Business relationships reflect the Korean family and social hierarchy. For example, a new business contact might refer to another by the last name plus the deferential title *sŏnsaengnim* [선생님], e.g. *Kim sŏnsaengnim*. Koreans feel more comfortable calling a Westerner by a deferential title, too, and may hesitate when addressing a Westerner even by a title such as Mr. or Dr. because of the lack of the deferential affix *nim* at the end. When a Korean knows another person's job or position in a company, the Korean calls that person by that job or position's title, or by the family name plus the title, e.g. Kim *wonjangnim* [원장님] (literally: 'the honorable director Kim'), Kim *kwajangnim* [과장님] ('the honorable section chief Kim'), or Kim *bujangnim* [부장님] ('the honorable office chief Kim').

With a superior

A Korean employee may bow upon greeting the superior, and in a meeting remain standing until told to sit down. He may keep a slightly stooped position to show humility and deference. The superior may simply wave his hand to greet or dismiss the employee. As mentioned in a previous section, superiors call their workers by titles such as Mr. Kim or Miss Park, but this is only to signify gender or status, not respect.

With a colleague

The behavior of Korean colleagues toward one another varies according not only to their status within a company, but also according to various other predictors of status such as age, gender, or marital status. Colleagues want to maintain a congenial, harmonious atmosphere, and so often use terms and manners of respect with one another. When meeting or when parting, Koreans say the same things to colleagues as when they meet a friend or family member, depending on the age and status of the colleague.

Do greetings and farewells vary between women and men?

American Ways

American men and women may have different ways to greet or part from one another, depending on the region and individual preferences. You may see American men and women embrace each other when they greet one another or part. This is true not only of family and friends, but also among colleagues and people meeting for the first time. For example, in some encounters a man may kiss the woman's cheek as an appropriate greeting for a colleague, a casual or social friend, or a family member. Women may hug women, and men may hug men. However, because of homophobia, men and men do not embrace as readily as women and women do. Women often shake hands with men or hug them. The differences between men and women are most distinctive when they are meeting strangers. Women are generally more careful about who they will smile at or talk to. When a woman is alone in a restaurant or other place, she may avoid eye contact or not smile at a stranger because of a fear that it is an invitation to friendship or a "come on." If a man smiles at a woman he does not know, the woman may interpret it as an invitation to friendship.

Korean Ways

Korean men and women generally do not embrace in public when greeting or parting, even among families unless someone has recently returned from a long trip. In the 1990's, many young couples may hold hands or hug in public, but it is still not widely acceptable socially. This display of affection in front of parents or others who are older may even be considered disrespectful.

Korean men and women friends or colleagues maintain a distinct physical distance. They seldom shake hands and would never hug unless the woman was much older than the man and initiated the hug as a motherly gesture. However, women may be physically affectionate toward women, and men may be affectionate toward men. Men often bow to each other or shake hands. Koreans generally do not hug when greeting or parting. Korean men and women use similar language when greeting or parting.

How do greetings and farewells vary between generations?

American Ways

Americans do not make age distinctions as strictly as Koreans do. To an American, someone is only a senior citizen after the age of 60 or 65. Americans also do not have strict distinctions of behavior other than common politeness. Therefore, Americans of all ages may hug, shake hands, and kiss one another regardless of their age.

Korean Ways

The basic distinction between generations in ways of greeting and parting in Korea reflect the age hierarchy there. Koreans not only make strict age distinctions — even a few months makes a difference — but they also have a tradition of respect and value for those who are older, especially senior citizens. Even though the Korean younger generation of the 1990's may not respect their elders as much as their parents did, the Korean age hierarchy is still strong. Therefore, greetings and leavetakings will involve a great deal of bowing and formality between the older and the younger. When the elders initiate it, there may also be hugging or shaking of hands.

acquaintance Casual friend, social friend, or someone we have been introduced to and may have some type of interaction with but do not know well. For example, my friend introduced me to her friend. Now her friend is my acquaintance. Or, I talk to someone regularly at the gym. She is my acquaintance.

best friend The most intimate friend.

browse To "eye shop"; to look around the shop or store.

boundaries of the individual The necessary respect for privacy according to each person. If you have just met an American and ask personal questions such as age or salary, you are crossing the boundaries of the individual.

cashier The person to whom a customer pays money. In many stores, the clerk may also be the cashier.

casual friends People one knows, but not closely.

cheeks The sides of the face.

civility Behavior according to general rules of courtesy.

clerk A person who helps others in a department store or shop.

close friends Intimate friends; friends with whom one shares feelings.

colleagues The people one works with. It can also refer to others in the same profession that one has not yet met.

courteous Considerate of the feelings of others according to polite norms.

cultural heritage The culture of the country that one's ancestors came from. Since the U.S. is a nation created by immigrants, it is made up of diverse cultural heritages. Many Americans identify themselves by this cultural heritage; for example, Afro-Americans, Korean-Americans, Italian-Americans, etc.

demonstrative To show one's feelings openly.

egalitarian Seeing all people as equal.

embrace A hug from the front.

encounter To meet; come across.

ethnic origin Cultural heritage.

family friends Friends that become similar to a family member. They are usually close friends.

first names The given name.

gender Sex, i.e. male or female.

geniality Friendly; easy to get along with.

good friend Close friend.

greet To say "hello" to; welcome.

gruff Rough; not showing geniality or courtesy.

homophobic Having a prejudice against homosexuals.

hugging To place one's arms around the neck or body of another and hold them close for a short time. There are many types of hugs.

leavetakings Activities and expressions related to departure

modest posture To stand or present oneself in a way that is not boastful or is considered humble.

nodding To move one's head slightly downward and then back up once or twice. This can be done in acknowledgment of the presence of another or in agreement with another.

occasion Situation.

prescribed Dictated by rules.

siblings Brothers and sisters.

small talk Chit chat; talking about general topics such as the weather, schools, children, etc.

"see you to the door" To walk with someone to the door when that person is leaving.

slap someone on the shoulder To place one's hand the upper back of another. It is a common gesture of informality and friendship among American men.

snub To purposely not speak or interact with someone. It is considered rude behavior and implies a feeling of superiority on the part of the person who snubs.

specialty shop A shop that sells specific items, such as greeting cards, flowers, etc.

social friends People one associates with in social activities, such as church, but not outside that environment.

socially stratified To have separation among groups in a society based on class, age, gender, or other factors.

solicitous To offer help or service to others.

superiors Those in a higher position in a company or in social relationships.

sweetie A term of affection.

take their leave (formal term) Depart.

touchy-feely (slang) Someone who likes to hug or otherwise touch others when talking to them or greeting them. It is also a term that can be used to describe someone who wants to discuss emotions. It can be used negatively or positively.

"You can see yourself out" In the U.S., usually a rude term indicating the person should leave the room without courtesy

wave A lifting and moving from side to side of the arm with the hand at a 90 degree angle and the fingers outstretched.

Glossary of Korean Terms

ajŏssi [아저씨] A general term used for an older male, but not a relative. It literally translates to 'uncle,' and is used to refer to family friends as well as to shopkeepers and strangers.

annyŏnghaseyo? [안녕하세요] A common Korean greeting which means "Hello. How are you?"

annyŏnghi kaseyo [안녕히 가세요] A common Korean expression which means "Goodbye."

ch'ŏŭm boepsŭmnida [처음 뵙습니다]: A common Korean expression which means "I am meeting you for the first time."

mannasŏ bangapsŭmnida [만나서 반갑습니다] A common Korean expression which can mean either "I am glad to meet you" or "I am glad to have met you."

mianhamnida [미안합니다] A common apology which means "I am sorry."

mom josimhaseyo [몸 조심하세요] A common expression used when saying "Goodbye," especially to people you know. It means literally "Watch your health."

sillyehamnida [실례합니다] A common Korean apology, it can mean both "Excuse me" and "I'm sorry."

sugohaseyo [수고하세요] A common leavetaking, especially with those of lower status, it means literally "Work hard."

Notes

[1] Americans have an expression that says, "It's not what you do, but who you know." They mean by this that personal contacts are sometimes more important than personal qualifications. But it is a cynical statement which contradicts the American ideal that one's own achievements are more important than personal influence.

"It's not what you do, but who you know" can aptly be applied to Korean relationships. This explains the great importance Koreans place on creating and maintaining friendships and gradually testing the friendship to determine the level of trust one can have for another. While Americans may consciously avoid creating an obligation between friends, Koreans see obligation as a basis for friendship. The friendships a Korean develops through elementary, junior high, and high school, in college, in the military, or through other associations are maintained and nurtured through regular meetings. These personal associations are invaluable connections for getting employment, making loans, and seeking out information or help. R. Saccone, the author of *The Business of Korean Culture* (Seoul,

Korea: Hollym Corporation; Publishers, 1994, p. 27), provides a good summary of the contrast between American and Korean attitudes toward friendship:

> Be careful not to mistake politeness and hospitality for friendship. Koreans are gracious and friendly hosts, and their kind manner is often interpreted by Westerners as a sign of close friendship. This can be a costly miscalculation. Koreans develop friendships slowly over a long period. Eventually, relationships become extremely close and most often last a lifetime. It's natural for such relationships to be used for personal advantage. Personal and professional relationships are closely intertwined in Korea while normally separated among Westerners. In the West, true friendships are often formed based more on personal attractiveness than advantage. Westerners are reluctant to conduct business with friends, whereas Koreans are uncomfortable conducting business with persons other than friends, after all, they feel that most people would not take advantage of a friend.

Whereas an American may go to a stranger rather than a friend for help, the Korean will rely on a friend for help. A Korean may even ask for favors or assistance as a measure of the strength of the relationship, or as a way of making it stronger and more trustworthy. To Koreans, friendships are very close bonds not to be treated lightly. According to an informant, even though two Korean business colleagues may seem to have become intimate friends, once the business relationship has ended, so does the friendship. What would appear as a friendship is actually the necessary cordiality required to maintain the harmony and cooperation that would allow the business relationship to grow and flourish. While this can happen in the U.S. as well, it is equally as common to continue a relationship with an individual after the business is completed because the two people liked each other personally as well as professionally.

CHAPTER 4

FAMILY LIFE AND EXPECTATIONS

FAMILY LIFE AND EXPECTATIONS

Introduction

Family life is the center of most societies. Yet each culture differs according to how family members interact and in what they expect of each other. This chapter discusses the differences in family life in the United States and in Korea. We discuss various aspects of family life throughout the text as family life relates to each chapter. In this chapter, however, we give a general description of family interaction and expectations.

What is the average modern family?

American Ways

In the U.S., the American family is centered around the nuclear family unit, which consists of the husband and wife and one or two children. Because divorce and remarriage have become increasingly common since the 1960s (the divorce rate in the U.S. is over 50%),[1] the modern average American family can take many shapes. In many cases it is a "blended family" or a single-parent family. A "blended family" is usually created by remarriage of one or both partners and includes children from previous marriages.

Along with other changes in society, the American family is experiencing a process of change. The high divorce rate has led to an increase in single-parent homes, which consist of a father or mother living with one or more children, and blended families, which consist of previously married men and/or women and their children from former marriages.

Even though the concept of family has changed over the past decade, the expectations of the married relationship has not. In general, in the U.S., the relationship of the husband and wife is based on affection, equality and togetherness. Even after children are born, the couple spends time and energy maintaining their love relationship. They do activities together both as a couple and as a family. Both the husband and the wife are expected to spend more time with each other than they do with friends. They also expect to share thoughts and feelings, and to enjoy each other's companionship. Ideally, the parents work together as partners in raising children, whose needs are given top priority within family structure.

The modern American family is also a nuclear family, and so there is very little extended family identity within the modern American family system. That is, it is not common for grandparents, aunts, uncles, or other relatives to live with married children. In the U.S., the parents of married children usually want to live separately from those children. They want to maintain their own independence after their children marry. They also want their children to become independent of them. This independence within the family is perhaps the greatest example of American individuality.

Even though the extended family is a minority, American families still communicate and cooperate with one another. Grandparents and their children visit one another's homes and keep in touch by phone, and the grandparents care about and take interest in their grandchildren's lives. However, the American parents of married children are expected not to interfere with the lives of their children and they have very little authority in married children's homes. The extended family — including grandparents, uncles, aunts, and cousins — often gather on special occasions such as weddings, funerals, birthdays, graduations, and holidays (especially Thanksgiving and Christmas). They also gather for family reunions, which are large events where all members of one side of a family (the mother's or the father's) are invited.

Korean Ways

The modern Korean family is in a stage of transition because of the rapid industrialization, urbanization, and Westernization the country has experienced over the last thirty years. With economic change has come geographic mobility, which has also weakened traditional societal structures. Thus, the boundaries of traditional culture are slowly changing, and respect for authority on all levels is being tested.

Societal changes have mostly affected the younger generation, and as a result family life and social relationships have been changing as well. While thirty years ago social and family roles were clearly defined, fixed, and inflexible, that is no longer true. Koreans — especially the new generation of Koreans — may be losing a clear concept of their own identity within the family structure.

Traditionally, Korean family life has depended on the extended family, in which the parents reside with the family of the eldest son after he marries. In addition, the extended family can include aunts, uncles, and cousins living in the same small town (village), or even in the same household. Indeed, the Korean language system reflects the nature of the extended family: cousins or in-laws can be referred to as sister, brother, aunt or uncle depending on the closeness of the relationship. Therefore, it may be difficult to discern who the actual nuclear family members are if based solely on their titles.

The Korean family is patriarchal and hierarchical, and thus the male older members of the family have the authority, respect, and responsibility. Although this is changing — recently inheritance laws were changed to allow oldest daughters to inherit from parents — age and position in families still determine one's role and responsibilities within the family. The greatest and most evident change in the modern Korean family has been the emersion of the nuclear family as a model, particularly in the cities.

Three of the five Confucian relationships define family relationships: Father-son, husband-wife, older brother-younger brother. The traditional Korean family is an extremely well-defined, close-knit, hierarchic-authoritarian system with the father at the head. The status of each person in the family depends on birth position or marriage. The father's main responsibility is to his father and mother, to his children (especially his sons), and to his wife — in that order. Each family member receives support, security, stability, affection, and love from one another, and in return, is loyal.[2] Family members show loyalty by fulfilling family-defined roles and meeting family obligations.

The extended family — including grandparents, uncles, aunts, and cousins — often gather on special occasions such as weddings, funerals, anniversaries of deaths, birthdays, graduations, and holidays (especially *Ch'usŏk* and New Year's Day). These gatherings, especially on holidays, focus on visiting each other's homes at intervals throughout the day rather than on one large gathering for a meal.

AMERICAN / KOREAN CONTRAST

The nuclear family is the American family model, and many of those families are blended families or single-parent families. The extended family is the exception rather than the rule in the U.S. On the other hand, the nuclear family has become more common in Korea, especially in the cities, but there are few divorced single parents or blended families. The extended family is still the Korean family model.

What do family members expect of one another?

American Ways

One distinction between the American family and the Korean family is based on the individualism inherent in American society. In the American family, the needs of each individual are of greater importance than the needs of the family as a whole.[3] An example of this would be the issue of education. While education is important to Americans, the family's honor or reputation does not depend on it. Instead, education is often seen as a way to economic advancement. So, if a child chooses not to attend college, the average American parent might be sorry, but would respect the child's wishes. The average family as a whole would not feel shamed by a child's choice of college or of career.

American independence and individuality is especially evident in the relationship of family members to one another. Children have no clearly defined obligations toward the extended family or even toward the immediate family as a whole. Instead, the child's responsibilities are to become independent and self-sufficient. Nevertheless, Americans show loyalty and love by helping other family members and remaining in contact with them. But they do not consider the whole family when making personal, individual decisions.

That is, although Americans consider the family important, they do not base decisions — such as attending college or marriage — on matters of "face" for the family. Instead, they are likely to base their decisions on the personal effect the decision will have on themselves or immediate members of a family. For example, if a father's new job would cause the family to move to another state, he would be expected to discuss the move with the nuclear family because they would be affected personally by it. Indeed, married couples expect to be able to make decisions together concerning employment, the spending of money, parenting, and other issues.

On the other hand, if a decision does not directly affect the daily life of another family member, such as which college to attend, Americans will likely not ask for, or expect, advice. That is, average Americans are not dictated to by the "best interests" of the extended family or "the family name." They resent and rebel against being told what to do by other family members.[4] Instead, they make independent decisions based on their own personal needs and desire for personal satisfaction.

For example, when unmarried Americans have a choice of a job — and the choice involves satisfying themselves or satisfying the family — they would be expected to base their decision on what was best for themselves as individuals. According to American thought, what is best for the individual is often considered to be best for the family as well because an unhappy and dissatisfied individual causes unhappiness and dissatisfaction in the family. Individuals are not responsible for improving their family's status as a whole, but only their own.[5]

Korean Ways

The Korean family is based on the collectivism inherent in Korean society. In the Korean family, the needs of the family as a whole —

including extended family — are of greater importance than the needs of the individual. This difference between family in the U.S. and Korea is highlighted if we use the same example of education as we did in the section on American ways.

Education is extremely important to Koreans, as level of education often represents one's hierarchical level in society. When a Korean attends college, it reflects on the family as a whole. The concept of *ch'emyŏn*, which we discuss throughout this book, extends to the entire family. The choice of school or the degree received, therefore, can be a matter of face for all members of the family, not just the student. So, economic advancement — although important — is not the primary factor in Korean education. Rather, family reputation is. A Korean child is under great family pressure to attend college, especially one of the top universities.[6] The family as a whole feels pride or shame by a child's choice of college or of career.

AMERICAN / KOREAN CONTRAST

In the U.S. attending a university is not restricted. Since equal opportunity is one of the philosophies underlying U.S. laws and social institutions, educational opportunity is available for all people. So, although there are "Ivy League" universities and universities have varying standards for admission, attending a university is generally less elitist than in Korea. Students also have the freedom to transfer from one university to another (without having to begin again), or to change majors several times while studying. In the U.S., it is also increasingly common for students to drop out of college and then return at a later date. It is also common for students to attend part-time while working full-time or to return to college full-time when they are over 30 years of age. These students are called "non-traditional students."

On the other hand, as of 1999, only a small percentage of Korean high school students were able to attend universities. Students have had to pass national college entrance examinations that dictate to which university they could gain admission. However, the goal of the Ministry of Education is to change this system by the year 2002. They are developing community and other open-admission two-and four-year colleges that will allow every high school graduate to attend college.

The Ministry of Education also aims to change another distinctive aspect of the Korean system of higher education: After attending a university, it has been difficult to transfer universities. Students have had to take the college entrance examinations again, and then begin at the new school as freshmen. This is changing. In Korea, it is also very rare for a person over thirty years of age to attend a university or to drop out and then return to school. Therefore, competition is keen for both admission and admission to the best schools.

Korean collectivism is also evident in the relationship of family members to one another. Children have clearly defined obligations toward the family as a whole. They are to fulfill a defined role, marry, have children and maintain family pride. They also have responsibility (especially the eldest son) for the economic prosperity and social stability of the family, and are expected to bring honor to the family name.[7] Thus, the concept of personal obligation of children to the parents (even after adulthood) and the subordination of personal goals and interests to those of the family are very much a part of the Korean family structure.

That is, a husband or father would likely make a decision — such as taking a job that would move a family to another city — based on the effect it would have on his own extended family rather than on the personal effect it would have on his immediate, nuclear family. He is also likely to make such decisions without discussing it with his immediate family, although he may have discussed it with his parents or others.

Honoring one's parents and family by perhaps sacrificing one's own happiness is not unusual even in modern Korea. A story can illustrate this. One young woman of marriageable age, around twenty-five, met and fell in love with a young man. But her parents disapproved of the relationship and told the young woman to end it because a marriage between them would not be good for the family. She was not to put her private and personal desires before the needs of the family, and so she gave up the young man. In another case, a professional woman of about twenty-eight was pressured to marry because her father was ill. She accepted an arranged marriage in order to satisfy her family. The husband then traveled to the U.S. to study while the woman continued her professional life in Korea. These situations may occur in the U.S., but they are rare. Importantly, they would be disapproved of in the U.S.

AMERICAN / KOREAN CONTRAST

Americans are likely to base such decisions as marriage, education, or career on the personal effect the decision would have on the individual or the immediate members of the individual's family. Family reputation is secondary to personal happiness and satisfaction. On the other hand, Koreans are likely to base such decisions as marriage, education, and career on the effect it would have on the reputation of the extended family as a whole. Personal happiness and satisfaction are secondary.

Finally, the father-son relationship is the focal point of the Korean family. The relationship to wife and other family members, such as daughters, is secondary. Daughters in general have traditionally had a low position in the family and society (although their status is changing progressively as Koreans limit their families to two or three children regardless of their gender). As we mentioned, duty and loyalty to the parents is paramount even after marriage. Still, women have authority within the home, and the wife of the eldest son can be quite influential within the larger family hierarchy. In the next section, we discuss individual roles within modern American and Korean families.

What are the defined roles within a family?

American Ways

American society has changed drastically since the 1950s, but there are still many defined roles within the family structure. Although the roles and responsibilities have changed, many of the traditional roles have remained the same. In general, we can say that within the nuclear family, the husband and father has the role of provider, disciplinarian, and **handyman**.

The husband is usually responsible for earning the primary family income, for punishing children, for maintaining the family car, for driving the family, for maintaining the outside of the home and the yard, and for maintaining the plumbing and electricity inside the home. The husband is also expected to maintain a good relationship with his wife.

In modern America, the husband-wife relationship is slowly becoming a partnership. In this partnership, the husband and children share with the wife the responsibility of taking care of the home. In this partnership the husband is not seen as ruler of the family. His role as father and husband is seen as supportive.

In contrast to the husband's role of provider, the wife and mother's role is of disciplinarian, provider of education, and **homemaker**. Almost half of the U.S. workforce is made up of women (46%).[8] So, the typical modern American wife will probably work outside of the home.[9] In addition to her job, the American wife and mother is usually responsible for taking care of the education, health, and after-school activities of the children. She is also usually responsible for the care of the home, for cooking meals, for shopping for food and clothes, and for writing letters and maintaining extended family relationships. As a wife, the woman's role is also to help maintain her romantic relationship with her husband.

In general, parents provide a home for their children and guide them through their lives. According to American thinking, the parent's job is to teach their children how to become independent. In response, the children learn to lead independent lives. It is the children's duty not to be dependent on their parents financially after they mature. Many parents think their own duty is not to be dependent on their children after the children have left home and the parents have retired. Thus, the ideal parent-child relationship is often based on mutual independence.

Within the framework of growing toward independence, American parents require their children to do household tasks. So many children take out the garbage, help with washing dishes or with the laundry, mow the grass, or sweep the floors. Some children get outside jobs such as mowing grass for neighbors, helping with farmwork, or delivering newspapers. Thus, it is common for teenagers to get part-time jobs while they are in high school, working for fast-food restaurants, gas stations or grocery stores. They also earn money by baby-sitting (taking care of other people's children for the evening).[10]

American children have chores or outside jobs in order to instill in them a sense of responsibility, independence, and the value of money. To Americans, dependence on the family is expected to diminish after childhood. Americans take pride in working hard to help finance their own education or lifestyle (whatever that lifestyle may be) and not depend on family for complete support. This is why many American teenagers or young adults work even though their parents could support them. They often work their way through college because they want to prove their independence, not just because it may be necessary. They want to "make it on their own" and "stand on their own two feet."[11]

Korean Ways

Although Korean society has changed since the 1950s, the defined roles in society are just beginning to change. Compared to the U.S., gender roles are much more rigid and defined in Korea, and there are fewer opportunities to break out of those roles. One of the changes, as mentioned above, is the gradual move away from the extended family to the nuclear family. However, the extended family still predominates in modern Korea.

The husband and father's role is of provider and authority. The Korean husband and father is usually the primary source of family income, and he is responsible for setting the rules within a family. In Korean, the husband is called *jibjuin* [집주인] (literally: 'housemaster'), and in that respect he is the house authority. For families with cars, the husband and father is responsible for maintaining the family car and for driving the family. In general, the father's relationship with his children is usually formal and distant. Love is rarely expressed through words or physical expressions of affection, and often an element of fear or awe exists.[12]

The wife and mother's role is of homemaker and intermediary with the father. The Korean wife and mother (in Korean, *jibsaram* [집 사람] or *ansaram* [안사람] (literally: 'houseperson' or 'inside person') will normally not work outside of the home, although the number of women in the workforce is increasing and Korean women are becoming more independent.[13] The Korean wife and mother is responsible for the care, discipline and education of the children, the care of the home, cooking, laundry, shopping, and for maintaining family relationships. Most of all, the Korean wife is responsible for handling the family finances. While the husband and father may have authority in terms of decision-making, the wife and mother has the financial authority and responsibility. Futhermore, the Korean wife and mother is an intermediary. That is, children do not usually go directly to their father when they want something. They go to their mother who acts as an intermediary with the father.

The roles of men and women in Korea are changing much more slowly than Korean society itself is changing. While the role of women has become less limited nowadays (especially in the cities), it still maintains many of its traditional boundaries. The role of the wife in a Korean family has always been subordinate to that of her husband, because the dominance of men over women derived from Confucian authoritarianism is still deeply rooted in society. This can especially be seen in the home. Even though Korean women can be highly educated, it is still often difficult for them to maintain their jobs after marriage, particularly if there is any family opposition. (This situation is slowly changing due to other societal changes such as economic development, smaller families, and economic need. Nevertheless, the current situation is that although women work in such fields as politics, business, and education, they are usually either single or married to men who have given them permission to work outside the home.) When women do have jobs or careers, they are usually confined to traditional roles as clerks, secretaries, or teachers. It is very difficult for Korean women to have a position of authority in business or elsewhere. Thus, the idea that a woman's place is in the home is still strong. The wife's role within the family is to serve her husband, produce children (especially sons), raise the children and take care of all the domestic chores. It is also to oversee the household finances and the children's education.

NOTE: In accordance with Confucian thinking, there is a saying about women: When single, they must obey their parents. When married, they must obey their husband. When widowed, they must obey their son. With other societal changes, this too is changing, but the new generation of Korean women still say it as a reminder of the changes that have taken place.

While modern day Koreans speak of "love marriages," many Koreans still have arranged marriages or base the marriage on family demands or other practical concerns. Furthermore, the complicated relationship between husband and wife retains many of its basic elements. There is still a delegation of roles: The husband is the breadwinner and the wife is the homemaker. On the surface, there is not much affection and togetherness evident in a Korean marriage, although this does not mean there can be no genuine affection and love. The nature of Korean society simply limits the situations and manner in which that affection can be expressed. In *Korean Patterns*, Paul Crane points out that because of arranged marriages, love was expected to follow marriage.[14] So, as we pointed out, in modern day Korea, there are many "love marriages," but arranged marriages are still popular.

AMERICAN / KOREAN CONTRAST

An American couple expects to maintain their romantic relationship and friendship throughout their marriage. A Korean couple usually leads independent lives and does not engage in "dating" each other (common in American marriages) after they have begun to raise children. However, the personal relationship of a Korean couple has begun to change with the influence of Christian and Western attitudes.

In Korea, parents are expected to provide a home for their children and to guide them throughout their lives. In return, children are expected to be loyal and obedient and take care of the parents in their old age. According to Korean thinking, the parents' job is to feed, clothe, educate, and house their children. The Korean family is built around mutual dependency — financial and emotional — and so the task of Korean parents is not necessarily to teach their children how to become independent, but instead to teach them their duties and dependencies within the extended family unit. Rather than financial, intellectual, and emotional independence as it is understood in the U.S., Koreans value just the opposite. Thus, unmarried Koreans may live with their parents or another relative (if they are attending school in another town or city, for example) at least until marriage.[15] They may be financially dependent long into adulthood.

As we have discussed, Koreans place a great deal of importance on education. Within that framework, Korean parents often do not require their children — especially male children — to do household tasks. So most Korean men, and some Korean women, have grown up without the experience of helping their parents take care of the home. Unless there is financial need, Korean children seldom hold outside jobs such as helping neighbors or selling newspapers. This type of job might affect the family's *ch'emyŏn*. It is not common for teenagers to get part-time jobs while they are in high school because they are studying long hours to prepare for their college entrance exams. However, college students may get part-time jobs (*arŭbaitŭ* [아르바이트] (from the German *arbeit*-'work') as tutors, or they may work for fast-food restaurants, in manual labor, or in grocery stores. Earning money by baby-sitting is not common in Korea, primarily because of the existence of the extended family.

> **NOTE:** There is still a great respect for age in Korea. Grandparents are given a great deal of deference. They are taken care of by the eldest son (or daughter if there is no son). In general, the first son is responsible for his parents when they get old. The wife must serve and take care of the needs of her parents-in-law as well as the needs of her immediate family. The fixed roles that closely knit a Korean family together, along with the mutual help within the home, provide a secure and happy life for the older people in the family. In the cities where there is a preference for nuclear families, one's loyalties are still to one's parents. However, where the loyalty to one's parents in the Korea of even twenty-five years ago was clear and distinct, in modern Korea with its emphasis on personal materialism, the sense of loyalty is vague and diffuse. So, you can see more older people living alone and caring for themselves in modern day Korea. Some people regret the gradual abandonment of the extended family.

What are the expectations of the husband/wife relationship?

American Ways

American couples have based their marriages on love for and physical attraction to one another. In general, American couples show this affection for one another outwardly and warmly, and the focus of their marriage is to maintain that affection. Throughout their marriage, most American couples work to maintain their close romantic relationship. They also enjoy each other's companionship and friendship. Most importantly, American couples see themselves as separate from their own individual families. When they marry, they are creating a new family. The American ideal is that the couple also establishes an emotional intimacy with each other and works as a partnership. An American wife or husband would be criticized for allowing family or friends to interfere with their marriage relationship.

An American husband and wife value and try to keep their pre-marriage relationship. They try to respect and take an interest in each other's hobbies and activities. They go out together in the evening either alone as a couple or with friends. Relationships, too, are based on mutual respect. The American husband shows respect by holding a door open for his wife, hanging up her coat in a restaurant, pulling her chair out before she sits down at the table, and holding the car ·door open for her when they leave. He may also show respect by praising his wife in public and private, listening to her without interrupting, or simply by asking her about her day and interests. The wife also shows respect for her husband by praising him in public and private, by listening to him without interrupting, and by showing interest in his activities.

Korean Ways

After a thousand years of Confucian influence which distinguished roles and stratified society, the husband-wife relationship in Korea is naturally based more on separation than intimacy as it is understood in the U.S. The relationship is one of separate roles within the hierarchic family structure which is divided by age and gender. That is, in Korea, a married couple focuses on fulfilling their responsibilities and duties toward family and each other first, and that becomes the focus of the relationship.

The focus on togetherness, companionship, and the cultivation of individual happiness between couples that is popular in the West is rare among Korean couples. Similarly, public displays of affection are traditionally conservative in general, but especially so between the sexes. Although holding hands and kissing in public is becoming more common among young people, it is not yet acceptable in Korean society as a whole. Affection between the sexes is still expressed more inwardly and privately than outwardly and publicly. This is true of married couples as well as of dating couples. So it may be common that children have never seen their parents kiss or show other physical affection.[16] Especially, children would not display such physical affection in front of their parents.

The separation between husband and wife roles is reflected in their social lifestyles. The social nature of Korean business requires the husband to meet after hours with colleagues or friends, and it is rare for husband and wives to go out alone together. Usually, the wife stays at home while the husband meets his friends immediately after work and eats and drinks with them until late in the evening. Wives also do not usually accompany their husbands to most non-family social functions. As Paul Crane[17] points out in *Korean Patterns*, taking the wife to social functions is a strain on the husband, and her possible candor in certain situations might cause him to lose face.

What is the hierarchy among siblings?

American Ways

The hierarchy in an American family is not always clearly defined. While it can focus around gender and age, it could also focus around ability and personality as well. Generally, the older child has the most responsibilities and the most authority regardless of whether the child is male or female. Sometimes, authority and responsibilities fall on the child who has the closest relationship with the parent or in adulthood simply lives closest to the parent. The first-born son in an American family does not automatically have authority and privileges, although this may occur in some individual families.

Americans generally believe the individual must earn respect through his/her actions. Thus, respect is given by siblings to those with whom they have developed a close respectful relationship. While in large families older brothers or sisters may take care of younger ones, an older sibling would rarely have the responsibility or authority to choose a university, job, or spouse for a younger one. In the U.S., family members in general help one another when needed, give emotional support, and respect the independence of each other.

Korean Ways

The hierarchy in a Korean family focuses around gender and age.[18] Thus, all children in a family are subordinate to the first son even if he is born the fifth child. Yet, as a son, he must assume a great deal of responsibility. If he is the oldest child, his responsibilities grow. Within the family hierarchy, younger children must show their older siblings respect, but they must especially respect the oldest brother. The oldest son is responsible for his parents as they age. He is responsible for his younger siblings if his father should become ill or die. In addition, he is responsible for conducting ancestor worship. Until recently, he also received all inheritance from the father.

Glossary of English Terms

handyman A person who can repair things inside the home.

homemaker The wife or husband who takes care of house cleaning, home decorating, cooking, child care, etc. for the family. In the U.S., many men take on these responsibilities.

Glossary of Korean Terms

ansaram [안사람] A husband uses this term to refer to his wife, and others can use it to refer to her in his presence. It literally means 'inside person.'

arŭbait'ŭ [아르바이트] Part-time job. It derives from the German word *arbeit* for 'work.'

jibjuin [집주인] A wife uses this term to refer to her husband, and others can use it to refer to him in her presence. It literally means 'house master.'

jibsaram [집사람] *Ansaram.*

Notes

[1] According to the Statistical Abstract of the United States: *The National Data Book* (Austin, Texas: Hoover's Business Press, 1996), p.104) in 1994 the divorce rate in the U.S. was 50%. According to the *Hankyǒreh* [한겨레] on-line newspaper of November 5, 1998, the number of Korean divorced couples in 1997 was about 2645 for every 11,000 couples compared to 1 for every 11,000 couples in 1990.

[2] See *Cross Currents* by Susan Pares (Seoul: Seoul International Publishing House, 1985), p.13.

[3] See *The American Way: An Introduction to American Culture* by E.N. Kearny, M. A. Kearny, and J. Crandall (New Jersey: Prentice Hall, Inc., 1984), p.202.

[4] Ibid.

[5] Ibid.

[6] The five most prestigious universities in Korea are Seoul National University, Korea University, Yonsei University, Ewha Woman's University, and Sogang University.

[7] See *The American Way: An Introduction to American Culture* by E.N. Kearny, M. A. Kearny, and J. Crandall (New Jersey: Prentice Hall, Inc., 1984), p.202.

[8] From the Statistical Abstract of the United States: *The National Data Book.* (Austin, Texas: Hoover's Business Press, 1996), p.396.

[9] We do not have statistics on how many of the 46% of women who work outside of the home are married or have children.

[10] See *Contact USA* by Abraham, P. and Mackey D. (Englewood Cliffs, NJ: Regents/ Prentice Hall, 1989), p.93.

[11] See *Korean Ideas and Views* by M. C. Kalton (Elkins Park, PA: The Philip Jaisohn Foundation, 1979), p.12.

[12] See *The American Way: An Introduction to American Culture* by E.N. Kearny, M. A. Kearny, and J. Crandall (New Jersey: Prentice Hall, Inc., 1984), p.202.

[13] See *Culture Shock: Korea* by S.V. Hur, and B.S. Hur. Singapore: Times Books International, 1988), p.32.

[14] See *Korean Patterns* by Paul Crane (Seoul: Kwangjin Publishing company, 1978), p.29.

[15] The common understanding from our informants is that the marrigeable age for women is from 23–25 (Korean age) and for men from 25–28 (Korean age).

[16] See *Communication Styles in Two Different Cultures: Korean and American* by M.S. Park. (Seoul: Han Shin Publishing Company, 1979), p.66.

[17] See *Korean Patterns* by Paul S. Crane (Seoul: Kwangjin Publishing Company, 1998), p.34

[18] See *Korean Ideas and Views* by M. C. Kalton (Elkins Park, PA: The Philip Jaisohn Memorial Foundation, 1979), p.12.

CHAPTER 5

CELEBRATING
FAMILY RITUALS

CELEBRATING FAMILY RITUALS

Introduction

There are many family rituals in both the U. S. and Korean. Family rituals are any family celebrations that bring the family together and help create or maintain its identity as a family. These rituals can be connected to daily life, to special events, or to national holidays. Some examples of such celebrations are:

*personal — birthdays, anniversaries, retirements
*social — weddings, funerals
*national — national holidays

Regardless of the reason for the celebration, the rituals themselves reflect both family and cultural traditions. These celebrations also become symbols of family life within both American and Korean societies.[1]

Families by their nature have habits and customs that they follow that bring meaning to their family life. In both the U.S. and Korea, most families create their own special rituals that bring special meaning to their lives as a family. Within both cultures, most of these rituals vary according to family, but there are some generalizations that can be made. In general, Americans may have an attitude of creating rituals, whereas Koreans may have an attitude of following rituals. The types of family activities may not vary, but the attitudes and expectations of Americans and Koreans may differ. Generally, Americans will put focus on family activities as a way of growing together and knowing about each other. Koreans may put focus on family activities as symbols of respect for the various individuals.

In this chapter, we give information about how specific events — personal, social, and national — are celebrated and discuss the specific rituals related to each occasion. We first discuss traditions and rituals connected to daily family life. After that, we discuss birthdays, graduations, and anniversaries. Next, we discuss customs and traditions related to weddings and funerals. Finally, we discuss the observance of national holidays.

What are the rituals of daily family life?

American Ways

The rituals of daily family life is another example of American individuality. There are some culture-based expectations of behaviors, but generally how each family interacts on a daily basis depends on the individual family. Some common rituals for many Americans that are part of their daily routine are:

*the family meal
*kissing a spouse goodbye in the morning
*greeting a spouse in the evening
*going on **family outings** on specific days
*a father and child **playing catch**
*a mother and child baking together

In general, the rituals of American daily family life focus around activities or actions that bring the family together emotionally. That is, Americans place value on doing activities as a family. Therefore, American families may have an attitude of creating rituals that are special to the individual family.

Korean Ways

The rituals of Korean daily family life may not differ very much from that of the American. Especially, Korean family life focuses on bringing the family together. It differs in some respects from American family life, however, in how it understands "togetherness." It also differs in how the Korean family may be more focused on following established ritual than in creating it. Some common rituals for many Koreans that are part of their daily routine

are:
*the family meal
*greeting a spouse in the evening
*going on **family outings** on specific days
*education of the children

How do families celebrate meals?

American Ways

It may seem odd to discuss "celebrating a meal" since people eat several times a day. Eating is an everyday necessity of life. But, traditionally, Americans have focused a great deal of attention around meals. Although many modern families may eat fast food, many other families still eat at least one meal together every day. Most importantly, it is an American ideal to enjoy meals together. On a special day of the week, such as Sunday, the family may invite extended family members (such as parents or brothers and sisters) to dinner. This Sunday dinner is usually a more special meal than other meals throughout the week.

Americans view mealtime as a time to share information about each other. Americans believe that the intimacy of the family as a group is a result of such regular activities and sharing of information.

Korean Ways

Korean family life has changed since the 1970s as Western values regarding family life have influenced the Korean family. More Koreans have adopted Christian values, which emphasize family life, as well.

Korean families enjoy meals together, but the family does not always eat the meal together. Traditionally, men ate together while the women ate at a separate table or after the men ate. Mealtime was not a time for men and women to share together. While most Americans have a regular time for meals, most Koreans are flexible about the time at which they eat. The father usually eats when he returns home from work, as in the U.S., but that may be at late hours.

Koreans do not generally have the view that mealtime is a time to share information about each other. But Koreans do enjoy sharing meals as a way of building community and friendship and family feelings, and such community is a result of such regular activities. Koreans may not insist on the regularity of such meals as Americans may.

What are some husband and wife rituals?

American Ways

Most American couples develop their own ways of showing affection and caring for one another. They may have **pet names** for each other. In the U.S., most couples have a ritual of kissing each other goodbye or hello. Two important times for these kisses are in the morning when at least one person is leaving for work and in the evening when one person is returning from work. Many couples have a ritual of going to bed at the same time. They may have a ritual of watching a movie together on Saturday nights after the children are in bed, or of washing the dishes together. Most of these rituals are for the purpose of showing physical affection for one another and for making time for the couple to talk and share activities that bring about **togetherness**. This is considered very important after the couple has children.

Korean Ways

Many modern Korean couples show more open affection and caring for one another than their parents or grandparents did. They may have **pet names** for each other, which are often based on the traditional terms for their positions in the family hierarchy. Most Korean couples refer to each other as *yŏbo* [여보] ('dear'), although many develop their own pet names, especially among the younger generation. Most Korean couples may have a ritual of kissing each other goodbye, but only if they are alone. A common ritual is the wife seeing the husband to the door. Newlyweds may have a ritual of going to bed at the same time, but after children arrive the married couple's relationship changes. Even modern, western-influenced couples will seldom have traditions of doing specific activities for the sake of togetherness.

What are some common family outings?

American Ways

To help the family grow as an intimate group, as well as to provide recreation for the children, the family may regularly do activities as a group. Some common family outings might be:

*eating out together
*traveling together on weekends or during summer vacation
*attending children's ball games or other sports events at schools
*going on picnics, especially at local parks
*visiting zoos, aquariums, or parks
*taking walks
*going to films

Korean Ways

Modern Korean families often only have one day a week to spend together, Sunday, because the husband and father's workday is often 12 hours long, and he may work 6 days a week. As modern young Korean wives try to involve the husband more in family life, Korean families, too, may regularly do activities as a group. Some common family outings might be:

*eating out at a restaurant
*traveling together to the beach or mountains for a short vacation
*going on picnics, especially at local parks
*visiting zoos, aquariums, or parks

*going to films

What are some rituals between parents and children?

American Ways

Many of the common rituals between parents and children involve teaching the child a skill and spending time with the child. One common ritual is for American parents to read to their children at night and to **tuck them into bed**. Another ritual is for them to kiss each child goodnight. A ritual between parents and very young children is to bathe the child. As children grow older, fathers and children may play catch together; mothers and children may bake cookies together. Some of the most common rituals may depend on the age of the child, such as the following:

*young children, about 6 years old: teaching the child to ride a bicycle. This usually involves buying the child a bicycle with **training wheels;** and then taking the wheels off and letting the child ride by himself or herself.

*young children, up to 10 years old: playing the "tooth fairy." As children lose their baby teeth, parents often tell children to put the tooth under their pillow. During the night, the parent takes the tooth and replaces it with a small sum of money.

Korean Ways

There are many common rituals between Korean mothers and their children. Most Korean mothers teach their children little songs or games from an early age. Modern Korean mothers may read to their children at night, but generally do not have a tradition of **tucking them into bed**. There generally is no tradition of kissing the child goodnight. Even though baseball is a popular sport in Korea,

Korean fathers and sons generally do not have rituals together involving sports. Although mothers may teach their daughters to cook, there is no general tradition of cooking together for fun and togetherness. Some of the most common rituals may depend on the age of children, and in Korea the rituals are often related to education, such as:

*young children, until puberty: reciting learning in front of the parents or guests.

Every culture has special events that relate to the individuals that make up a family. In this section, we discuss births, birthdays, graduations, promotions, and retirements.

How are births celebrated?

American Ways

In the U.S., Americans first acknowledge a pregnancy by congratulating the new mother and father. In congratulating the new parents, they usually:

*say "congratulations"
*ask about the mother's health
*ask if the parents want a boy or a girl
*ask the due date
*ask what the parents plan to name the baby

Before the birth, the friends or family of the couple (usually of the mother) will give her a **baby shower**. A baby shower is a party (usually only attended by women), to show support for the mother and to celebrate the impending birth. It is also practical because all of the guests bring gifts for the baby.

At the time of the birth, it is a tradition for American men to pass out cigars to their friends or co-workers. This applies regardless of whether the new baby is a boy or a girl.

Most American children are born in the hospital, and after the birth family members often visit the hospital. For several months after the birth, friends and family continue to give the child gifts. Usually within the first month after the birth, the couple send out **birth announcements** which give information about the child and include a picture. Sometimes families make these announcements themselves, especially on a home computer. Sometimes families buy them. Friends and families often send cards of congratulations as well as presents. Although the child is named at birth, there are also certain customs regarding the naming of children that are related to religious beliefs such as baptism or christening. [2]

Korean Ways

In Korea, there is some gift-giving before the birth of the child, but there is no tradition of baby showers. Koreans may proudly announce the impending birth of a child (especially if it is a first child). As in the U.S., they will tell the family members first. In congratulating the new parents, Koreans usually:

*say "congratulations" (*ch'ukha hamnida* [축하합니다])
*tell the mother to be careful of her health (*mom josimhaseyo* [몸 조심하세요])
*say they hope it is a boy

At the time of the birth of the child, the father will announce the birth to friends and co-workers and often take them out for a drink, especially if it is a son. However, it is possible for the father not to tell co-workers if the child is a daughter. Family members prepare a traditional seaweed soup (*miyŏk kuk* [미역국]) which they take to the mother for her to eat for the week immediately after the birth.

Only immediate family members visit the mother and child immediately after the birth of the child. However, Koreans will have a large celebration to honor the hundredth day after birth (*paekil janch'i* [백일 잔치]). The guests bring presents for the baby, with the most traditional gift being a gold ring. Korea is a patriarchal society that especially celebrates the births of boys.

Thus, parents often have a special photo of the child taken at this time, especially of boys (in which the boy is often undressed).

How are birthdays celebrated?

American Ways

Most Americans celebrate birthdays with a cake and candles. This is especially true for children, but also true of adults as well. Many parents often give birthday parties for the children every year until the teenage years. The child's friends are invited to these parties and they bring gifts. The question of gifts is an important one. This is especially because Americans try to avoid obligation from others when giving gifts. In general, except to children or to special family members or spouses, Americans do not regularly give gifts for birthdays. The degree of the celebration generally depends on the level and type of relationship and the occasion. We have provided a short list for you below: ·

*casual friends - do not acknowledge the birthday or simply wish the person a "happy birthday."
*close friends - may send a card, make a phone call, invite the person to dinner, or give a gift with a card
*adult family members - may send a card, have no acknowledgement, make a phone call, or send a gift
*children of relatives - depends on the relationship
*parents - usually a card and a gift
*husband/wife - usually dinner, a card, and a gift

In the U.S., some birthdays are celebrated specially as milestones in a person's life. Some of these special birthdays for Americans are:

*a child's first birthday
*the 16th birthday (for girls it is called "Sweet Sixteen") - becoming 16 is primarily important because most Americans can

get their driver's license at that age.

*the 18th birthday for both young men and women - Americans are considered **legal adults** with adult responsibilities at this age. They can vote, get married without a parent's permission, and join the armed forces.

*the 21st birthday - in many states, young people are not allowed to buy alcoholic drinks until the age of 21.

*the 30th birthday - most people begin to take life more seriously at this age.

*the 40th birthday - this is considered the beginning of "mid-life" and the end of youth. A lot of humorous cards and activities refer to this as the age of becoming "**over the hill**."

*the 65th birthday - this is the age of retirement for the average American. Most people think of themselves as "**senior citizens**" after this age.

Korean Ways

Many modern Koreans celebrate birthdays with a cake and candles, but this is a tradition that they have adopted from the West. Most Koreans celebrate their birthdays by having their favorite food. They also usually serve rice-cake soup ([*ddŏk kuk* [떡국]]) as a special birthday meal. Traditionally, children especially get their favorite meal but do not have a party in the Western sense. (However, in recent years some wealthier families are beginning to have birthday parties for their children.) Parents often give children money for their birthdays, but generally there is no expectation of special birthday presents (except for the first birthday). Koreans generally do not give gifts for birthdays, but they may celebrate birthdays with impromptu parties that would include a cake and drinking. Friends may buy each other a meal if they know it is the other's birthday. But large, planned birthday parties as we know them in the West are not generally celebrated with the exception of the 60th. Therefore, a list of celebrations according to the relationship of the people involved is not necessary in this section. However, there are special important birthdays for Koreans, and this list we provide below:

*a baby's hundredth day (*paekil nal* [백일날]) - this is a day to celebrate the birth of the baby after the first (perhaps fragile) few months of life. Immediate and extended family members, as well as friends gather for a large meal. Gifts are exchanged as well.

*a child's first birthday[3] - this is a large family celebration similar to *paekil nal*. Usually, the parents have a portrait taken at this time with the child, and a photograph of the child alone among rice cakes and special food.

*the 20th birthday (*sŏnginsik* [성인식]) - most Koreans are considered legal adults with adult responsibilities at this age.[4] It is often celebrated by drinking, especially for young men.

*the 60th birthday (*hwangab* [환갑]) - the age of retirement for the average Korean, and the age after which they are considered "senior citizens."[5] The birthday celebration itself is an extravaganza of food, entertainment, and presents attended by family and friends.

How are anniversaries celebrated?

American Ways

An anniversary usually refers to the wedding anniversary. Married couples usually celebrate this event in an intimate manner, with a dinner, cards to each other, and gifts. After a certain number of years, they may also celebrate with a party and invite friends or family to help them celebrate. Friends and family may give the couple cards on their anniversary, but they usually do not give them gifts.

Two important anniversaries are the **silver wedding anniversary** and the **golden wedding anniversary**. The silver wedding anniversary marks 25 years of marriage, and the golden wedding anniversary marks 50 years of marriage. The couple usually has a party, or their children have a party for them to celebrate these anniversaries. This is especially true for the golden wedding anniversary. The common type of party for this anniversary is an **open-house**. That is, it is not a formal dinner. Many couples also renew their wedding vows at the time of these important anniversaries.

NOTE: The term anniversary can be used for a variety of situations that can be commemorated, including deaths and employment.

Korean Ways

There is no annual celebration of the wedding anniversary in Korea as there is in the West. However, couples may decide to remember that special day privately. There is a tradition of celebrating the 25th anniversary by some couples (*jinhonsik* [진혼식]). On the other hand, the anniversary of deaths is celebrated.

How are graduations celebrated?

American Ways

The most important graduations in the U.S. are from high school and college. In the past, graduation from elementary school (eighth grade) was celebrated, but that is not as common nowadays. The customs and traditions surrounding the two primary graduations are discussed below:

High School: During the **senior year** of high school, American students have special photographs taken, called their "senior picture." During the fall, they order name cards and invitations. They also often buy a class ring upon which is engraved the initials of their school and the year of graduation. About one month before the graduation date, the graduate sends invitations (usually with a name card and a senior picture enclosed) to friends and family. Few family members beyond the immediate family attend the graduation, but they often send a card of congratulations and a present of money. For high school graduation, $10.00 - $20.00 is an average gift, depending on the financial status of the individuals and their relationship to the graduate. The parents may give the child a larger gift, such as a trip or a car, depending on the financial ability of the parent. Often, the family will hold an open-house reception for the graduate one or two days after graduation.

College: The customs related to college graduation are similar to those of high school graduation. Although students can have senior pictures taken, the emphasis on such pictures is less than it is in high school. However, there may be more emphasis on buying a school ring. As with high school, few family members beyond the immediate family attend the graduation, but they often send a card of congratulations and a present of money. For college graduation, $20.00 - $50.00 is an average gift. The parents may give the child a larger, such as a trip or a car, depending on the financial ability of the parent. Often, the family will hold an open-house for the graduate one or two days after graduation.

Korean Ways

Education is highly valued in Korea. This is evident in the fact that graduations from all levels of school — from elementary to college — are formally celebrated. The customs and traditions surrounding the two primary graduations are discussed below:

Elementary and Secondary School: Koreans hold a formal graduation ceremony for every level of their children's education, beginning with kindergarten and proceeding up through middle and high school. Koreans have a tradition of taking school photos, but this tradition reflects both their economic history and the society's collective nature. That is, they take group photos instead of individual photos, which are most often taken after the graduation ceremony. In particular, there is no tradition of a "senior picture," nor is there a tradition of sending invitations to graduations. There is no tradition of a class ring. Friends and family members attend the many different graduations and bring small bouquets of flowers to give to the graduate as well as to the teachers. To celebrate, the family will often take the graduate to a meal after the graduation and give small gifts of money. However, an open-house to celebrate a graduation such as is known in the U.S. is not a Korean tradition. Depending on the financial ability of the parents, they may also give the child larger gifts as well.

College: Customs related to college graduation in Korea are similar to those of high school graduation. There is no tradition of senior pictures, but there is a tradition of group pictures, especially according to school and department, which are collected into a school album. There is also no tradition of sending out invitations. Family members and friends attend the graduation and give the new graduate gifts of money and flowers. It is not uncommon to see new college graduate of both genders holding many small bouquets of flowers and other small gifts such as books, etc. They also receive money. The new graduate will then celebrate with family or friends by having a meal, usually in a restaurant.

AMERICAN / KOREAN CONTRAST

Americans have a tradition of sending greeting cards on many occasions, including birthdays, graduations, retirements, births, weddings, anniversaries, deaths, and many holidays. There are specialty stores that sell only cards for these many occasions, and department and grocery stores also have a section only for cards. There are a variety of cards – both humorous and serious – one can choose. These cards usually contain a special verse or saying that expresses the sender's feelings. Sometimes, Americans write their own message inside as well. When an American gives a gift, it is custom to include one of the cards. Koreans, on the other hand, do not have the custom of sending cards for various occasions. They will sometimes give a card with a gift, but the card will usually be blank inside and have a short personal message from the sender. Such cards are sold in specialty shops or in the stationery section of department stores.

How are getting a new job and retirements celebrated?

American Ways

In the U.S., there is no specific custom related to getting a new job. Sometimes a person who has gotten a new job may buy a dinner for another as a way of celebrating, but generally there is little formal acknowledgment.

Retirements, on the other hand, are celebrated. They are often celebrated at the person's place of employment with a party and presents (provided by one's co-workers, not the employer). They are also often celebrated by the retiree's family or friends with an open-house.

Korean Ways

Koreans have a custom of the persons beginning employment giving gifts of new underwear to family members and special friends when they begin a new job. Often, this gift is given as a thank you for continued support — emotional, financial, or in practical ways that helped the person obtain a job — but it is also a handed-down tradition.

Retirements are not generally celebrated, except in the form of the birthday celebration of *hwangab* [환갑].

AMERICAN / KOREAN CONTRAST

Americans often celebrate such events as retirements, graduations, and special anniversaries with an open-house. An open-house can be held either in a person's home or at a special location, such as a social room at a church. The open-house is usually an informal gathering during a specified period of time, e.g. from 2 to 4 p.m. Guests are welcome to visit at any time in that two-hour time frame. Usually light food is served, such as sandwiches and a cake. Koreans, on the other hand, do not have a tradition of an open-house. When Koreans celebrate special events that involve many people, they usually celebrate at a sit-down dinner at a restaurant.

How are weddings celebrated?

American Ways

Americans see a marriage as the uniting of two individuals who become a new family unit with their marriage. The family may encourage and support them emotionally, but they are essentially creating their own new family with the marriage.

In discussing weddings, we refer to a **traditional wedding**. Because Americans admire individuality as much as tradition, there are many cases of changes within the traditional wedding framework. Many couples also choose to have non-traditional weddings as well. In this section, we describe traditional weddings, but we also discuss variations on the traditional wedding. We also discuss the role of religion in weddings.

The stages of an American wedding are engagement and wedding.

Engagement

Normally the man asks the woman to marry him. He buys an engagement ring for the woman. The couple then go about the process of planning the wedding and **setting a date**. Some couples do not immediately set a date, but others usually set a date for within six months to one year of the engagement. If the couple wishes a traditional church wedding, then they may have to wait for a time when the church will be available. There is no specific engagement party or other event, although the couple may choose to do something special to celebrate.

Before the wedding

Invitations: One to two months before the wedding, the couple sends out invitations. Most wedding invitations are RSVP, which means you must inform the couple whether you are attending. It is not appropriate to go to a wedding if you are not invited. It is also not appropriate to bring an extra guest. Normally, children do not attend weddings because they will make noise. Sometimes, people choose to attend only the reception which follows, but not the wedding itself. Sometimes, the wedding is very small, and so guests are only invited to the reception.

AMERICAN / KOREAN CONTRAST

Americans plan ahead and so have specific ways they ask their guests to help them in this planning. For formal events such as weddings or a special party, Americans especially like to know how many guests to expect so that they can prepare an appropriate amount of food, etc. So, for special events, Americans often send special invitations in the mail many weeks in advance of the event. At the bottom of the invitation will be written some information about whether you need to reply to the invitation, i.e. to tell them whether or not you will attend. Most commonly, you will find the letters RSVP at the bottom. This is a request for you to reply. Sometimes you may find the words "regrets only," which means you need to reply only if you are not planning to attend. Koreans, on the other hand, tend to be more spontaneous about even large events such as a wedding. One of the foundations of Korean society is a promotion of personal modesty. To extend invitations well in advance of an event might seem boastful and self-important. Therefore, Koreans often extend invitations only a few days before an event. Americans send invitations in advance as a consideration of others so that they may plan their schedules. Whereas Koreans do not send invitations in advance as a consideration of others so that they will not be embarrassed.

Bridal Shower: Usually a week or so before the wedding, the friends or family of the **bride** give her a **bridal shower**. They have light refreshments, cake, and games. The guests bring practical gifts for the home. Often, people who are not invited to the wedding will be invited to the shower.

> **NOTE:** Gift-giving is an important part of the wedding. Many couples will register their names at specific stores and ask for specific items, such as dishes or small appliances. People who wish to give them gifts then go to that store and ask if the couple had any special requests. They then either buy a gift certificate or purchase a gift which the store will send to the couple. Gifts, generally, are for the home and do not include large appliances or homes.

Bachelor Party: During the week before the wedding, the friends of the **groom** will give him a **bachelor party**. The bachelor party usually has a lot of drinking and entertainment. The friends of the groom usually make a lot of jokes about the groom losing his freedom with his marriage.

Marriage License: At least three days before the wedding (depending on the state), the couple must apply for a marriage license from their local court house. This is legal permission to marry. In less than half of the states, the couple must also have blood tests before they apply for the license. After the wedding, they will have a marriage license which is signed by the person who performed the wedding (**officiated**), and shows that they are legally married.

Wedding Rehearsal: The evening before the wedding, the couple and the **wedding party** gather at the wedding site and practice the wedding.

Rehearsal Dinner: After the rehearsal, the groom's family takes the bride's family to dinner at a restaurant. Traditionally, the bride's family pays for the wedding, but in recent years many couples have also begun to pay for themselves.

The Wedding

A traditional wedding is seen as having two parts: The wedding ceremony itself and the reception. We discuss each one separately.

Wedding: A traditional wedding usually has the following form:
*the bride is dressed in a special, white dress. She carries a large bouquet of flowers and wears a veil or a special headdress.
*the groom is dressed in a suit or a tuxedo.
*there is usually **a matron of honor** and **bridesmaids** for the bride. (The number of people who **stand up** for the bride varies according to individuals. At some weddings, there is only a matron of honor and a best man; at others, there may be a matron of honor, several bridesmaids, etc.). The people who stand up for the bride and groom wear formal dresses, usually of the same color and design. They usually all carry flowers. The matron of honor stands closest to the bride and helps her before, during, and after the ceremony.
*there is a **best man** and **ushers** for the groom. They are all dressed in matching tuxedos or suits. The best man stands closest to the groom and helps him before, during, and after the ceremony.
*music is played before the ceremony. There are often special songs sung at different times during the ceremony. The groom waits for the bride, who walks up the aisle. Traditionally, the bride walks up the aisle to "Bridal Chorus from Lohengrin" by Wagner. She and the groom leave the altar after the ceremony to "The Wedding March" by Mendelssohn.
*the church or home where the wedding takes place is specially decorated with flowers and ribbons. If it is a church, the bride's guests usually sit on one side; the groom's guests sit on the other.
*a minister or justice of the peace officiates at the wedding. The wedding itself centers around the words of the person who officiates. During this part of the ceremony, the couple exchange vows. At the end of the ceremony, they exchange wedding rings. Since the 1960s, many couples write their own vows or ceremony, which is then interwoven with a traditional

ceremony. In many denominations, the minister may encourage the couple to write their own vows or to choose appropriate words to describe their relationship.

*after the rings are exchanged, the bride and groom kiss. They then walk down the aisle together. Often, the guests applaud them.

*before and after the ceremony, pictures are taken. After the pictures, the bride and groom leave the wedding site. The guests have been waiting for them outside of the chapel. Traditionally, as the newly married couple left, the guests threw rice on them. Nowadays, the guests more often throw bird seed. There are also new traditions, such as ringing small bells or blowing soap bubbles. The couple leave the wedding site in a car that has been decorated. Usually "just married" is written on the car, and shoes or tin cans have been tied to it.

NOTE: The text for a civil ceremony and a traditional church ceremony can vary. In addition, the texts for ceremonies vary by religion. Futhermore, a religious service may be added to the actual stating of the vows (the ceremony). For example, many Catholics have a full Mass before the exchange of vows. Some protestant churches may follow this form as well by having a religious service (but not a Mass).

After the wedding—the reception

Receptions vary according to the size of the wedding. At smaller weddings, the reception is often held immediately following the wedding.

Gifts: If gifts have not been sent in advance of the wedding, the guests usually bring their gifts to the reception. There is seldom a table for gift giving immediately before the wedding. Rather, gifts are usually brought to the reception. At some receptions, the couple opens their presents in front of their guests.

Food: Some receptions provide a full meal. At these dinners, there is a head table where the couple and their wedding party sits. Other receptions may provide a buffet. Others yet, may provide only snacks or sandwiches.

Cake: Regardless of the type of refreshment offered, one essential aspect of the reception is the wedding cake. The cake usually has several layers and traditionally has a small model of a bride and groom on the top. Toward the end of the reception, especially if it is a dinner, the bride and groom cut the cake together with one hand. They then feed a piece of cake to each other. Everyone applauds when this is done.

The bouquet and the garter: During the reception, usually close to the end, the bride will throw her bouquet over her left shoulder. The woman who catches it is said to be the next one to get married. The bride will have a blue garter on one leg. During the reception, the husband will take off that garter and pitch it over his left shoulder to his male friends. The man to catch it will be the next to get married.

The first dance: The first dance at the wedding is for the groom to dance with his mother and the bride to dance with her father. During this dance, the father will give the bride to her new husband. Other guests will not dance until after this dance.

At some point during the reception, the couple may leave for their honeymoon. Some couples stay for the reception and do not leave for the honeymoon until the next day.

Korean Ways

Koreans see a marriage as the uniting of two families. It is very much a family occasion and a family decision. Often, the new couple may live with the groom's parents, especially if he is the oldest son. Regardless of whether the couple lives with the husband's family, the bride is seen as joining the husband's family and leaving her own.

In Korea, there are two types of wedding ceremonies: a **traditional wedding** (which is modeled on Yi Dynasty customs) and a white wedding (which is modeled on the Western marriage ceremony). Regardless of the origin of the tradition, a wedding ceremony in Korea is a way of announcing the marriage to the public, but it is not the legal ceremony. That is, in the U.S. the formal marriage ceremony and the legal ceremony take place at the same time. In Korea, the marriage is not official and legal until it has been processed in the district office and until the marriage has been entered into the family records. So, often, the couple may have already been legally married for some time before the actual wedding ceremony.

The stages of a Korean wedding are engagement and wedding.

*Engagement (*yakhonsik* [약혼식])

A marriage is agreed upon and the couple announce it. Often, the families are involved in this process, too. They set a date. There can also be an engagement party at which food and drink is served.

*Wedding (*kyŏlhonsik* [결혼식])

The wedding has several stages.

Before the wedding

Invitations: Invitations are usually extended orally close to the wedding date. Everyone is invited who knows the couple and is not inappropriate for these guests to bring an extra guest. Children attend weddings, and sometimes whole families come. The wedding hall can sometimes become very noisy with people talking and visiting outside and inside the wedding hall, even during the actual ceremony. As in the U.S., sometimes people choose to attend only the reception, but not the wedding.

Gift-giving: There is an elaborate and extensive tradition of gift-giving between families to celebrate a Korean wedding, with many of these gifts exchanged between the families in the months prior to the ceremony. The richer the family, the more elaborate the gifts.

However, most gift-giving follows this pattern:

Husband's family: The husband's family usually provides the new couple with an apartment and gives the bride several sets of jewelry. They also give the bride some new clothes for her wedding trip, and they buy new clothes for her parents. The groom, several days before the wedding, will come to the bride's house with some of his friends carrying a box (*ham* [함]) of clothing and other gifts for the family. This is a fun tradition that includes lots of joking and lots of food and drink.

Bride's family: The bride's family often provides the new couple with furniture and with appliances. Wealthier families may also buy a car or set their new son-in-law up in business. Thus, Koreans often talk about the wedding gift being comprised of three keys: keys to an apartment, keys to a car, and keys to a place of business (in cases where the groom is a doctor).

The couple: The couple usually buy each other watches and rings. Rings are currently exchanged as part of the wedding ceremony, but it is not a traditional Korean custom. They wear the rings unless they are poor or if they want to keep them safe for some reason. Newlyweds can often be identified not only by the wedding ring, but also by their new watches and jewelry.

NOTE: Gift-giving is an important part of the wedding. Outside the wedding room, a table is set up and a placard bearing the names of each family hangs from the table. Guests bring their gifts to this table, and someone writes the name of the guest down. The most common gift is money, and it is given in a white envelope. A common amount is between 30,000 and 50,000 Won. Small practical gifts for the home are not common. Some couples arrange for gifts for the guests as well.

The Wedding

A traditional wedding is seen as having two parts, the wedding ceremony itself and the reception. We discuss each one separately.

Wedding: Because the Western-style white wedding is more common in recent years, we describe that wedding first. Then we describe a traditional wedding.

White Wedding: A white wedding usually has the following form: *the bride is dressed in a special, white dress. She carries a large bouquet of flowers and wears a veil or a special headdress. The bride does not smile during the ceremony. If she does, it is said that she will have daughters.

*the groom is dressed in a suit or a tuxedo and white gloves. The groom also is not supposed to smile.

*the bride and groom stand at the front of the room with a presider or master of ceremonies (*juraeja* [주례자]). If it is a religious ceremony, the minister, monk, or priest is the presider.

*music may or may not be played during the ceremony. The groom usually walks up the aisle, then waits for the bride, who walks up the aisle after he is standing at the front of the room. Koreans will often play the "Bridal Chorus from Lohengrin" by Wagner during this part of the wedding, but may choose some other type of Western music as well.

*unless the couple is Christian and has specially arranged to be married in a church, the wedding takes place in a wedding hall, which has many rooms designated for this person. In fact, many large companies have wedding halls for their employees to use. There may be large bouquets of flowers near the front where the couple stand, but the hall room itself is not specially decorated with flowers and ribbons. As in the West, the bride's guests usually sit on one side; the groom's guests sit on the other.

*a person officiates at the wedding as an announcer (*sahwoeja* [사회자]). This person announces who the people are and what will take place. After some bowing, some short speeches by friends, or some music and entertainment, the *juraeja* — usually an older, married friend, teacher, or someone else of distinction — will make a longer speech about marriages or give advice to the couple. But there is no specific text for a ceremony that every wedding follows. Depending on the ceremony, the couple may exchange vows (*sinlang sinbu matjŏl* [신랑 신부 맞절]) and rings. They normally do not kiss. At the end of the ceremony, following the longer speech by the *juraeja*, the couple is presented together. They then bow to the guests, who applaud.

*before and after the ceremony, pictures are taken. It is an important part of the ceremony to have different sets of friends and family in photographs with the couple.

*after the pictures, the guests leave the wedding hall for the banquet site. The bride and groom then change their clothes into traditional Korean clothes for an important ceremony known as "*p'yebaek*" [폐백].

Korean traditional wedding: Some modern young couples choose to have a ceremony modeled after the traditional wedding of the Yi Dynasty. While traditionally the wedding was in the yard of the bride's home, most modern young couples celebrate the traditional wedding in a wedding hall. They often modify the ritual. In a traditional Korean wedding:

*the bride is dressed in a green and red *hanbok* [한복]. Over the *hanbok* is another short dress with long, multi-colored sleeves. She has a large red circle in the middle of her forehead and one on each cheek. She wears her hair in a large elaborate bun in the back, with a large wooden hairpin through it. She wears a small black hat decorated with sequins. On her feet, she wears traditional rubber shoes. She carries a large white cloth, which she holds over her forearms which are clasped one inside the other. She holds this cloth in front of her face during the ceremony. She was traditionally carried to the wedding site in a palanquin. She must keep her face hidden by the white cloth over her forearms before and during the ceremony. She does this by holding her forearms up to her forehead.

*the husband is dressed in blue silk. He wears a black felt hat and black felt boots. He traditionally entered on a white pony. He brings a pair of wooden ducks to the ceremony (which symbolize fidelity). (Both his and the bride's clothing are based on the dress of the noblemen of the Yi Dynasty because everyone is royalty on their wedding day.)

*during the ceremony, the bride and groom sit opposite each other separated by a table piled high with rice cakes and fruit. The master of ceremonies tells the couple what they should do and extolls the virtues of marriage. That is, he discusses certain virtues and periodically tells the couple to bow to each other. The bride makes three *k'ŭnchŏl* [큰절] (large bows), several times throughout the ceremony, for each time the groom bows once. Two women assist the bride with these bows. The bride and groom each take a drink of rice wine and a ceremonial bite of rice.

*a respected person will give a speech of advice.

*finally, the couple turn and bow to their guests, who applaud. At this point, the bride can lower her white cloth and show her face to her new husband.

*while the guests enjoy a reception, the bride and groom retreat to perform the *p'yebaek*.

After the wedding — the reception

P'yebaek: *p'yebaek* is a traditional ceremony in which the bride is brought into the husband's family. The bride's family do not attend the ceremony.

*the bride is dressed as she would be in a traditional Korean wedding ceremony. She is in a green and red **hanbok**, over which is another short dress with long, multi-colored sleeves.

*The husband is dressed in blue silk. He wears a felt hat.

*The husband's parents, siblings, and other important members of the extended family are seated. The bride (assisted by two women) and groom perform three *k'ŭnchŏl* to the parents and to each of the family members in turn and give them wine to drink. After each bow and cup of wine, the relatives give money to the couple (in envelopes). The groom's mother also throws jujubes and peeled raw chestnuts into the bride's lap. The number of daughters and sons is said to be measured by how many jujubes (daughters) and chestnuts (sons) the bride catches in her skirt.

Guests: While the couple performs the *p'yebaek*, the guests go to a local restaurant or reception hall and eat usually seated at long tables. The bride and groom may join them for a short time to thank them for coming. Then they retire to the husband's home or leave directly for their honeymoon. Before the honeymoon, they may open their gifts in private or with the family.

AMERICAN / KOREAN CONTRAST

Americans view weddings as both a public and private celebration that the couple shares. Publicly, the couple celebrates with wedding showers and other parties. Privately, the couple celebrates by usually inviting only family and special friends to the wedding ceremony itself. Some American couples even choose to have a small ceremony just for themselves and may even exclude family members. On the other hand, Koreans view weddings as both a family and a community event. They often celebrate the pre-wedding period with an engagement party and several traditional activities, such as the bridegroom delivering a *ham* to the bride's home. The wedding is often open to whomever would like to attend and is a social event that includes business associates of parents and other family members.

For both Americans and Koreans, the period before the wedding is a time for the families of the bride and groom to become acquainted. For Koreans, this acquaintance takes on a greater importance than it does it the U.S. since the wedding is a merging of families, not merely a private event for the couple.

What are the rituals surrounding deaths and funerals?

American Ways

In the United States, there are specific behaviors related to responding to the death of someone. Americans
*send sympathy cards or a short letter.
*say, "I was very sorry to hear about (the name of the person)" or "Please accept my **condolences**. Is there anything I can do to help?"
*send flowers to the funeral home or to the individual (for family members, colleagues, etc.).
*take food to the family's home or to a location for the dinner which follows the funeral.

The family in the first hours after the death will:

*contact a funeral home.
*arrange to buy a plot of land for the burial.

*arrange for an **obituary** (a notice in the newspaper of the person's death). This obituary will announce the death to the community and give information about the surviving family members.

*arrange for the funeral service.

*select clothing the deceased will be buried in.

*notify other family members.

Most funerals occur about three days after the death of a family member. This is for practical reasons — it takes time to prepare the body, and there is often a viewing of the body.

Viewing of the body: Normally, bodies are taken to **funeral homes** to be prepared for burial. Then, the bodies are **embalmed**. The family buys a **casket** from the funeral home to bury the body in. The family brings special or favorite clothing to dress the **deceased** in.

For one or two evenings, the body in its casket is shown for people who want to come to the funeral home and see it. The family stays at the funeral home during these calling hours, and friends and family come to **pay their condolences**. These visitors often stay for thirty minutes or an hour and talk to each other or to family members.

At the funeral home will be a visitors' book for mourners to sign. They can usually also pick up a small pamphlet which gives information about the deceased and the funeral service. After the funeral, the family writes thank you notes to the visitors, especially to those who brought flowers.

NOTE: The atmosphere at a funeral is very quiet, which Americans consider respectful. Americans value self control during these times. While there may be quiet weeping, they avoid loud outpouring of emotion. For persons who scream or cannot control themselves they say, "They are not taking it well." Persons who can control emotions are "taking it well."

Also, Americans often visit graves, especially on holidays such as Memorial Day, on the anniversary of the person's death, or on the person's birthday. When they visit, they often bring flowers or they decorate the grave (especially at Christmas).

There is no ancestor worship and no specific ceremony that accompanies the visit to the grave.

Funeral Service: Before the body is buried, there is usually a funeral service. Often, this a religious service, and in some religions the body is taken from the funeral home to a church for the service.[7] Most often, a religious representative, such as a minister, priest, or rabbi, officiates at the funeral service, which the immediate family has arranged in advance. A Christian religious service is usually comprised of:

*a prayer or meditation.
*quiet music before the service, some singing once or twice during the service, and music or singing at the end. Sometimes the music is something special that the deceased would have liked.
*readings from Bible passages or some special, inspirational quotes.
*a short sermon talking about the deceased and about life and death. This is followed by a prayer or meditation.
***eulogies** (in which the family or friends talk about the deceased).
*all of the **mourners** walking in single file in front of the casket to **pay their last respects** at the end of the service.

The Burial: If the body is being buried, the procedures after the service are usually comprised of:

*the mourners leave the church or funeral home, and the casket with the body is carried out by **pallbearers**. It is placed in the **hearse** and driven to the cemetery.
*some of the mourners will follow behind the hearse in their cars in a **funeral procession**. The mourners will have a little flag on the top of their cars. As they drive slowly to the cemetery, they turn on their lights. A policeman accompanies the funeral procession, and traffic stops for them until they have passed.
*at the burial site, flowers are placed by the casket, which sits beside or above the **grave**. Seats are arranged for the immediate family members.

*after a short prayer or speech, the family will leave. Many people take a flower from some of the bouquets to keep.

*the body is lowered into the grave and buried after the mourners have left.

*there is usually a reception at a church or in the immediate family's home following the burial. The food has usually been provided by members of the community, and all mourners are invited to eat after the service.

NOTE: Some families have a private funeral and do not have viewing. Instead, after the funeral there may be a memorial service. The memorial service may follow the format of the funeral service, but have more eulogies and there will be no viewing of the body. Furthermore, some individuals may desire to have their bodies **cremated**. In these cases, their families may have memorial services for their friends and family, or may choose to have only a private service. Some families keep the ashes of the deceased. Others may distribute the ashes at a special place.

Korean Ways

Koreans do not view the body as Americans do, but they do have days of mourning in which family, friends, and colleagues visit the family of the deceased.

In the following we detail the period of mourning after a death, the funeral service and burial, and the Korean "memorial service" known as *chesa* [제사].

Period of mourning: Traditionally, Koreans prefer to die at home partially because they believe that the spirit of the deceased stays in the place where the person has died. Another reason they prefer to die at home used to be lack of choice: Hospitals were not readily available. With industrialization since the 1950s, however, has come an increase in hospitals and a change in the custom of dying at home. When people do die in the home — and it is still common — the days of visitation and mourning usually occur in the home, even though most Korean homes and apartments are small. If someone dies in the hospital, then the days of visitation occur in a special area of the hospital set up for that purpose. Indeed, some modern hospitals are building an entire wing for mourning.

After the death, the body of the deceased is prepared within a day for the mourning period to begin, but there is no tradition of viewing the body as there is in the U.S. (There are three, five, or seven days of mourning, depending on the wishes of the family.) If the person has died in the home, the body is placed in a coffin which is then placed in an important part of the house. The body is cremated after the days of mourning and the funeral ceremony. During the days of mourning, a small altar is set in front of the coffin that contains:

*a photograph of the deceased with a black ribbon draped over the upper two corners.
*a bottle of rice wine, seasonal foods, stacks of rice cakes (*ddŏk* [떡]), dried pollack, and fruit. At mealtimes, freshly cooked rice and soup (or a bowl of water) is served on the table as well. Chopsticks are symbolically put in the bowl of rice and a spoon is put in the soup as an offering for the deceased. (These foods represent sustenance for the deceased as they pass on to the next world. The women family members have usually cooked the favorite foods of the deceased.)
*incense.

The family members stay up all night during the several days of mourning. During this time, family and friends may come at any time to pay their condolences. The family of the deceased — usually the male members — sit by the altar with sad faces to receive the visitors.

These mourners make two *k'ŭnchŏl* [큰절] ('large bow') and a half bow to the altar, and then bow to the family. They may leave an envelope with money on the altar or in front of the family members. (This money helps the family with the funeral costs.) The mourners then retire to another room to eat.

Traditionally, white is the color of mourning in Korea. So, during the days of mourning, the family dress in white clothing made of hemp, but visitors are not expected to. In recent years, however, some male family members wear black suits with a white band on the sleeve.

AMERICAN / KOREAN CONTRAST

In the U.S., self control is valued in times of grief. While Americans may expect the family to cry at a funeral, they also expect most of the crying to be done privately in the home. On the other hand, Koreans expect both men and women to grieve quite openly with much crying and wailing, and even loss of self control.

There is no obituary column in a Korean daily newspaper as there is in the U.S., and notification of the death is usually done by word of mouth. However, in recent years wealthier families often put a death announcement in the newspaper. Wealthier families also have a family plot of land in a mountainous/hilly area away from the family home in which the family members will be buried (or entombed).

However, the majority of Koreans do not have family plots, and in these cases the deceased is cremated. The ashes are either kept in small urns in Buddhist temples (if the family was Buddhist), put inside a tomb (of wealthy families), or spread without specific ceremony on a hillside or in the river.

Funeral Service and Burial: When a person has a mountainside burial mound (there are no cemeteries), the funeral service is a procession by the male family members with the body to the burial site or throughout the village/neighborhood. Before the procession to the grave site, the women say their goodbyes through tears and wailing. When it is time for burial, traditionally the pallbearers carry the wooden coffin in a decorated palanquin.

At the grave site, the family performs a special rite, known as *hakwansik* [하관식], before lowering the body into the shallow grave.

During the burial, the coffin is broken open and the body placed in the grave. It is then covered by a large mound of earth that makes a small hill on the mountainside. Afterwards, the family members return to the family home for a meal. (In modern Korea, many women may choose to accompany the body to the grave site as well.) If there is no burial, the casket is quietly taken to the crematorium after a quiet short ceremony by immediate family members.

Related to Korean funeral and burial rituals is the custom of *chesa* [제사]. It is an important part of Korean life related to the honoring of ancestors, and thus to one's cultural heritage. There are two types of *chesa*: In the home and at the grave site.

Chesa at home: *Chesa* is performed in a large room at the home of the eldest son (or oldest family member), where all the family members gather. An altar is set up that is very similar to the one used during the time of mourning: A small table laden with a photo of the deceased, food, drink, and incense. After performing *k'ŭnchŏl* twice before the table and then standing and doing a half bow, each person in turn takes a drink of wine, offers a drink to the deceased in the form of a filled glass, and bows two and a half times again. Finally, everyone bows together two and a half times toward the deceased and then eats and drinks the food and alcohol they have given up in offering. *Chesa* is performed at home on the birthday of the deceased for the first three years after death, on *Ch'usŏk*, on the anniversary of the death, and on New Year's Day. Koreans believe that the spirit of the deceased is in the home, and thus will bless the home if honored regularly through *chesa*.

Chesa at the grave: On the anniversary of the family member's death, the family gathers together and goes to the grave site (usually male members, but sometimes whole families go as well) to pay honor to the deceased. They take a small table and place food and drink on the table for the spirit of the deceased. After bowing (*k'ŭnchŏl*) twice before the table and then standing and making a half bow, each person in turn takes a drink of wine and then pours a drink for the deceased over the grave. Each person then bows again two and a half times. Then, they clean around the grave. Finally, they bow again, and eat and drink the food and alcohol they have given up in offering. *Chesa* at the grave is performed for *Hanshik* Day, *Ch'usŏk*, and sometimes at New Year's.

What are the important holidays and how are they celebrated?

American Ways

There are two categories of holidays in the U.S.: Legal and traditional. A **legal holiday** means that the post office, bank, etc. are closed on that day. The legal holidays are New Year's Day, President's Day, Martin Luther King Day, Memorial Day, Independence Day, Labor Day, Columbus Day, Veteran's Day, Thanksgiving Day, and Christmas Day. The most well-known traditional holidays are Valentine's Day, St. Patrick's Day, Easter, and Halloween. In this section, we briefly discuss these holidays and the rituals or traditions that are related to them as well as to religious holidays.

NOTE: Many legal holidays are celebrated on a Monday to allow Americans to have a 3-day weekend.

Legal Holidays

Martin Luther King Day: January 15. Established in 1983 to honor the great civil rights leader, there is no specific custom yet established to honor this day. It is celebrated as a legal holiday on the third Monday in January.

President's Day: February 21. This holiday honors two important American Presidents, George Washington and Abraham Lincoln (both were born in February). The holiday is celebrated either on a Monday before or after February 21, so that Americans can have a three-day weekend. Oddly, many stores choose that day to have large sales, especially for furniture and home products.

Memorial Day: Originally May 31, it is always celebrated the last Monday in May. On this day, people who have died, especially in wars, are remembered. The U.S. President hangs a wreath at the Tomb of the Unknown Soldier in Arlington National Cemetery in Virginia. People take flowers to graves, and there are special articles in the newspapers about previous wars. Many small towns have parades and families have picnics. Many people believe summer begins with the Memorial Day Weekend.

Independence Day: This holiday is always observed on July 4. It is in honor of the signing of the Declaration of Independence in 1776. Usually, families have picnics. In small towns there are parades. Every town and city has fireworks on this day to celebrate.

Labor Day: This is always held the first Monday of September. It is not in honor of labor workers, but rather marks the end of the easier summer months and the beginning of the harder winter months. On this day, families have picnics. Many people believe summer is over on Labor Day Weekend.

Columbus Day: The traditional day of Columbus's birthday is October 12, but the holiday is celebrated on the Monday previous to October 12. The day is to honor the explorer and his discovery. There are no special customs on this day.

Veteran's Day: The designated day for this holiday is November 11. Veteran's Day is in honor of all soldiers who have fought in wars. In small towns, there are often parades. There are also special television programming and articles in the newspaper about previous wars and issues related to veterans.

Thanksgiving Day: Thanksgiving is a very important American holiday. It is celebrated on the fourth Thursday of November and honors European immigration to the North American continent. The story is that the Pilgrims (immigrants) to New England had a very bad winter in which many of their group died. They survived only with the help of the Native Americans. At the end of their first year and after their first successful harvest, they sat down together for a feast. They gave thanks for the food and for their survival. Thanksgiving is considered a family holiday, when most families get together for a large meal and have time together. The common food for Thanksgiving is a baked turkey, mashed potatoes, sweet potatoes (yams), cranberry sauce, and pumpkin pie. These are all foods indigenous to New England. The Thanksgiving holiday extends over a 4-day weekend, but only Thanksgiving Day itself is a legal holiday. Many people begin shopping for Christmas the day after Thanksgiving, and so the holiday is said to mark the beginning of the "holiday season" which lasts until at least Christmas Day.

Christmas: December 25 is the legal holiday and the day Christmas is celebrated on. However, for many people Christmas is associated with the weeks between Thanksgiving and Christmas Day, called "the holiday season." (For many others, it extends beyond Christmas Day to New Year's.) During the holiday season, many people have parties. Many people make special cookies, candies, and cakes, which they often give as gifts. During the Christmas season, money and gifts are collected for the poor. There are special songs of the season, Christmas carols. Some people go to the houses in their neighborhoods and sing these carols. People give gifts to family members, friends, and co-workers. Family members usually open gifts on Christmas morning, but it depends on the family tradition. Christmas began as a religious holiday, and for many it remains so. But for the majority of Americans, Christmas has become a traditional holiday separated from its original religious meaning. One tradition especially for children is that of Santa Claus. American children believe that Santa Claus lives in the North Pole and rides a sleigh on Christmas Eve to bring toys and other gifts to good little boys and girls. Children leave cookies and milk on a table for Santa Claus to eat when he comes down their chimneys to leave presents. Many families gather on Christmas Day for a large meal of turkey or ham and lots of delicious vegetables, breads, and cakes.

New Year's Eve and New Year's Day: New Year's Day is the legal holiday, but it is quietly celebrated. The common meal on New Year's Day is pork or roast beef, depending on the area of the country. New Year's Eve is a time of celebration, and many people have parties to welcome in the new year.

Traditional Holidays

Valentine's Day: February 14. This is considered a day of romance and love. Husbands and wives and boyfriends and girlfriends exchange cards and give each other gifts of chocolate or flowers. Family members and friends may also exchange gifts on such days. Many people wear red and white on these days, and women wear heart-shaped pins or earrings. Hearts and red roese are the symbols of Valentine's Day.

St. Patrick's Day: March 17. This is a holiday in honor of the patron saint of Ireland. It is celebrated with parades in areas with large populations of Irish-Americans. Many bars will color their food and beer green, and many people wear green on this day. Two symbols of St. Patrick's Day are clover and **leprechauns**.

Halloween: October 31. Halloween is based on All Hallow's Eve, when it was believed in ancient times in Great Britain that evil spirits came out. And so the people would dress in costumes to frighten away the evil spirits. In the American version, children dress in odd costumes (often as monsters, witches, or skeletons) and go door-to-door. They knock on the door and say "trick-or-treat," and the resident gives them candy or fruit. For fun, many adults dress up on this day and celebrate it as well with parties.

Religious Holidays

Easter: Easter is a Christian holiday in which the resurrection of Jesus Christ is celebrated. It is not a legal holiday, and its date changes from year to year according to the religious calendar. However, it usually falls at the end of March or the beginning of April. Many people celebrate Easter by buying flowers, especially lilies, and new clothes. Many Christians who do not regularly attend church do attend at Easter. Many families gather for Easter dinner, where the most common food is ham or turkey. Traditional aspects of Easter are that children color hard-boiled eggs, which their parents hide. The children then have an Easter Egg Hunt. Parents also give their children Easter baskets, which are filled with candy and toys. They tell their children that the Easter Bunny brought the baskets.

Christmas: This has been dealt with in the section on legal holidays.

NOTE: Some holidays have special greetings or expressions. The most common ones are: "Happy Valentine's Day," "Happy Easter," "Happy Fourth of July," "Happy Halloween," "Happy Thanksgiving," "Merry Christmas" and "Happy New Year."

Korean Ways

Until after World War II, Korea followed the Lunar Calendar (*ŭmnyŏk*) [음력]), a system of setting dates by the cycles of the moon rather than the artificial imposition of fixed dates on a calendar. Following the Lunar Calendar, then, would mean that dates fall on different dates of the year according to the Western Calendar (*sŏyŏk* or *yangnyŏk* [서역, 양력]). It is a system that is sometimes confusing to Westerners and often to Koreans as well, especially modern Koreans who have become accustomed to the Western calendar. However, the Lunar calendar is still used especially by farmers to help them decide when to plant and harvest crops.

The most important Korean holidays are New Year's Day and *Ch'usŏk*, which are also family-centered holidays. During these holidays, city dwellers try to return to their home villages to perform *chesa* and have a family reunion. Each of these holidays lasts for about three days, and most shops and other public conveniences are closed for business. New Year's Day and *Ch'usŏk* are considered family holidays, with special foods and family and friends enjoying the leisurely pace of the holiday. On most holidays, the government may arrange special performances of traditional Korean performing arts in the national theaters.

The list of holidays compiled here provide fixed calendar dates as well as the general time of year that the holiday is celebrated according to the Lunar Calendar.

Legal Holidays

New Year's Day: January 1, or late January to mid February (Lunar Calendar). This day is celebrated both according to the Western and the Lunar Calendars. The legal holiday falls on the Western Calendar, and two to ten weeks later New Year's is celebrated again according to the cycle of the Lunar Calendar. (Many Koreans expect that as the old generation familiar with the Lunar Calendar passes away, so will the celebration of the Lunar New Year.)

Regardless of whether it is celebrated according to the Western or the Lunar Calendar, the traditions remain the same except that no New Year's Eve is celebrated for the Lunar Calendar. New Year's Day has several traditions:

*as a family holiday, it requires family visits with bows of respect (from a sitting position) (*sebae* [세배]) to the elders of the household.

In one's home, the *sebae* are performed before breakfast. Later, family members may visit each other's homes to perform *sebae*. Children especially look forward to going from house to house because they receive money (*saebaeton* [세배돈]) for their bows.

*the family eat special foods such as *ddŏk* [떡] and *ddŏkkuk* [떡국], *sikhye* [식혜] (a sweet rice punch), *sujŏngkwa* [수정과](a persimmon punch), *makkŏli* [막걸리] (a mild, thick rice wine), and *dongdongju* [동동주] (a special kind of strong rice wine which is essentially a better quality of *makkŏli*).

hanbok is often worn, especially by older Koreans.

*traditional games are played, particularly *yutnori* [윷놀이]. *Yutnori* is comprised of a playing board, pieces to move around the board, and 4 pieces of rounded wood about 4 inches long and flattened on one side. Players throw the wooden pieces up in the air and move their pieces on the board according to how the pieces of wood have landed. The first person to circle the board with all pieces is the winner.

chesa is performed to one's ancestors

NOTE: New Year's Eve: December 31. In Seoul, the large bell (*jongkak* [종각]) on Chongro, a large avenue that runs through downtown Seoul, is rung at midnight. In addition to the ringing of the bell, Koreans have also traditionally gathered for parties to welcome in the new year.

Independence Day: March 1. This day is in honor of the attempted independence from Japanese Colonization on March 1, 1919. In honor of the day, the Korean Proclamation of Independence is read. People gather in Pagoda Park in Seoul. There may be special performances of Korean traditional performing arts. There is often special television programming and articles in the newspaper recalling the Japanese occupation and the bravery of the leaders of the independence movement. Often there are parades.

Arbor Day: April 5. Public officials and private citizens plant trees on this day. The planting of trees is especially significant since much of Korea's forestry was destroyed during the Korean war.

Children's Day: May 5. Parents give presents to their children. Parks, zoos, and amusement parks are often free of charge to children and provide a lot of special programming for children.

Buddha's Birthday: the eighth day of the fourth month according to the Lunar Calendar (usually in May according to the Solar Calendar). On this day, Buddhists and non-Buddhists alike visit temples. At the temple, they hang lanterns with the family name attached to it. Along the street, colorful paper lanterns can be seen hanging from houses or on balconies, and in Seoul there is a parade from Yoido to Chokaejong (on Chongro in downtown Seoul), one of the most famous Korean Buddhist Temples.

Memorial Day: June 6. This day honors those who have died in wars or in other service to their country. A special memorial service is held at the Korean National Cemetery in Seoul.

Constitution Day: July 17. This day is to commemorate the adoption of the Constitution for the establishment of the Republic of Korea in 1948. There may be special television programming or newspaper articles detailing the history and events that led up the establishment of the constitution.

Liberation Day: August 15. This day celebrates both the liberation from the Japanese Occupation in 1945, and the beginning of the Republic of Korea in 1948. There may be special television programming or newspaper articles commemorating Korea's independence.

Ch'usŏk [추석]: August 15 according to the Lunar Calendar (which usually falls in late September or early October according to the Solar Calendar). Also called the "Harvest Moon Festival" or the "Korean Thanksgiving", *Ch'usŏk* is celebrated over a three-day period. Held during the full moon, it is a time to return home to perform *chesa*, and so it is a time of extended home visits, of returning to one's roots. For this reason, the roads and railways are jammed with holiday travelers trying to return home, so if you want to travel during this time you should buy your bus or train ticket well in advance. *Ch'usŏk* is also a time of elaborate and generous gift giving. The specialty food associated with *ch'usŏk* is *songp'yŏn* [송편], a rice cake shaped like a half moon and filled with sweetened sesame seeds or mashed red beans and steamed over pine needles. A Seoul tradition during *Ch'usŏk* is to climb or drive to the top of Namsan mountain in Seoul to admire the moon. *Ch'usŏk* in essence, then, is a quiet family-oriented holiday full of food, gifts, family, and friends.

National Foundation Day: October 3. This day celebrates the mythical founding of Korea in 2333 B.C. by Tangun, God's son who came to earth and mated with a bear.

Hangŭl **Day:** October 9. This day celebrates the establishment of the Korean alphabet, *Hangŭl*, in 1446 by the Great King Sejong. The creation of their alphabet, *hangŭl*, represents for Koreans independence and the establishment of their own personal identity separate from Chinese. It marks the beginning of literacy in the indigenous language of Korean.

Christmas Day: December 25. Christmas was brought to Korea by Western missionaries and is celebrated by many Koreans in a style adapted from the West. Some Koreans buy Christmas trees and others decorate their homes. Some Koreans give gifts and Christmas carols have made their way onto the radio. Korean Christians (about 25% of the total population) celebrate Christmas as a religious holiday.

Traditional Holidays

Borŭm [보름]: First full moon of the lunar new year. On this day, for luck throughout the year, families abstain from meat and instead of plain white rice eat a mixture of rice, millet, soy beans, kidney beans, and tapioca (sweet rice).

Hanshik [한식] **Day:** 105 days after the winter solstice according to the Lunar Calendar. On this day, Koreans eat cold food and attend to the graves or shrines of ancestors.

Parent's Day: May 8. This day began as a tribute to mothers but gradually evolved into a day for both parents. Children give a corsage (usually a carnation) to their mothers and a gift to their fathers. It is not unusual, however, to give a corsage to the father as well.

Teacher's Day: May 15. In Confucianist Korean tradition, teachers have an honored position in Korean society. On this day, elementary and secondary students may give their teachers a flower or a small gift. College students may give the same kind of gift to their teachers or take them to lunch.

Armed Forces Day: Oct. 1. Formerly a national holiday, this day honors the military, which celebrates it.

NOTE: Some holidays have special greetings or expressions. The most common ones are: (New Year's) "*saehae bok manhi badŭseyo*"[새해 복 많이 받으세요] (literally: 'at the New Year, receive much good luck/fortune'); (Christmas) "*Sŏngt'anchŏl ch'ukhahamnida*" [성탄절 축하합니다] (literally: 'congratulations during the Christmas season').

Glossary of English Terms

baby shower Party given before the birth of a baby. Cake and snack food is usually served, and every guest brings a gift for the new baby.

bachelor party A party for the groom usually given the night before the wedding. The bachelor party is supposed to celebrate the groom's last night of freedom, and so the party may include a lot of drinking and even women.

best man The best friend or brother of the groom. He represents the person who will advise and support the groom during his marriage. He also carries the ring that the groom will give to the bride at the end of the ceremony.

birth announcements A small card that usually contains a picture of the newborn and information about it: Its name, weight at birth, and length at birth.

bridal shower A party for the bride before the wedding.

bride The woman getting married.

bridesmaids Married or unmarried friends and relatives of the bride who stand by the bride during the ceremony. They represent the people who will support and help her during her marriage.

casket A box, usually of metal or wood, in which people are buried.

civil ceremony A marriage performed by a judge or justice of the peace. It is usually conducted in an office. It provides the legal bonds of marriage but does not have any of the celebration or formality of a traditional wedding.

condolences Show their sympathy to the surviving family members for the death of a loved one.

cremate To burn a dead body. This is done in a crematorium.

daily routine What a person does regularly every day; for example, most people wash their face and brush their teeth as part of their daily routine. They also collect their mail or put out the trash as part of their daily routine.

deceased A term of respect for the person who has died.

embalmed Filling the dead body with fluid to prevent it from rapid decay.

eulogy A short speech telling about the deceased and especially the good qualities the person had or the person's virtues.

family outings Short trips a family makes together, such as trips to a local park for a picnic.

funeral homes Mortuaries. They are businesses that specialize in the preparation of bodies for burial.

funeral procession Cars going from a church or funeral home to a cemetery.

grave Where a person is buried.

groom The husband at the wedding.

golden wedding anniversary Fifty years of marriage.

hearse A special car with a long back area used only for carrying dead people.

legal adult The age at which a person can make personal commitments without consent of the parents. These ages vary according to states and according to the activity.

legal holiday Holidays on which the banks, post office, and government offices are closed.

leprechauns In Irish tradition, these are very small people with magic powers.

matron of honor A married woman who stands close to the bride and helps her during the ceremony. She represents the person who will support and advise the bride the most during her marriage.

mourners The people who attend a funeral.

obituary An announcement in the newspaper of a person's death which lists information about the person. For example, the names of the person's family members and any special achievements might be listed in an obituary.

officiate To be in charge of a ceremony.

open-house A party where food is served and guests may come within a restricted time span; for example, from 2-4 p.m.

over the hill An expression that implies that a person is no longer in the prime of fitness or ability.

pallbearers Usually six men (family or friends of the deceased) who carry the person's casket from the funeral home and from the hearse to the grave site. It is considered an honor to be a person's pallbearer. Husbands or parents are usually not pallbearers.

pay last respects Whenever someone makes a visit to a person's home, it is to "pay respects." When a person dies, then we visit to "pay our last respects."

pet names Unusual names or special words that show a couple's affection for one another. Some examples of these "terms of endearment" are "sweetheart," "honey," or "darling."

playing catch Throwing a softball or baseball back and forth to each other.

RSVP These initials stand for the French *répondez s'il vous plaît*, which translates 'please reply.' Americans use these letters on invitations, and have even turned them into a verb meaning to reply, (e. g.) "Did you RSVP?"

senior citizens A general term for all elderly. It is especially used after the age of 65.

senior year The twelfth (and final) year (grade) of school, or fourth year of high school. The ninth grade is called **freshman;** the tenth grade, **sophomore;** and the eleventh grade, **junior**. This is true of the college years as well.

silver wedding anniversary Twenth-five years of marriage.

stand up for the bride/groom Support the couple by being an active part of the wedding.

togetherness Time deliberately spent together in an activity for the purpose of becoming emotionally closer together.

three-day weekend To have a Friday or Monday on which one does not work.

traditional wedding For Americans in such a wedding the bride wears a white dress and the groom a suit or tuxedo.

training wheels Two small wheels attached to the back wheels of a two-wheel bicycle. The training wheels help the child to maintain its balance on the bike.

trick-or-treat This is what children say at Halloween in order to get candy.

tuck someone in to bed To make sure the covers are arranged over a person. This term is especially used with children, but adults may use it too.

ushers The male version of bridesmaids. They are family and friends of the groom who will support him and advise him during his marriage.

wedding party The members of the wedding, including the bride, the groom, the bridesmaids and the ushers.

Glossary of Korean Terms

chesa [제사] A ceremony which honors ancestors. It involves the ritual offering of food and wine to the spirit of the deceased.

ch'ukh'ahamnida [축하합니다] 'Congratulations.' This term is appropriate for almost all occasions.

ddŏk [떡] Rice cakes. They come in various sizes and shapes.

ddŏkkuk [떡국] A soup made of sliced rice cake in a beef broth. It is served for birthdays and at New Year's. While it is eaten at other times as well, eating it on these special days symbolizes the passing of a year.

dongdongju [동동주] A clear and strong rice wine.

hangŭl [한글] The Korean alphabet.

hanshik [한식] According to Korean tradition, Koreans eat cold food and attend to the graves or shrines of ancestors on this day.

ham [함] A large wooden box containing gifts for the bride and her family.

hanbok [한복] A general term for traditional Korean clothing.

hwangab [환갑] The sixtieth birthday. It is a major event in the life of Koreans when they officially become senior citizens.

k'ŭnchŏl [큰절] A large bow which involves the person going from a standing to a sitting position, bending over at the waist, and touching the forehead on the forearms which are outstretched.

kyŏlhon [결혼] Marriage.

makkŏli [막걸리] A thick rice wine.

miyŏkkuk [미역국] A soup made of seaweed in a beef broth. It is eaten every day after the birth of a child to build up the mother's blood.

mom josimhaseyo [몸 조심하세요] A term used in response to a sign of illness, such as a sneeze, or to someone who is departing. It means literally 'be careful of your health.'

p'yebaek [폐백] A ceremony after the wedding ceremony in which the bride bows to the husband's immediate family members. *P'yebaek* signifies the wife being brought into the husband's family.

paekil janch'i [백일 잔치] A large party to celebrate the hundredth day of a child's life. A large meal is served, and the guests bring gifts.

sebae [세배] The new year.

saebaeton [새배돈] Money given to children after they give a New Year's bow to their elders.

sillang [신랑] Groom.

sikhae [식혜] A sweet dessert drink made of sweet rice and sweetened with sugar.

sinbu [신부] Bride.

songp'yŏn [송편] Rice cakes shaped into half moons, and steamed over pine needles. They are served especially at *Ch'usŏk*. *Songp'yŏn* are often of different colors and are filled with sweetened sesame seeds, sweetened red mashed beans.

sujŏngkwa [수정과] A sweetened dessert drink made of dried persimmons, honey, cinnamon and pine nuts.

yakhon [약혼] Engagement.

yŏbo [여보] A term used by husbands and wives for each other. It may translate as the English 'dear.'

yutnori [윷놀이] An indigenous Korean game traditionally played at New Year's. The game is comprised of four *yutnori* sticks which are rounded on the top and flattened on the bottom, a game board, and game pieces to move around the board. In *yutnori*, players throw the sticks up into the air and then move their game pieces according to how many sticks have fallen with the rounded side up. The first person to move all the game pieces around the board wins.

Notes

[1] We use a variety of terms such as celebrations, traditions, and rituals to describe group actions related to different occasions. The word **ritual** is used both to describe informal daily routines and formal events. A ritual can be the form given to a celebration. A celebration can be an expression of a tradition that is repeated annually.

[2] There are certain customs regarding the naming of children that are related to religious beliefs. For Catholics, there is often a baptism within the first six months of life at which the child is given a name and presented to the rest of the Catholic community. For Protestants, there is often a christening, at which the child is given a name, but not baptized.

[3] In Korea, traditionally a baby is considered one year old when born, and then adds a year on the following New Year's day. (Koreans add a year to their age at the new year rather than on their actual date of birth.) Thus, it is sometimes hard to determine a Korean's age without knowing the year in which the person was born. Nowadays,

many Koreans have adopted the Western approach to determining age, but many others maintain the traditional approach. A shorthand way to determine a Korean's age in Western terms may be to subtract one year from the age given. In the case of celebrating a child's first birthday, it would be celebrated 365 days after the child's birth. See *Through a Rain Spattered Window* by M.J. Daniels (Seoul: Taewon Publishing Company, 1983), p. 43, for a brief discussion of how Koreans calculate personal age.

[4] Legal ages in Korea vary according to gender and activity. For example, the legal age to marry without a parent's consent is twenty. The legal drinking age is twenty; for the bars with women, it is twenty-one. The legal age for employment is fifteen; for entering the military nineteen. Retirement varies according to the organization. Every Korean must graduate from elementary school, but there is no other age limit regarding quitting school. The legal age for smoking is twenty. All of these ages are in actual chronological years based on a person being zero years of age at birth rather than according to the traditional Korean way of calculating age.

[5] In the rhythm of life according to the lunar calendar, days in the calendar are divided into cycles of sixty. When a person turns sixty years of age, it means that person has lived the full cycle of life. The lunar calendar cycle has run its full course, as well. See *Through a Rain Spattered Window* by M. J. Daniels (Seoul: Taewon Publishing Company, 1981), pp. 42-43, for a complete discussion of this concept of time and age.

[6] Information in this and the following section have two sources: *Culture Shock! Korea* by Sonja V. Hur and Ben S. Hur, (Singapore: Times Books International, 1988; *The Folklore of American Holidays* by Hennig Cohen and Tristram Potter Coffin (Eds.),(Detroit: Gale Research Company, 1987).

CHAPTER 6

FOOD AND DRINK

FOOD AND DRINK

Introduction

Most people are interested in eating. Whenever two people talk about travel or foreign countries, they usually talk about the meals they have enjoyed. Interest in eating is **universal**, and people usually identify countries with the foods popular there. So, when they discuss cultural differences, they often begin by talking about food. For example, whenever either of us met Koreans for the first time, Koreans would show their knowledge of the United States by telling us they had eaten fried chicken, hamburgers, or pizza. Whenever Americans meet Koreans, they may tell them how much they like rice or *kimch'i*. Food is the great connector. Thus, we begin this chapter with a section on customs related to food, including social drinking.

In the next section of this chapter, you will then read about eating habits and **table manners**. When Koreans eat with Americans — or Americans with Koreans — they may have a long discussion about using chopsticks. How should I eat fried chicken? *Kalbi* [갈비]? Do I take food from a communal bowl or take some out and put it on my plate? Do I serve others first, or serve myself first? Is it all right to blow my nose at the table? These are just a few of the common questions we answer in this section. We also discuss customs related to eating in restaurants, including how to treat the **server** and how to pay the bill.

In the final section of this chapter, you will read about the concept of **hospitality**. It is important for you to know what to eat and how to eat it. But it is equally important for you to know who is paying for the meal or if you need to **reciprocate** the invitation. How do Americans and Koreans differ in their concepts of hospitality? Knowing this may help prevent you from innocently offending an American or a Korean. Knowing what kind of meals are eaten in the U.S. and in Korea, expected table manners and behavior at meals, and how to be hospitable will make you more comfortable and confident on a social level. This knowledge is also a first step toward cross-cultural understanding between us. If you know the eating customs and expectations of Americans and Koreans and the types of food that they eat, you may be better prepared to visit the United States or Korea. Or it may make you more comfortable to invite an American or Korean to dinner. But there is a third component to enjoying meals as a way of crossing the bridge between our two cultures: Individual customs. So, remember, as you read our descriptions that every custom is situation dependent — people behave differently according to the individual and according to the situation.

What comprises a meal?

American Ways

There are ideals and there are realities. Ideally, the American family eats meals together. In reality, the contemporary American family may not always eat together. You might see the ideal in the media: Most films of American family life you see will show the family gathered around the evening meal. Most American advice books on how to have a healthy family will emphasize the importance of sharing at least the evening meal together. However, the lifestyle of the modern American family does not allow time for cooking big meals, and often meals are eaten "**on the run.**" So, you may encounter Americans who regularly eat together or you may meet some families who seldom sit down for an evening meal together. Also, many American men share in the cooking duties in the home. Some men are even the primary cooks in the home if they enjoy cooking.

Many Americans rely on **fast food**; in general, American cooking today is generally simple and quick. Americans maintain busy lifestyles, and nearly 50% of American women work outside of the home.[1] Because many women work outside of the home, they have less time than in the past to cook several large meals a day.

In past years, many American families had a tradition of eating a large meal together on Sunday. Some families still keep this tradition, but often they go to a restaurant rather than cook. Even though many American families are no longer able to eat together, it is still an ideal that many families aspire to. Americans especially consider the evening meal as a time to talk to one another and become closer. Indeed, if you see a family in a film that does not eat together, it usually means the family is not emotionally very close. Apart from the family meal, eating together is generally considered a way to become closer to others. For example, there are community festivals which center around food. Friends and colleagues have lunch or dinner together as a way of becoming more familiar with each other.

American meals can also be diverse. There are many regional differences. The U.S. is also a land of immigrants, and they have all brought their food with them: Korean, Italian, Chinese, German, French, Mexican, etc. The most popular of these **ethnic** foods are Italian, Chinese, and Mexican. They are so popular that in nearly every city there are Italian, Chinese, and Mexican fast food restaurants. Another type of food is known as "American home cooking." We describe in this next section some aspects of the ideals and realities of "American home cooking."

> **NOTE:** American meals can be flexible and diverse. You may meet someone who eats pizza for breakfast, for example. But in general, we can say that Americans eat three meals a day. Each of these meals has its own distinct menu and regional flavors.

Generally, compared to Korean cooking, "American home cooking" is rather **bland** and involves meat, potatoes, a vegetable, and bread. The most popular vegetables are corn, green beans, peas, and carrots. Americans eat sweet desserts such as ice cream, pie, or cake. They also eat a lot of **pasta** or noodles as a replacement for potatoes. Americans generally do not eat a lot of rice except in some parts of the South. Most large supermarkets, however, sell a wide variety of vegetables — canned, frozen, or fresh, which Americans eat in a variety of ways. Common vegetables are lettuce, tomatoes, varieties of cabbage, spinach and other greens, varieties of squash, varieties of onions, brussels sprouts, asparagus, broccoli, and cauliflower. Even though Americans often eat more potatoes, bread, and meat than they do vegetables, they are taught from elementary school onward to eat from four food groups as a way to stay healthy.

The four food groups are:

> grains
> meat, fish, poultry, and legumes (beans)
> fruits & vegetables
> dairy products

These four food groups represent a "balanced diet," which is the ideal combination of foods to eat. Here are some sample menus for breakfast, lunch, and dinner. We list some common menus — examples of American home cooking — but also include some of the more realistic things that Americans eat. Not every American eats these dishes — or has a "balanced diet"—but most Americans would agree these are the models most nutritionists or doctors suggest.

Daily Menu

BREAKFAST		
1) **scrambled eggs** bacon, sausage, or ham toast with butter and jam a glass of orange juice coffee	2) **pancakes** with butter and syrup bacon a glass of orange juice coffee	3) a donut and coffee or a bowl of cereal with milk

LUNCH	
1) soup and sandwich fruit or cookies milk or **soda pop**	2) hamburger french fries milk shake

DINNER		
1) **meatloaf** / a meat dish mashed potatoes & gravy sweet peas **rolls** **green salad** ice cream milk or soda pop	2) spaghetti with meat sauce green salad garlic bread cake or ice cream milk or soda pop	3) pizza soda pop

As you can see, in the U.S., different foods are served for breakfast, lunch (also called "dinner" in some parts of the country), and dinner (also called "**supper**"). Americans usually drink milk, water, coffee, iced tea, or soda with their meals. Breakfast can be a small meal, such as cereal with milk or a sweet roll, or it can be much larger, usually eggs, bacon or some other meat, bread and maybe potatoes (especially in restaurants). Fruit or fruit juice is popular at breakfast, as is coffee.

Lunch is often a small meal, such as soup and a sandwich, or something else they can prepare at home and take with them, such as leftovers. It is eaten around 12 o'clock in the afternoon. Often raw vegetables or a salad are part of the meal, with fruit or a cookie for dessert. Many Americans who work outside the home will eat fast food, such as a hamburger and french fries, for lunch. Others may eat only a salad or a container of yogurt (especially if they are dieting to lose weight). If eating at a restaurant, Americans may have a beer or a glass of wine with the meal. But generally, most Americans will wait until dinnertime to have an **alcoholic beverage**.

AMERICAN / KOREAN CONTRAST

Americans and Koreans both commonly take their lunch to work or to school. Americans call this a "sack lunch," a "brown bag lunch," a "dinner bucket," or a "lunch pail." They also sell lunch kits, made of plastic, metal, or insulated vinyl which both children and adults use. A typical brown bag lunch usually includes a sandwich, potato chips, fruit, and cookies. It could really contain anything, but some other common items for a sack lunch include boiled eggs and raw vegetables. A Korean lunch packed at home is also named after its container, a *toshirak* [도시락]. A *toshirak* is a small plastic case with compartments for rice and *panch'an* [반찬] (side dishes). In addition to rice and side dishes, a popular lunch is *kimbab* [김밥], which is rice and vegetables rolled in dried seaweed, and then cut into decorative bite-sized pieces. Koreans will also carry a pair of chopsticks in a little case, or the *toshirak* will have a space especially for the chopsticks. The American lunch is meant to be conveniently eaten with the hands; a Korean lunch is eaten with chopsticks. Koreans generally do not eat with their fingers.

For Americans, the evening meal is usually the largest meal of the day, the most elaborate for most people, and eaten between 5 and 8 p.m. Americans have a lot of food choices and eat a variety of combinations. However, an average American supper is usually comprised of some kind of meat, a starch such as potatoes or pasta, and a vegetable. Sometimes, salad is also served. Bread is usually served, as is dessert. Coffee is often served with dessert. An average American family would serve milk, soda pop, or water, and some people might enjoy a beer or a glass of wine with the meal — particularly if it is a special occasion. The meal may also vary according to whether it is a "family dinner" or a formal dinner party with guests. Many families on busy nights may just order a pizza for dinner.

NOTE: These are examples of some popular combinations for these meals, but not every meal matches these descriptions. Indeed, every region of the U.S. has its own variations and characteristics. Here are some of them:

*The **Northeast:**(Maine to Maryland) and the **Pacific Northwest** (Washington & Oregon): seafood

*The **South** (from Kentucky to Alabama and Mississippi): fried chicken, cornbread, greens (mustard, collards, etc), and black-eyed peas

***Midwest** (from Ohio to Kansas to North & South Dakota): breads and pastries

*Mountain States (Wyoming, Colorado, etc): wild game such as deer and pheasant, as well as beefsteak

*The **Southwest** (Texas to Arizona): barbecued meat, Mexican food

In addition, some cities or states have specialties that reflect their cultural heritage (such as gumbo in Louisiana) or particular agricultural products (such as citrus fruit in Florida). Chinese food is popular everywhere.

Korean Ways

Korea is a culturally homogenous country, and thus its food represents that homogeneity although there are many regional specialties. You will find, too, that Korea is a resourceful country, and its foods represent the many imaginative ways in which limited resources and a few ingredients can be creatively applied. You will also discover that there are Chinese and Japanese restaurants that serve some favorite dishes. Since the 1970s, there has been an increase in American fast food chains in the larger cities — mostly for chicken, hamburgers, or pizza. There are also cafeterias, especially at large supermarkets, and restaurants in department stores. However, with the exception of Chinese restaurants and some coffee shops, there are few "take out" restaurants and no "drive-thrus." Furthermore, in recent years Koreans have also adapted some American dishes to their menu. Part of the reason for this is practicality — American food can be simple and easy to prepare in contrast with Korean food. Another reason is diversity — Koreans enjoy the variety and newness of other foods.

Koreans serve the same basic types of food for breakfast, lunch, and dinner, but there may be some variations according to convenience. That is, each meal is usually comprised of rice, soup, and assorted side dishes (called *panch'an*), but for lunch, some Koreans popularly eat a big bowl of noodles instead of rice and soup. The noodles show the Chinese influence on the Korean diet, and different varieties of noodles are favorites at Chinese restaurants. At all meals, *kimch'i* and a variety of vegetables are common side dishes, as well as some type of fish or dried seaweed.

Compared to Americans, Koreans do not eat a lot of meat although they do enjoy beef (marinated or flame-broiled), chicken, and pork. The most common meat dishes are marinated beef (*bulgogi* [불고기]) and marinated beef ribs (*kalbi* [갈비]). Koreans also commonly eat meat cooked in soups (*kuk* [국] or *t'ang* [탕]) and stews (*tchigae* [찌개]). There are several delicious specialty soups which are served in a very large bowl and with rice and *kimch'i* are considered a meal in themselves: *Kalbit'ang* [갈비탕] (rib soup), *sŏlŏngt'ang* [설렁탕]

(tripe soup), *yukgyejang* [육계장] (a very spicy beef soup), *komt'ang* [곰탕] (a beef dish made from cooking beef bones overnight), *haejangkuk* [해장국], (a spicy vegetable soup in pork or beef broth), or *sŏnjikuk* [선지국] (a beef blood soup), *kamjat'ang* [감자탕] (a potato and pork bone stew), and *maeunt'ang* [매운탕] (a very spicy fish soup).

If you are treated to meat dishes — especially beef in a Korean home or at a restaurant, it is not as special as it was in the past, but it is still a sign of Korean generosity and hospitality.

The most common ingredients for flavoring in Korean cooking are soy sauce, sesame oil, sesame seed, green onion, garlic, ginger, and red pepper. Koreans also enjoy the more expensive pine nuts and ginkgo. A soy bean paste — known as *toenjang* [된장] — and anchovies are common soup bases.

Koreans eat a variety of vegetables and roots, but the most common are spinach, squash, eggplant, carrots, daikon radish, napa, bokchoy or celery cabbage, cucumber, and bean sprouts. These vegetables are rarely mixed together, but instead are steamed and mixed with seasonings such as onion, garlic, and sesame.

Served as side dishes, vegetables are collectively called **namul** [나물]. Squash, particularly zucchini squash, is often dipped in an egg batter and fried. Potatoes are eaten as a side dish or served in some soups.

Roasted chestnuts or peanuts, corn, and sweet potatoes are traditionally eaten as snacks, especially from street vendors, but Koreans also have a variety of snack foods which can be bought at the supermarket, such as potato chips, seasoned peanuts, chocolate and other candy, ice cream, and a variety of corn and other grain snacks. Pizza, noodles, peanut butter and jelly sandwiches or hamburgers are also normally seen as snack foods rather than meals in themselves.

To a Korean, a meal is not a meal without two **staples**: Rice and *kimch'i* [김치]. Although Koreans may sometimes call *kimch'i* "Korean salad," it may best be described as a hot, pickled relish. Any variety of pickled vegetable is called *kimch'i*, but the most common type is made of cabbage, red pepper, garlic, green onions, and ginger. Radish is also a common ingredient in *kimch'i*. (*Kkaktugi* [깍두기] is the name of the most popular radish *kimch'i*, which is made of radish cut into small squares, but there are many varieties of radish *kimch'i*.)

There are many regional varieties and types of *kimch'i* as well as types of *kimch'i* according to the season, such as water *kimch'i* in the summer (radish and onion in a salty water broth, served chilled) or spicy cabbage *kimch'i* in the winter.

Koreans do not eat desserts after the meal in the way that Americans do. You will rarely see cake, pie, cookies, or ice cream at the end of a meal. Instead, they are eaten as snacks or at parties. However, you will likely be treated to fresh fruit, such as apples, pears, tangerines, strawberries, persimmons, or melon (depending on the season).

For apples, pears, and melons, the fruit will be peeled or sliced and divided among the guests. Koreans also have two delicious sweetened drinks that may be served after the meal and considered a dessert: *sujŏngkwa* [수정과] and *shikhye* [식혜]. *Sujŏngkwa* is a drink made with dried persimmons, honey or sugar, cinnamon, and pine nuts. *Shikhye* is made of tapioca and sweetened with sugar or honey. They are both served chilled and are quite refreshing, especially in the summer. Water is normally drunk after the meal.

You can see both the variety and sameness of the Korean diet from the sample menus for breakfast, lunch, and dinner that we list below. We list both the model menu and the meals that may reflect Western influence.

Daily Menu

BREAKFAST	

1) fried egg
   rice
   fish
   kimch'i
   assorted vegetable combinations as side dishes
   toasted dried seaweed
	2) milk
	   sweet roll

LUNCH	

1) a bowl of beef rib soup (kalbit'ang)
   with noodles
   a bowl of rice
   kimch'i
	2) a bowl of thick noodles in black
	   bean paste
	   kimch'i

3) kimbab (rice and vegetables rolled in dried seaweed) kimch'i	4) a sandwich, hamburger or pizza

DINNER		
1) rice soup fish kimch'i assorted vegetable combinations as side dishes toasted dried seaweed	2) rice marinated beef kimch'i assorted vegetable combinations as side dishes toasted dried seaweed	3) pork cutlet salad rice

As you can see, Koreans eat rice and *kimch'i* at nearly every meal. Within this framework of basically the same foods, there is still great imaginative variety in the types of foods prepared.

NOTE: We have listed examples of some popular combinations for these meals, but not every meal matches these descriptions. Although Korea is generally a culturally and racially homogenous country, there are also many regional varieties of foods as well. As in the U.S., these varieties are usually related to the geography and special agricultural products in the region, such as seafood in port cities or apples in Taegu and the surrounding area. Some of the most well-known regional specialties are:

***Jonju bibimbab:** a special type of *bibimbab* [비빔밥] (which originated in the city of Jŏnju).

***Pusan, Mokpo,** and **Inchon** (port cities): seafood, especially raw, and very spicy fish soups and stews (*saengsŏn maeun t'ang* [생선매운탕] or *tchigae* [찌개]).

***Ch'unch'on:** *mak kuksu* [막국수], homemade buckwheat noodles in a beef broth

***Zedong** (in Kyunggi Province): *kalbi* [갈비], marinated beef ribs

AMERICAN / KOREAN CONTRAST

American meals and Korean meals are very similar in that they each have a starch (potatoes, pasta, or rice), some meat or fish, and vegetables. They are different in the portions of these foods that they eat and in how they prepare them. There may also be only three or four dishes at an American meal, and Americans take large individual servings. On the other hand, there may be many dishes of great variety on a Korean table, but the Koreans take small servings from communal dishes (except for rice and soup). They are also different in the fact that Koreans have rice at almost every meal.

In what order is food served?

American Ways

In an average American home, the meal is served all at once, with the table full of large bowls and serving dishes. The bowls and serving dishes are passed around the table so that each person can take some onto his/her plate. Dessert is usually put on the table after the other dishes have been cleared away. In a restaurant, soup or a salad may be served before the rest of the meal. Dessert has to be ordered. Americans generally do not eat sweet things before the meal.

If you look at a menu in a nice restaurant, you will see the heading "appetizers." **Appetizers** are small portions of food to eat before the main meal. In a home, the family may eat crackers, nuts, or potato chips while waiting for dinner. At a restaurant, soup, salad, or some specialty dishes may be eaten before the main meal is brought to the table. These appetizers usually have to be ordered, and they cost extra. However, most restaurants serve bread along with water or other drinks for the guests to enjoy while they wait for their meal.

In homes, food is usually served in large bowls or on platters which are passed around from person to person. Every person then takes food onto their plates from these larger dishes. Americans never eat directly from the larger, communal dishes. Often, Americans begin to eat only after everyone has filled his or her plate.

NOTE: In very informal households, the family may dish the food out of the pot they have cooked in. At very formal dinners, the meals are served in a prescribed order, so that different dishes of food are on the table at different times. Each part of the meal, called a "course," is eaten before the next one is served. At community dinners — such as at churches or other meetings with large gatherings of people — everyone might bring a dish of food. This is called a "potluck." At a potluck, the food is placed on a large table (with main dishes, vegetables, salads, and desserts separated, but usually in that order), and then the guests stand in line and walk down the table taking whatever food they desire.

As we have mentioned, Americans drink **beverages** during the meal — soda pop, fruit juice, water, milk, iced tea, and coffee. Many Americans also drink coffee after the meal.

AMERICAN / KOREAN CONTRAST

Americans often drink beverages directly from the can or bottle. They also eat or drink beverages while driving or while walking along the street. Bottled water is quite popular, and you can see many people carrying their bottles of water with them wherever they go. Modern Koreans have developed some Western habits of eating while walking on the street — especially ice cream — but generally, Koreans still do not eat or drink liquids while walking along the street or driving. They also generally pour the liquid into a glass before drinking it or drink with a straw. However, Koreans have traditionally had food stands where the Korean can stand and enjoy a snack or a quick meal of noodles.

Korean Ways

In Korea, too, all of the food is served at the same time except for dessert. Food is served at a restaurant with little variation from how it would be served in the home. Appetizers are not served; however, *kimch'i* or other side dishes may be placed on the table before the food arrives.

Dessert might not be served at all. At a restaurant, dessert is not ordered separately but is usually given **gratis** at the end of the meal. When dessert is served it is usually a piece of fruit **in season**. The fruit has been peeled and sliced so that each **diner** may have one individual slice. The fruit is served on one communal plate, and each diner takes a slice.

Although rice and soup are served in individual bowls, the side dishes are communal. Everyone takes and eats from the same bowls of *panch'an* (side dishes), from a large fish on a serving plate, or from some stews or other soups on the table. Koreans eat most food with chopsticks but use a large spoon for soup.

AMERICAN / KOREAN CONTRAST

Americans have a tradition of baked goods and other sweets, which are most often eaten for dessert. Koreans have some specialty sweets — especially a wide variety of rice cakes (*ddŏk* [떡]), which are made from sweet rice pounded into a doughy consistency — but do not have a tradition of ovens and baked goods. As a result of Western influence, however, there are many bakeries which sell donuts, bread, cakes and other baked goods. These are usually eaten as in-between meal snacks. In most large cities, there are also Dunkin' Donuts outlets and several American ice cream franchises.

What about social drinking?

American Ways

Social drinking means drinking alcoholic beverages at social gatherings such as dinners, picnics, and parties. While Americans usually drink a non-alcoholic beverage with their meal — water, soda pop, fruit juice, or milk — sometimes, adults will drink beer or wine with their meal as well. Hard **liquor**, such as whiskey, is usually drunk before or after the meal, at parties, or at special parties for meeting people called **cocktail parties**. Hard liquor is also drunk in bars.

NOTE: In the U.S., the term "drinking," as in "Will there be any drinking at the party?" or "I don't drink," or "Would you like a drink?" normally refers to drinking alcoholic beverages. The phrase "He's a heavy drinker" usually is a polite way to say the person may be an alcoholic. In Korea, the term for drinking is "*hanjan hada.* [한잔 하다]" The Korean host may say, "*hanjan hapsida*" [한잔 합시다] ('Let's have a drink!'), and this drink may be beer, rice wine, or stronger alcohol. The Korean term for alcoholic beverages is "*sul masida*" [술 마시다]('drink alcoholic beverages').

American customs and expectations regarding social drinking vary somewhat from that of Koreans. In terms of customs, Americans expect to drink primarily in the late afternoon or evenings, i.e. at the end of the working day. Sometimes they eat nothing with their drink or they may eat chips or nuts. Many people may have a beer as a simple refreshment at home. At a cocktail party or other social event where there is drinking, they may eat appetizers, such as chips, nuts, or cheese and crackers, but not a full meal.

You may find that American attitudes toward drinking alcoholic beverages differ from those of Koreans, too. Because of the conservative religious influence on the development of American culture, Americans are conservative in their attitudes toward drinking. Most Americans admire **moderation** and self control, and it is usually considered embarrassing if a person becomes drunk in public. That is not to say that all Americans are moderate drinkers and never become publicly drunk. Drinking in moderation is an American ideal, and those who drink too much are generally criticized. Indeed, it is considered admirable if someone can "hold his liquor," i.e. drink but not become drunk.

Another American attitude toward alcohol is that Americans do not force drinking on others. There are perhaps two reasons for this. First, they do not force drinking on others out of respect for individual choice. Second, they may be sensitive to recovering alcoholics who are trying not to drink. There is generally no social stigma against women drinking. However, for health-conscious modern Americans, there is a general trend away from social drinking.

> **NOTE:** Among American college students there is a trend called "binge drinking." Binge drinking is drinking a great quantity of alcohol in a short time. This is quite dangerous and can even cause death. Some U.S. colleges do not allow alcohol to be served — or in some cases even drunk — on campus; others restrict drinking to specific locations or dormitories that admit students only over the legal drinking age. Some schools issue permits to allow drinking at certain parties.

There are several laws in the U.S. regarding drinking. One of the most **prevalent** laws is a **legal drinking age** in every state.[2] That is, people under a certain age cannot purchase or drink alcoholic beverages either in stores, bars, or restaurants, or even drink it in the home. In some states, the age is eighteen; in others, it is twenty-one. Most young people think of becoming twenty-one as their chance to drink legally and, therefore, often make a ritual of buying beer or other alcohol and getting drunk on their twenty-first birthday. Either eighteen or twenty-one is the age at which young people are considered legal adults (depending on the state). If you are under this age, you are considered by law a minor, or underage, and cannot buy alcohol. If you buy alcohol for a minor or allow a minor to drink with you, you may be breaking the law. Three other laws related to alcohol include 1) buying alcohol, 2) driving while drunk, and 3) drinking in public (as in a park or at the beach).

First, it may not be easy for you to purchase alcohol. There are restrictions on where you can purchase alcohol — including beer and wine. Many restaurants do not serve alcohol because they do not have a "liquor license" from the state. There are liquor stores that sell a variety of alcohol, and many supermarkets also carry alcohol. In many states, there are "blue laws," which prohibit the sale of alcohol on Sundays. There are also "dry" cities or counties, especially in the South, where the sale of alcohol is illegal at any time. Furthermore, at any time — in a restaurant, a bar, a liquor store, or a supermarket — you may be asked to show your identification to prove you are the legal drinking age. Finally, in some states, such as Ohio, hard liquor is sold only in state-owned specially stores.

NOTE: Each state has different laws related to purchasing and drinking alcohol. If you are traveling to the U.S., be sure to find out what the laws and regulations are in that state.

Second, you should never drive a car in the U.S. if you have been drinking. Driving after drinking (also known as "driving under the influence" (DUI) or "driving while intoxicated (DWI)) is against the law. In many cases, there are large fines for being caught while driving under the influence, and in some cases you can have your driver's license **revoked** or be required to spend time in jail. The media gives much attention to car accidents caused by people who drink and drive. Currently in many states, it is considered a murder, termed "vehicular homicide" or "manslaughter," if someone dies as a result of an accident caused by drunk driving, and the driver often has to spend time in prison.[3] It has now become common practice to designate someone who will stay sober (not drink) when people go out for the evening. That person is called the "designated driver."

A final law related to drinking involves drinking in public places. Many states have laws against open containers of alcohol — including beer — on the street or in parks or other locations. To be safe, if you are visiting the U.S. and want to drink, you should drink in a home or in a restaurant. Be careful about drinking in parks or other public places.

Korean Ways

In Korea, there is a great deal of emphasis on social drinking, especially among men.

Koreans usually drink only water with their meal (which is drunk primarily at the end of the meal), but there are also special occasions when beer or *soju* [소주] (a strong, cheap undistilled liquor that resembles vodka) may be drunk. Koreans eat while they drink —

from dried fish and peanuts to noodles to a full dinner — which can occur either in the home, in a restaurant, or at the many special bars or drinking houses in every village and city. Nightclubs have also become commonplace in the cities.

NOTE: Korean restaurants and drinking houses tend to be specialized and restricted to only certain types of food or drink. For example, there are specialty restaurants for marinated beef, for beef ribs, for fish, for the different soups, for serving certain types of wine, etc. A Korean tea house (*tabang* [다방]), does not sell food, but only beverages. For alcoholic drinks, there are *makkŏllijib* [막걸리집], which sell an indigenous, thick rice wine (*makkŏlli*); *maekjujib* [맥주집], which sell beer (*maekju*); *sojujib* [소주집], which sell *soju*; and *suljib* [술집], which sell all kinds of alcohol, including Western hard liquor (*yangju* [양주]). These specialty houses also serve certain foods that are typically eaten with these different beverages. A *makkŏlli jib*, for example, may sell *bindaeddŏk*[빈대떡], a pancake made with ground mung beans and vegetables. There are also stands along the street, called *p'ojangmach'a* [포장마차], where people can stop for a quick bowl of soup and some *soju* or other alcoholic drink. Some people may stop for hours at these friendly little stands.

Koreans do not have a tradition of cocktail parties. Instead, the Korean tradition is to go to a specialty house and drink together, especially small groups of men. If you are doing business in Korea, you can expect to spend many evenings after dinner at some specialty house drinking with your colleagues until late in the evening, rather than spending a few hours before dinner enjoying a drink or two. You may also be treated to the more expensive nightclubs.

AMERICAN / KOREAN CONTRAST

In the U.S., there is no stigma against women drinking in public. In Korea, drinking — especially in public — is an activity that has been primarily reserved for men although this is changing. In recent years, many women have begun to drink publicly as well. However, women drinking in public is still not looked upon favorably by Korean society at large.

Korean customs and expectations of social drinking differ from those of Americans. In terms of when they drink, Koreans may drink whenever it is sociable to do so, although they normally do not drink before lunch time.

While Americans may have appetizers or even nothing to eat while consuming alcohol, Koreans always eat while drinking — noodles, dried fish, nuts, *kimch'i*, and rice cakes. As a result, there are many specialty foods traditionally associated with drinking such as sweet and sour pork or noodles. Drinking may occur before, during, or after the meal, and is often ritualized. In Korea, drinking is a way for people to bond together. It is quite common to have a meal together, and then begin drinking and bring on more food to accompany the drinking. If you are invited to a Korean home as a couple, the wives normally leave the table while the men stay and drink.

Social drinking in Korea reflects the group-oriented Korean focus on building relationships and being concerned about *ch'emyŏn* ('face'). Thus, to show his hospitality and generosity, a Korean host — either in the home or at a public place — may be continually forceful in encouraging his guests to drink or eat. If you are the guest of a Korean and drinking is present, you will want to show appreciation for your host's hospitality and help maintain the host's good feelings. To be a gracious guest, you may do one of three things:

1) drink everything you are offered, even to the point of drunkenness;
2) politely take the drink and then sip it;
3) take the drink, pour it out into another container and offer to fill the glass for the host. The alcohol itself is not important, but accepting your host's hospitality and protecting his feelings are.

Rarely would a Korean decline the offer of the host. When a Korean wishes to stop drinking, he must do so in a way that will not cause any discomfort or embarrassment to the host or other guests that are continuing to drink. That is, he must not break the general mood that has been created. Some examples of how to decline a drink without offending the host would be to say you cannot drink for medical reasons or that alcohol makes you sick. These are perfectly acceptable reasons and give your host the opportunity to further show generosity and hospitality by ordering you another type of drink.

You may find that Korean attitudes toward drinking alcohol differ from that of Americans in other ways as well. Koreans are generally not as conservative as Americans in their attitudes toward drinking. Also, Koreans often drink to excess to show their appreciation of the host's generosity or to maintain the mood of the evening. This show of appreciation is considered more important than the abstract notion of "self control" or knowing one's limit. Koreans are also not generally embarrassed by becoming drunk in public. Their focus is more on pleasing the immediate group than on individual concerns. Furthermore, Koreans tend to be more forgiving of drunkenness than Americans are. Whereas moderation may be an American ideal, abundance and generosity in hospitality — both giving and receiving it — are Korean ideals.

The legal drinking age in Korea is nineteen. Restaurants, bars, etc. are not supposed to serve to minors. There are few restrictions when purchasing alcohol in stores, however, and alcohol can be bought at any time. As in the U.S., Korean young people may make a ritual of drinking on their nineteenth birthday.

NOTE: Among both American and Korean college students, drinking is a common activity for students after class or as part of on-campus group activities. In the past, drinking was mostly for the young Korean men, but in recent years it includes women as well. Drinking on campus is quite open and accepted, and Korean students do not need special permits to do it.

Koreans also have strict laws against driving while drunk but none about drinking in public (as in a park or at the beach). If a person causes an accident while driving under the influence of alcohol, he may face a prison term, especially if injury is involved. Koreans do not yet have the tradition of designating a member of a group to drive or help others home. However, many drinking establishments may employ a "designated driver" — someone who drives drunken guests home for a fee. Many friends may help another reach home; others may leave the drunken friend to stagger home on the bus or subway alone.

AMERICAN / KOREAN CONTRAST

Americans and Koreans both drink as a way to socialize. They differ mainly in their attitudes toward such drinking: Americans generally do not drink to get drunk and reserve the right to decline a drink; Koreans may show their appreciation of hospitality by getting drunk and are careful in how they refuse a drink so that the host will not be offended.

What are appropriate table manners?

American Ways

Every culture has a concept of table manners, the term for polite behavior when eating. American customs and expectations of ideal table manners range from how to pass the food, to how the food is eaten, to how the food is appreciated. In general, American table manners reflect the American concern for the comfort of everyone and equal opportunity for eating at the table.

If you are a guest in an American home, you will notice that it is good table manners to wait to dish out your food until the host offers food. Generally, you do not begin eating until everyone has food on their plates and is ready to eat. Usually, the father or the mother in the home will signal when everyone can begin eating. Americans help themselves to **seconds** only after everyone has eaten. If there is only a small amount of an item on the table, they ask if anyone else wants that item. Then they may share it or offer it to the other person.

NOTE: Some American families begin their meal with a blessing. This can be done either before food is passed around or after everyone has food on their plates. If it is after the food has been passed, then they say the blessing — or grace — before they begin eating.

If Americans are at a restaurant and not everyone has received their food, those who have received food will wait to eat. This is related to the American concept of fairness — it is not polite to eat in front of someone who cannot also eat. Therefore, the person who has not received food needs to tell others to begin eating ("Please, go ahead.") Americans may also not be formal about passing the food around. Instead, they may tell the guest to "help yourself," that is, to reach out for bowls, etc. and put the food on your plate.

AMERICAN / KOREAN CONTRAST

Both Americans and Koreans judge people's educational or social levels by how good their table manners are. Americans may focus on the manner in which food is eaten or how someone treats the servers (in a restaurant). A Korean may focus more on hospitality and graciousness. In addition, when a guest or in their own a home, Americans wait until everyone is ready to eat. When a guest, Koreans wait until they are urged to eat.

In addition to waiting until everyone is ready before beginning to eat, Americans also have some other specific rules of good table manners. You may find from this list that many behaviors which Koreans accept are considered bad manners by Americans. Similarly, Americans may behave at the table in some ways that Koreans may consider bad manners. Generally, the following are considered acceptable table manners for Americans:

1) Do not reach across the table. If you need something that is not near where you are sitting, ask someone to pass it to you. For example, "Please pass the salt."
2) Do not make noise while eating soup or other food. That is, do not slurp your food or noodles.
3) Keep your mouth closed when chewing food.
4) Do not talk with your mouth full.
5) Do not smack your lips while eating.
6) Do not belch/burp loudly during or after the meal. If Americans do burp/belch, they say "Excuse me," and sometimes laugh in embarrassment.
7) Do not pick your teeth at the table.
8) When not using the fork or other utensils, lay them on your plate or other dish.

Many Americans place napkins on their laps before eating, and regularly wipe their mouths while eating. They usually do not pick up the soup bowl and drink from it. However, they may eat certain foods (such as fried chicken or pizza) with their fingers. It is not impolite for Americans to blow their nose at the table. If you drop food or a napkin on the floor, you pick it up.

AMERICAN / KOREAN CONTRAST

Americans tend to eat slowly to savor the taste of the food. (They also eat slowly to help with digestion.) They often stay at the table after finishing the meal to talk or drink coffee. Koreans, on the other hand, may eat quickly to show their appreciation of the good taste. They also do not stay long at the table, but get up as soon as they have eaten and leave. The exception to this rule is when drinking is involved.

Americans often comment on the good taste of the food, ask questions about it, and engage in discussion while eating. In many families, children are taught to ask to be excused from the table if they want to leave before others have finished eating. That is because everyone generally leaves the table at the same time. As always, these are ideals of behavior, and not everyone follows these ideals.

NOTE: Regarding cigarettes or cigars, most cities and locations in the U.S. support a smoke-free environment. If you are a smoker, you need to ask permission to smoke in someone's home. Many families do not smoke or allow smoking at the dinner table. Many restaurants are smoke-free or have smoking and non-smoking sections. Public places, such as university buildings and office buildings, have designated locations for smoking.

Korean Ways

Korean customs and expectations of ideal table manners range from how to pass the food, to how the food is eaten, to how the food is appreciated. Korean table manners reflect a concern for the comfort — emotional and physical — of everyone at the table. They also involve a loud and active appreciation of the food that has been served and vary according to the status of the individuals who are eating together. Therefore, good table manners may have less to do with the manner in which food is eaten (as they do in the U.S.) than with the personal relations of those involved in eating. In many cases, what Americans consider bad table manners may not be bad manners in Korea. And what Koreans find unacceptable may be acceptable to Americans.

If you are a guest in a Korean home, you will notice that it is good table manners to wait until the head of the household encourages you to eat. However, generally, you do not need to wait until everyone has food to begin eating. Food is not passed around a Korean table, as in the U.S., but instead individual portions of rice and soup are brought to the table where side dishes are already waiting. In some cases, you may be brought a little table with enough food for you and your host.

NOTE: Many middle-class Korean homes have a table and chairs in the Western tradition. However, the majority of Koreans still sit on the floor for meals and eat from a low table (*bapsang* [밥상]), which usually can be folded up after the meal and stored away. These tables come in many sizes. Some families choose to eat from these small tables even when they own a larger, Western-style table.

At a restaurant, everyone will usually be served at the same time, and so there is little need to wait for others. This is because many dishes are communal dishes, or everyone is eating the same thing at a specialty restaurant. Koreans always encourage others to eat. If for some reason not everyone has received their food, those who have not received food may apologize and then wait for you to tell them to go ahead.

Generally, the following are considered acceptable table manners for Koreans:

1) It is acceptable to reach across the table rather than ask that something be passed. (When there are many communal dishes, it may be selfish to ask for one specific dish. However, if the host notices that you prefer a certain dish, the dish will be moved closer within your reach. If you are a special guest, all of the more delicious dishes may have been placed in front of you when you sat down.)

2) It is acceptable to make noise while eating soup or other food. Koreans eat many soups and bowls of noodles while they are very hot, and so slurp the food as a way to get it cool. Furthermore, they show appreciation of the food's taste through the noise they make.

3) Many Koreans do not necessarily keep their mouths closed when chewing food.

4) Many Koreans may talk with their mouths full. They will usually put a hand over their mouths when doing so, however, especially women.

5) Koreans often smack their lips while eating to show appreciation for the food.

6) Koreans may belch/burp loudly during or after the meal to show appreciation. They then may comment on how delicious the meal was.

7) Koreans may pick their teeth at the table, but will usually cover their mouth with their hand while doing so.

8) Korean men may loosen their belts before sitting down to the meal, during the meal, or after the meal is over.

9) Koreans either hold their utensils in their hands when not eating, or lay the utensils on the table. They do not put the utensils in the dish.

This list focuses on what Koreans do while eating in contrast with American expectations. There are also other manners in enjoying a meal that involve personal interaction more than the manner in which food is eaten. Here is a list of some general rules, some of which may apply differently according to the situation:

1) Do not leave your chopsticks stuck down in a bowl of rice. [This is done only for the dead.] Do not leave the spoon inside

an empty bowl.
2) Do not blow your nose at the table. If you need to blow it, get up and go to the bathroom to do it.
3) If you are eating with someone older or of superior status, defer to that person. Many Koreans may turn their heads while drinking or eating in such situations.
4) Do not smoke in front of someone older or of superior status.
5) To show generosity, take some food and put it in the rice bowl of another person.
6) Wait to be dismissed or to eat if eating with someone older or of a superior status.

NOTE: Koreans have different expressions related to eating depending on the status of the individual:
*For someone of a higher status: *chinji chapsusida* [진지 잡수시다].
*For someone of equal status (respectful): *shiksa hasida* [식사 하시다].
*For someone familiar or of lower status, including children: *bab mŏkda* [밥먹다].

These three expressions all translate to the same meaning: 'Help yourself to food.'

In addition, as we mentioned in the previous section on food, Koreans generally do not eat with their fingers, even such things as fried chicken or pizza, although this is changing with the younger generation. They may, however, pick up the soup bowl and drink from it. If you drop food or a napkin on the floor, you leave it there, especially in a restaurant. It will be cleaned up at the end of the meal. Furthermore, Koreans may loudly proclaim that their stomachs hurt because they are so full as a compliment to the host or hostess or to show their own hearty appetite.

NOTE: Koreans do not have a tradition of using napkins as Americans do. However, many homes will place paper napkins on the table or set a box of kleenex or a roll of toilet paper nearby. Restaurants may have napkins on the table with the spoon or chopsticks or have them in a little basket on the table.

AMERICAN / KOREAN CONTRAST

While eating, Americans place their utensils in their plates or dishes when taking a break or talking. When they are finished eating, they leave the utensils in the plate or dish. On the other hand, Koreans do not leave their utensils in their plates or dishes when taking a break or talking. Instead, they place the utensil on the table or hold it in their hands. When finished, they lay the utensils on the table.

Americans may blow their nose at the table if it is necessary or while talking to someone, but this is considered very bad manners for a Korean. Koreans may sniffle for a long time rather than blow their nose. If they must blow their nose while eating, they will often get up from the table to do so. If they are talking to someone, they will turn away from that person or even leave the room. This is especially true when a Korean is with someone older or of a higher status. Both Americans and Koreans may also say "excuse me" in these circumstances.

Koreans generally do not have much discussion while eating, but they do make a point to comment on the taste of the food and perhaps to discuss it. Koreans may explain the foods to you if you are enjoying the company of Koreans hosts. In a home, Koreans may leave the table as soon as they are finished, regardless of whother others are still eating. In a restaurant, they may all stand up abruptly as soon as the meal is over.

What can I generally expect in a restaurant?

When eating in a restaurant in the U.S. and Korea, manners and attitudes toward guests and etiquette are generally the same as at home. But there are some differences in practical matters. This section addresses some the practical aspects of eating in a restaurant, including ordering meals, interacting with the servers, and tipping. We differentiate between types of restaurants in both countries when it is appropriate.

American Ways

Americans follow the same rules for table manners in a restaurant as at home, but the situation may be more formal. Very often, the server will take orders for beverages before the guests order the meal. In this case, the guests can read the menu and make choices while their beverages are being brought to them. As we stated in the section on social drinking, at some restaurants Americans may drink a cocktail before or with their meal. Sometimes, the restaurant will have a bar, and the guests will wait there and have a drink while waiting for a table. But not all restaurants are able to offer alcoholic drinks or they can only offer beer or wine.

In some restaurants there may not be a server to **take the order** for the meal. This is especially true in a **salad bar** or a **cafeteria-style** restaurant. In a salad bar, you normally pay a fee to the cashier as you enter the restaurant. You then can eat as much of the various foods made available as you wish.

In a cafeteria-style restaurant, you will go stand in line and pick out your meal from dishes of food which you can see, pay the cashier, and then find a seat. Some restaurants combine these two styles, and some restaurants and fast food places also offer salad bars. In all kinds of restaurants there will be people who bus the table — take the plates and clean the tables. In some cases, they are the individuals who bring the drinks as well.

After you enter a restaurant, you may have to wait to be seated (depending on the type of establishment). Many restaurants have a sign that says "Please wait to be seated" at its entrance. As we mentioned in a previous section, there are usually smoking and non-smoking sections, and you will be asked which one you prefer. After you are shown to your seat, the server will bring you a menu and glasses of water. Nowadays in the U.S., it is common for the server to introduce him or herself to you. You are given time to decide on your food order; then the server returns, and you place your order. Many people sit and talk a while after eating before asking for the check and leaving.

NOTE: Although it depends on the restaurant loud noise or any drawing of attention to oneself in a restaurant is generally seen as bad manners. You are expected not to make loud noise or otherwise disturb the other patrons at the restaurant. Some restaurants may ask you to leave if you become too noisy. If you want to have a party that may be noisy, you can request a separate room at some restaurants.

Korean Ways

As stated, Koreans generally practice the same table manners in a restaurant as at home. The server will bring water to the table and take the order for the meal. The menus and prices are normally written on the walls in Korean, especially in specialty restaurants. There are servers in all Korean restaurants except fast-food and cafeteria-style ones. The server is also the person responsible for taking the dishes and cleaning the tables. Koreans may have to wait to be seated.

If it is a more formal or Western-style restaurant, the server may bring menus with the water. (The menus may have English translations, especially in the larger cities.) In this case, the guests can read the menu and make choices while their beverages are being brought to them. The order board and menus in fast food restaurants will be written in English and Korean. In cafeteria-style restaurants in supermarkets and in some other, more Westernized shopping areas where you can see what you are getting, you can just point to what you want. The meal is usually ordered quickly and brought quickly. Koreans then eat quickly and leave quickly. Often, they go to a coffee shop or other location after leaving the restaurant. Coffee is not served at most non-Westernized Korean restaurants, but alcoholic beverages may be.

NOTE: The campaign against smoking in public places has reached Korea, and there are an increasing number of restaurants that now have no-smoking areas. In general, however, smoking is still allowed in all environments, especially after the meal. Korean men (who are the majority of smokers) seldom ask for permission to smoke.

While Koreans normally eat quickly and leave quickly, there are exceptions to this rule. Koreans value conviviality in gatherings and enjoy parties. If there is a party — which will involve drinking — they may stay at the restaurant for many hours and become rowdy with singing and other activities. There are specific restaurants which specialize in accommodating such parties, but it may occur at any location. So, you may find a somewhat noisy atmosphere in restaurants or other public establishments.

How do I interact with the server, order the meal, and pay the bill?

American Ways

In the U.S., the customs and expectations for interacting with the servers and other restaurant staff are both friendly and business-like. As we described in the previous section, the server will bring drinks and a menu. Before taking orders, the server may ask if the order is all on one check ("Will this be all together or separate?") when there are two or more people ordering. The server takes the orders from each individual patron, even if one person is **treating** the others. This allows for individual special requests if there need be and a sense of confidentiality and individuality.

The customers and the servers are expected to treat each other with respect. If you are hosting others, you may establish a special relationship with the server, who will recognize you as the person in charge. In general, you are expected to speak to the server quietly. You get the server's attention by 1) looking in the server's direction and **making eye contact**; 2) gently reaching out, or otherwise catching the server's attention when the server is passing by; or 3) looking in the server's direction and making a movement with your head or slightly raising your hand. You can expect the server to regularly return to the table to check on you and see if you need anything, usually by asking "Is everything all right?"

NOTE: In terms of general restaurant etiquette, patrons should not snap their fingers or shout for the server. Americans also are not expected to complain about prices on the menu to the server. It is generally bad manners to complain too much about the prices in general, but it is acceptable to talk about how reasonably priced a restaurant is.

American restaurants normally have printed menus, except for fast food restaurants or other special restaurants such as salad bars. The price is not negotiable but sometimes there are specially priced items that are not on the menu (**specials of the day**), or the price is lower than that printed on the menu (this is printed on a separate sheet of paper). The server normally informs you of these options. If the server does not, you should ask. Usually different courses and appetizers are all priced separately, and you can order some food **a la carte** (separately from a full meal). Americans tend to discuss all of the meal options, and one person may recommend items to his/her companions if he/she is familiar with the restaurant and its food. If the restaurant is too expensive, the patrons may decide as a group to leave and go to another restaurant.

AMERICAN / KOREAN CONTRAST

Most Americans expect to pay for their meals separately ("Dutch treat"), unless they are special guests or have been invited for a special occasion. If an American wants to treat you to dinner, he/she usually says, "I'd like to treat you to dinner," "I'd like to take you to dinner," or "Let's go to dinner. It's my treat." Otherwise, there is an expectation of paying separately.

In Korea, one person is expected to pay for the group, and there may be some good-natured arguing about who pays. Sometimes, this arguing can become quite strong.

At the end of the meal, you can quietly ask the server for the check, or the server brings the check automatically, often after asking "Will there be anything else?" or "Would you care for any dessert?" Where you pay for the meal depends on the type of restaurant. Sometimes the bill (check) is paid at the door, and sometimes the money is given to the server. In salad bars and some other restaurants, it is paid at the time of ordering. Usually, Americans leave a **gratuity** (also known as a "**tip**") for the server on the table when they leave (if you have paid by credit card, you can mark in an amount for the tip on the credit card). The tip is usually 15-20% of the total bill. U.S. servers pay special attention to customers in order to earn their tips.

> **NOTE:** There is no tipping in fast food restaurants such as McDonald's, but you may be expected to tip in a salad bar if the server brings drinks and otherwise takes care of you. Many restaurants will include the gratuity in the check. Some restaurants will have a sign that tells you that the gratuity is included in the price of your meal. You will need to pay attention at the restaurant, or even ask the server, to discover what the practices are.

Korean Ways

As in the U.S., Koreans customarily expect to interact with the servers and other restaurant staff in both a friendly and business-like manner. But there are some subtle differences. As a reflection of the collective nature of Korean society, Koreans usually establish a kind of **rapport** with the server, and very often one person takes charge for everyone at the table. The rapport that is established often represents the hierarchical nature of Korean society in that the customer is in a superior position to the server. (If the server is also the owner, this distinction may not be as clear.) The customer is demanding, yet personable; the server is solicitous, yet businesslike.

There is no custom of separate checks in Korea, and the expectation is for one person to pay for all, particularly for the evening meal. However, there are occasions when "Dutch treat" is practiced, such as at lunchtime when colleagues generally pay separately or occasionally at dinner (depending on the relationship of the diners). When taking orders, the server assumes that all orders will be on one check and that one person is in charge. Korean servers generally do not often return to the table to check on you, and so you can expect to have to be aggressive to get the server's attention. Therefore, it may be acceptable in a Korean restaurant for you to snap your fingers to get the server's attention or to yell loudly across the room for the server. However, in recent years this interaction with the server has become less aggressive.

AMERICAN / KOREAN CONTRAST

The custom and expectation of tipping strongly influences the difference in service in American and Korean restaurants. In the U.S., the customer is expected to leave a tip for the server. The server works hard to earn this tip — by being friendly, by returning to the table often, by being helpful. If the service is slow, the tip may be small.

Korean restaurants do not have the custom or expectation of tipping, and so their servers are usually not as solicitous as American servers — they are paid the same whether the service is slow or fast. You also should not expect the Korean server to return often to your table to refill glasses or otherwise check on you.

Korean restaurants customarily have the menus printed on the wall, except for more Westernized restaurants. However, in the past ten years, printed menus have become more common. When menus are available, usually only appetizers and main dishes are printed. Seldom is food offered a la carte; usually the whole meal is one price. Except for drinks, the price is usually inclusive. In some cases — especially with large parties — the price may be negotiable. There are seldom specials of the day or other such specially-priced items. Western liquor is generally not served except in more expensive restaurants, although some common Korean strong liquor such as soju may be available as well as Korean brands of beer.

Paying the check can be both simple and complicated in Korea. As in the U.S., payment is normally made at the end of the meal, but Koreans usually do not ask for the check. Instead they stand up and begin to exit the restaurant. The server will then either bring the bill to the cashier or tell the cashier (if they are not the same person) what you ordered. Thus, there may or may not be a bill presented — depending on the type of restaurant it is. Most commonly, you pay the bill to a cashier as you exit. As we mentioned, there are no separate checks, and rarely does everyone pay for his own meal separately. Usually, one individual will discreetly and quietly pay for all the meal, sometimes while you are still eating. Sometimes, however, one person may fight and argue for the privilege of paying for another. The greater the argument, the greater the gift of the meal. Koreans leave a tip only if there has been special treatment by the restaurant, such as bringing in special food or allowing an all-night party.

AMERICAN / KOREAN CONTRAST

Americans do not begin to leave until they have the check. Koreans get up and begin to leave as a sign that the check should be brought or for the server to tell the cashier.

What is hospitality?

American Ways

At Home

As a Korean, you may be surprised by the nature of American hospitality. Americans can be very hospitable, but they have limitations that reflect the American expectations of respect for individuality and respect for individual rights. American hospitality is shown in how food is offered, when food is offered, and expectations of how a guest should respond. Hospitality reflects a person's family upbringing more than a national cultural attitude.

If you visit an American home, you may or not be offered something to eat or drink during the visit. However, the majority of Americans are likely to offer you a glass of water, a cup of coffee, or a soft drink. Americans will give you a choice. Rather than automatically bringing you a refreshment, they will ask you if you would like something to drink. As a Korean, you may refuse the offer out of politeness. But if you refuse, do not expect to be offered a second time: Americans expect you to answer the question with a direct yes or no. American hospitality gives you — the guest — choices. American hospitality also respects your right to say "no." American guests, therefore, expect to be given choices and to have the opportunity to say "no." They do not expect a host or hostess to insist on the guest's eating or drinking because that will make an American guest uncomfortable.

American guests may also ask for something to drink or eat after declining the initial invitation. Similarly, American hosts may say to the guest, "If you want anything, just tell me." Especially in an **informal setting**, they may tell the guests to help themselves: "If you want anything, just help yourself." So, sometimes the guest may be expected to pour his/her own wine or dish out food without asking others. At other times, the guest may need to ask if they may have some more of a particular dish.

NOTE: Customs of hospitality vary according to regions and are — as are most customs — situation dependent. Southerners have a reputation for gracious and generous hospitality. In the South, too, the host may indeed force food on you as the guest and offer the food many times. The Mid-West has a reputation for helping strangers and neighbors, especially if they are in trouble (a car has broken down, there is a flood, etc.).

AMERICAN / KOREAN CONTRAST

Americans and Koreans are both concerned with the comfort of the guest and with being good, generous hosts. In both cases, the type and level of hospitality may vary according to the level of the relationship or the nature of the business. However, there are important distinctions in terms of the host's expectations of the host's and guest's responsibilities. In the U.S., a good host allows the guest personal freedom and offers many choices. The host expects the guest to state if anything is needed. "I can't know if you don't tell me" is a common expression and attitude. On the other hand, in Korea a good host anticipates your needs, which may include making the choices for you. A good host also offers food and other refreshments many times. A good guest in Korea eats or drinks abundantly to show appreciation, or at least tastes the food or sips the drink out of politeness.

You may have to wait before food or drink is offered to you when visiting an American home. Americans commonly offer something to drink immediately after the guest has arrived; however, many people prefer to sit and talk awhile before they offer drinks. When you visit an American home, you may need to wait thirty minutes or more before your meal is served to you. During that time, you usually have something to drink and eat appetizers. It is polite to compliment the host/hostess on the drinks and appetizers, but you are not required to eat them.

NOTE: It is impolite to complain loudly about being hungry or ask when the dinner will be ready when a guest in a home (unless you are a very close friend or family member), even in a joking manner.

A good guest in the U.S. regularly compliments the host/hostess on the meal by making polite comments, such as "This is really delicious." Although it is welcome to see guests eating heartily, a good host takes no offence if the guest declines the food. The guest can say, "No, thank you," and add politely, "But it looks delicious" or "I'm on a diet." For Americans, stating that they are on a diet or have a preference for certain foods is another expression of respect for American individuality.

AMERICAN / KOREAN CONTRAST

Americans expect to talk about their different daily activities during the meal. For business people or other professional colleagues, sharing a meal is an opportunity to discuss business in an informal setting. They have small talk while waiting for the meal and discuss business during the meal. On the other hand, Koreans do not expect to talk a lot during the meal; the meal is not necessarily a time for togetherness or conversation. When business and professional colleagues meet, they wait until after the meal to discuss business.

In a Restaurant

In a restaurant, the issue of hospitality focuses on who is paying for the meal and when it is paid.

As we stated in the previous section, Americans generally pay at the end of the meal. Often, both friends and colleagues ask for separate checks at the time they order. The server will often ask if it is "all on one check or separate" as well. When you ask for separate checks, it indicates that everyone is paying for his or her own meal. This is a common and expected practice. If you wish to treat others to the meal, then you should tell the server that it is on one check. You can also choose to quietly pick up all of the checks at the end of the meal. Americans generally make only a quiet, short protest about payment because any argument about payment is considered embarrassing to the host and guest. You can expect the person being treated to say "You don't have to do that" or to simply say "Thank you." They may also tell you that they will look for an opportunity to **respond in kind** sometime.

NOTE: If Americans wish to avoid obligation, they may not allow you to treat them to a meal.

Korean Ways

At Home

Koreans are famous for their generous and abundant hospitality. Korean hospitality reflects the Korean collectiveness, as well as the concepts of *ch'emyŏn* and *nunch'i*. Korean hospitality is shown in how food is offered, when food is offered, and expectations of how a guest responds to hospitality. You can generally expect Koreans of all social backgrounds to respond with the same spirit of hospitality.

If you visit a Korean home, you are an honored guest, especially as a Westerner.

NOTE: Koreans do not entertain much in the home, but rather entertain in restaurants. If you are invited to a Korean home, it is a very special occasion for them, and you should treat it as one as well.

A good Korean host is expected to anticipate the needs and wants of the guests and so serves special foods or drinks that may be expected both from your and their status, as well as according to the level of relationship you have. Generally, for a short visit, you can expect a soft drink or a cup of coffee to be brought to you or even some whiskey or other strong drink. If you are brought coffee, the host may already have stirred in cream and sugar while preparing it in the kitchen. You can also expect fruit, cookies, or other snacks. Rather than asking you if you would like something to eat or drink, the Korean host will bring it to you automatically as a sign of generosity and hospitality. You do not have to drink or eat what is offered, but it is polite to take at least a sip or a nibble and to praise the generosity of your host.

AMERICAN / KOREAN CONTRAST

When Americans decline food or an invitation, they are usually sincere. When Koreans decline food or an invitation, they are usually being polite and need to be asked a second or third time.

A good Korean host shows hospitality by encouraging you to partake of food. The host may insist several times and even put food onto your plate or in your hand. You are expected to show appreciation for your host's generosity and hospitality by eating with great appetite and by verbally showing your appreciation at the taste and the amount of the food.

Dinner is usually served right away in a Korean home and eaten quickly, and so there is little wait. Depending on the occasion, more food may be brought in after the main meal is taken away. If you have spent several hours visiting, then you may be encouraged to eat again before leaving. It is important for you to remember that your Korean host may spend a great deal of money and effort in preparing a special meal for you. Good Korean guests not only eat abundantly, but they also compliment the host regularly and profusely.

Likewise, Koreans will usually not wait until everyone is ready to eat before beginning to eat. Rather, the host or hostess tells the guest to eat a lot ("*Manhi chapsuseyo*" [많이 잡수세요]) when serving the dish, and the Korean begins to eat right away to show enthusiasm and appreciation. Korean manners, then, reflect a focus on the feelings of the host instead of a focus on arbitrary and objective rules.

Koreans are famous for their great hospitality, and this is partly due to the great concern they show for the comfort of their guests. But Korea is a communal, collective society, and as a result the guest also adjusts his behavior to show consideration for the host or hostess as well. They show this consideration through their enthusiasm for the meal. As we discussed in the section on table manners, good table manners reflect communality as well. For example, rather than dishing out individual portions of the many side dishes at a meal onto individual plates, side dishes are usually eaten from a communal bowl. Also, rather than disturbing someone to pass something at the table, Koreans reach across the table to take food from a dish with their chopsticks. A good host may use *nunch'i* to anticipate a guest's favorite dishes and move them closer to the guest or place the best dishes near the guest at the beginning of the meal.

AMERICAN / KOREAN CONTRAST

In the U.S., guests often offer to help the host or hostess. In informal situations, they may even help with clean up. This custom does not apply to Korea, and so Korean guests may not offer to help in any way when visiting a home.

Although as an American you may be accustomed to declining food because you are on a diet or just do not want to eat, in Korea this is considered rude and individualistic. In general, a polite way to decline food in Korea is by accepting a small portion and then leaving it on the plate. This shows appreciation for the host's feelings and preserves both the host's and guest's face through consideration and mutual understanding of each other's feelings. It shows an anticipation of the feelings of others, as well as a respect for the communality of the meal (instead of demanding a respect for one's individual tastes and desires.) If you must refuse food, you need to do so in a way that appeals to your Korean host's generosity. For example, you can apologize profusely and say that you are sick.

NOTE: Do not be surprised if a Korean guest complains about being hungry or asks when the dinner will be ready. This is usually done in a joking manner and shows the Korean's appreciation of hospitality.

In a Restaurant

In Korea, the person who has invited you to a restaurant will expect to pay for the meal.

NOTE: If several people together have suggested eating at a restaurant, one person is expected to fight for the opportunity to treat the others. In some cases, the one with the most income may be expected to pay.

The host decides the level of the restaurant according to your relationship and the importance of the business. As we stated in the previous section on paying the bill, Koreans generally pay at the end of the meal. Separate checks are uncommon in Korea, even among friends, and may be considered rude. To avoid confrontation about paying, the Korean host may get up in the middle of the meal to use the restroom and pay the bill while away from the table.

In a restaurant, as in a home, anticipating the guests' needs and being aware of their needs is the focus of Korean hospitality. Thus, a host or hostess anticipates that a guest may feel shy or modest about being too eager to accept seconds or may need encouragement to join in the atmosphere of the group. The guest, too, is aware of the host's desire to show hospitality. To that end, Koreans generally will not accept a refusal of food or drink the first time. Instead, a Korean host or hostess will continually offer food until a very firm refusal is given, or until the guest takes some more. Furthermore, the Korean host may order additional dishes for everyone to share together in addition to individual meals that have already been ordered.

Glossary of English Terms

a la carte To order items from the menu individually. For example, you can order a meal and then add a salad a la carte, or you can order a salad or a potato a la carte and not order a full meal.

alcoholic beverage Any drink containing alcohol.

appetizers Small amounts of food served before the meal begins. Cheese and crackers are a common appetizer.

beverages Liquids, such as water, coffee, soft drinks (soda pop), etc.

bland Without many spices or flavorings.

cafeteria-style A type of restaurant in which the diners go through a line and receive food directly from a server. The diners then carry the food themselves to tables.

cocktail parties Parties where alcoholic drinks and appetizers are served. They are usually early in the afternoon before dinner time, e.g. 5-7 p.m. and are for the purpose of socializing.

diner The person eating.

dutch treat Each individual pays for his/her own meal.

ethnic Belonging to a distinct race or nationality, such as Italian, Chinese, or Mexican.

fast food Food that can be ordered, served, and eaten in a very short time. Very often, the food can be ordered from the car and served from the restaurant window in about 5 minutes. This is called "drive-thru."

gratis Free of charge.

gratuity The tip (usually 15-20% of the total bill).

green salad Usually a mixture of different kinds of fresh lettuce, sometimes mixed with other vegetables such as cucumbers, green peppers, or green onions.

hospitality Inviting someone and making him/her feel comfortable and welcome.

informal setting A relaxing atmosphere, such as in one's home and in many family restaurants.

in season When a vegetable or fruit naturally becomes available according to the season of the year, such as tomatoes in August and corn in September.

legal drinking age In the U.S., young people cannot buy alcoholic beverages or drink them in public places. In some states, the legal drinking age is 18; in others it is 21.

liquor Any alcoholic drink that contains more than 40% alcohol, such as whiskey. Beer and wine are not considered liquor.

making eye contact To look at someone's eyes and have them look at yours at the same time.

meatloaf A dish made of ground beef and pork mixed with onions, egg, and spices. It is a common dish in the American Midwest.

moderation Not extreme.

on the run Eaten very quickly. Very often the food is eaten in the car or while walking somewhere.

pancakes A mixture of eggs, flour, and milk that is poured into a pan with a small amount of oil and fried lightly on each side. They are usually served for breakfast and are eaten with butter and syrup. There are a wide variety of pancakes.

pasta There are many varieties of pasta. The most popular are spaghetti and macaroni.

prevalent Common.

rapport A close understanding and feeling of mutuality.

reciprocate To do the same for someone; pay back. For example, if someone buys you lunch, then you reciprocate by buying him/her lunch the next time you meet.

respond in kind To give someone a gift or treatment of the same or similar value that one has received.

revoked Taken away; canceled.

rolls Rolls are made of the same ingredients as bread but are small, individual servings. Dinner rolls are normally not sweet, but breakfast rolls are. Breakfast rolls are often called "sweet rolls."

salad bar A large area where lettuce, raw vegetables and prepared salads, such as potato salad, are located together. The diner then helps himself to as much of these foods as the diner wishes.

scrambled eggs Eggs that are stirred when being cooked.

seconds After you have eaten all of the food on your plate, you take a second helping of some of the dishes.

separate checks To receive individual bills in a restaurant.

server Rather than the gender-specific waiter/waitress, most restaurant employees are called "servers."

smoking section In the U.S., smoking is restricted in most public places. Most eating establishments have separate sections where smoking is permitted. Most other establishments, such as factories and schools, have designated areas for smoking.

soda pop A regional name for carbonated drinks such as Coke.

specials of the day A meal with a special price that has been prepared in large quantities and served only on specific days of the week.

staples The main ingredients/foods of any diet.

supper The evening meal. It is called "dinner" in some areas.

table manners The rules of behavior while eating.

take the order To write down the food items that the patron is requesting.

treating To pay for the meal of another person.

to tip To give someone extra money for services (above what the item costs).

universal Something related to all human beings regardless of their country of origin, gender, or race.

Glossary of Korean Terms

bibimbab [비빔밥] A special one-dish meal in which quantities of side dishes are placed over rice. There is usually an egg on top. The whole dish is usually then mixed together with red pepper paste. It is a common dish for lunch. Koreans often jokingly call it "Korean leftovers."

kalbi [갈비] Marinated beef ribs cooked at the table over charcoal. The ribs are usually cooked in a strip and then cut into smaller pieces by the server.

kimch'i [김치] Any pickled vegetable. The most common variety is a combination of cabbage, radish, onions, garlic, seafood, and red pepper. There are many other combinations as well depending on the season and the region.

kuk [국] A soup with a small amount of vegetables and a meat or fish broth. It is usually served in a soup bowl at a meal where there are other side dishes and rice.

namul [나물] A generic term for vegetables, especially the vegetables that have been steamed and seasoned and are served as side dishes.

panch'an [반찬] Any side dish served at Korean meals.

soju [소주] A strong, unfermented alcoholic drink indigenous to Korea. It is similar to vodka and very cheap to buy.

shikhye [식혜] A "dessert drink" made from sweet rice.

sujŏngkwa [수정과] A "dessert drink" made from boiled dried persimmons and flavored with honey or sugar, cinnamon, and pine nuts.

t'ang [탕] A soup made from boiling pieces of meat for a long time with the meat served in the soup. Popular examples of this are *sŏllŏngt'ang* [설렁탕] (made from tripe), *kalbit'ang* [갈비탕] (made from ribs), *samgyet'ang* [삼계탕] (made with chicken and ginseng), and *maeunt'ang* [매운탕] (made from boiled fish and very spicy). There is also a related version, called *jang* [장]. The most popular type of *jang*, is *yukgyejang* [육계장], which is made up of beef, green onions, and red pepper.

tchigae [찌개] A thick soup with many vegetables, which Americans might call a stew. The most popular *tchigae* is made up of a soybean paste base, with vegetables added (especially squash).

Notes

[1]Statistical Abstract of the United States. *The National Data Book* (Austin, Texas: Hoover's Business Press, 1996).

[2]An example of the enforcement of the legal drinking age is this sign at a bar in a restaurant:

Warning!

IF YOU ARE UNDER THE AGE OF 21
You are subject to a fine of up to $1000 or imprisonment up to 6 months, or both, if you furnish false I.D., order, pay for, share the cost of, attempt to purchase or possess or consume in any public place any alcoholic beverage.

[3]Until the 1980s, laws regarding drunk driving could be lenient. However, as a result of campaigns by family members of people killed by drunk drivers, the laws have become stricter. Currently, In many states, a death caused by drunk driving is tried in court as a homicide (murder). The term for this is *vehicular homicide*, and the severity of punishment varies by state. Penalties for repeatedly being caught drinking and driving can also be severe. The most common penalty is having one's driver's license revoked. Perhaps related to these laws, a critical mood has developed in recent years in the U.S. against drinking alcohol.

CHAPTER 7

MONEY, EMPLOYMENT, AND BUSINESS

MONEY, EMPLOYMENT, AND BUSINESS

Introduction

Everyone likes money. Or at least, everyone needs money. Money is important in every culture. However, attitudes about money — earning it, saving it, loaning it — vary from society to society. As you may have experienced, attitudes about money can interfere with or otherwise play an important role in your relationships with others. This is especially true when dealing across cultures and languages.

Since money must usually be earned, employment plays an almost equal role in society with money. If you are reading this book to know more about working with Americans or Koreans, then their attitudes toward employers, employees, salaries, and general work relationships are important to you.

Finally, since people in both societies spend and make money, business is related to the use of money. You may be reading this because you are currently doing business with Americans or Koreans. You may be reading this to understand the shopkeeper. In these cases, you are likely interested in how best to get others to cooperate with you, and to do that you want to know their attitudes toward doing business. Business is, after all, the process of making money.

So, in this chapter, we address issues related to money — the making of money, using money, and spending money. First, we look at American and Korean **currency** and specific terminology related to money. Then we discuss what each culture thinks about money.

What currency is used in each country?

American Ways

The United States uses **dollars and cents**. Currency comes in both paper, which is called a **bill,** and coin. Americans have special terms for their coins. (These terms refer to the coins themselves, not to the amount.) Here is a list of those terms:

*penny = one cent piece
*nickel = five cent piece
*dime = ten cent piece
*quarter = twenty-five cent piece
*half-dollar = fifty-cent piece
*a silver dollar = a one dollar coin

The amounts of currency are:

*the one dollar bill
*the two dollar bill
*the five dollar bill
*the ten dollar bill
*the twenty dollar bill
*the fifty dollar bill
*the one hundred dollar bill
*the five hundred dollar bill
*the one thousand dollar bill

Fifty-cent pieces, dollar coins, and two-dollar bills are not commonly used. All paper bills are of a uniform size, regardless of the **denomination**, but coins vary in size. The dime is smaller than the penny or nickel because it was originally made of silver. The coins a person has in a **purse** or pocket is called "**change**" or "**small change.**"

Most Americans do not carry large sums of **cash** with them, but instead deposit their money in banks in a checking account. When they pay for something, they often write a check. Checks have the person's account number and name and address printed on them and require the person's signature. For this reason, only that individual can use the check. At the end of every month, the bank sends a **statement** which shows the number of checks written and the amount of each. The check writer then must **balance his/her account** to be sure that they have kept good records of what was drawn from the bank. Americans also regularly use credit cards or buy money orders from the bank or the post office.

NOTE: Americans have quite a few slang words for money. A common slang word for dollars is "bucks." It is often used for emphasis and can have a connotation of surprise or unhappiness at the cost of something. Other slang terms are "smackers" (dollars), "clams" (dollars), and "moolah" or "dough" (money in general). Someone who is making a lot of money is said to be "rolling in the dough." One thousand dollars is called "a grand." One hundred dollars is called a "C-note." Someone who is not making very much money or someone who will not spend a lot of money on something is said to be "nickel and diming it."

Korean Ways

Korea uses the *won* [원]. Currency comes in both coin and paper, which vary in size and color according to the denomination. *tchari* [짜리] is a generic suffix used to denote the price or value of an item, e.g. *ch'ŏn wŏn tchari* (valued at 1000 *won*). *jang* [장] is the suffix used for counting, and denotes a piece of paper. *jŏng* is a term written on Korean checks and is equivalent to the English term "only." Koreans do not have special terms for their coins as Americans do, but instead name the amount plus the suffix *tchari* [짜리]. Here is a list of those combinations:

*sip won tchari [십 원 짜리] = **ten** *won* **piece**
*ohsip won tchari [오십 원 짜리] = **fifty** *won* **piece**
*baek won tchari [백 원 짜리] = **one hundred** *won* **piece**
*ohbaek won tchari [오백 원 짜리] = **five hundred** *won* **piece**

The amounts of currency are:

*ch'ŏn won [천 원] = **1000** *won* **bill**
*ohch'ŏn won [오천 원] = **5000** *won* **bill**
*man won [만 원] = **10,000** *won* **bill**

Coins, especially the coins a person has in a purse or pocket, are called *janton* [잔돈] (literally: 'small money').

Koreans may carry large amounts of cash, especially if they are wealthy. However, when they must pay a large sum, they may use checks (*chagiap sup'yo* [자기앞수표]) issued by a bank. These checks are in specific amounts, the most common of which is 100,000 won, and are in exchange for cash. They do not contain the person's account number or name on them, and so if lost can be used by anyone. While a system of checking as is known in the U.S. has been established in Korea, it is still not popularly used. Rather, they deposit their money in a savings account and draw out money as they need it. They also have money orders through the postal service (*wup'yŏn hwan* [우편환]).

AMERICAN / KOREAN CONTRAST

American paper currency has the same physical size. Korean paper currency has different sizes depending on the amount of the currency. Both American and Korean coins vary in size.

What are general attitudes towards money?

American Ways

The United States has a capitalist economy, and compared to other countries, the majority of its citizens live relatively financially profitable lives. The U.S. was founded on conservative beliefs, and in general that conservatism about money still holds true today. But it holds true more in people's ideals of how people should be or behave than in what they actually do.

For example, Americans admire people who are careful about money. In general, they respect a person who is "good with money" — that is, someone who can save and use money "wisely." That means Americans respect the person who does not waste money, who saves well, and who does not need to borrow money. However, the reality is that many Americans overspend; they just may feel guilty about it.

Although Americans also separate the financial from the personal, they consider money a personal matter. That is, Americans consider their **income** and their use of money a private matter.

Here are some common **maxims** regarding money that reflect the conservative nature of American attitudes:

*a penny saved is a penny earned ("It's hard to save money, but saving even a small amount can make a difference.")
*money is the root of all evil ("Money causes the harm in the world.")
*it's important to live within one's means ("Don't spend more than you earn.")

Americans appreciate **frugality** and investment, but they also appreciate money spent. Two common maxims from the twentieth century that show Americans respect money and wealth are:

*he's small change ("He is not an important person.")
*money talks ("Money is what is important and what will get respect.")

There are many contradictions, however, because Americans will also often disapprove of extravagance.

Korean Ways

Korean society has always been socially and economically stratified, but especially so during the Yi Dynasty (1392-1910). During that time, most of the wealth was in the hands of the royalty. The merchant class was the last in the hierarchy, following scholars (*yangban* [양반]) and farmers. The largest portion of the population, the peasant class, had the smallest portion of income. Many Korean attitudes about money still revolve around this social structure which disappeared during the early part of the twentieth century.

Koreans ideally have a conservative attitude towards money in that they value saving money. They also, however, have an attitude of the necessity of spending money. One distinctive Korean attitude about money is the importance of demonstrating generosity. Although Korean attitudes are changing, Koreans have always appreciated and respected generosity, especially in the form of gift-giving. They have expected it of themselves and of others in a position to afford generosity. For example, in the past a Korean would spend a great portion of his income to show hospitality to a guest, even if that meant eating poorly the rest of the month or borrowing money. Currently, such attitudes are changing, and Koreans may be more economical, even when showing hospitality. Koreans value saving, which is the responsibility of the wife. In addition to money in savings accounts at banks, Koreans have special accounts for housing or other special needs. A traditional approach to saving which focuses on the community is the village *kye* [계]. A *kye* is a neighborhood group which pools money together for various purposes. For investments a *kye* involves bringing together the capital for a trading venture, and has been described as a "hopeful get-rich-quick money club."[1] In another type of *kye*, the members each pay a specific amount to one member of the group. Over a period of time, each person will receive this total amount. Other types of *kyes* are for the purpose of collecting money for community needs, such as fire prevention, burials, and weddings. While the *kye* originated in the villages, it still thrives in the communities and neighborhoods of large cities.

Most Korean proverbs related to wealth and money are stated indirectly and can be applied to other situations as well[2]. Regarding saving Koreans say:

t'ikkŭl moa t'aesan [티끌 모아 태산]: A mountain is made up of small clumps of dirt. (Which is equivalent to "A penny saved is a penny earned" in English.)

Many other Korean proverbs reflect the power and pleasure of wealth. For example:

toni jegallyang [돈이 제갈량]: Money is as powerful as Marshal Cheko Liang.

tonman issŭmyŏn kwishinto purilsu itta [돈만 있으면 귀신도 부릴수 있다]: Even the spirits will work for you for money.

tonae ch'im baetnŭn nom ŏpda [돈에 침 뱉는 놈 없다]: No person spits on money.

toni jangsada [돈이 장사다]: Money is power.

tonman issŭmyŏn kaedo mongch'ŏmjida [돈만 있으면 개도 몽첨지다]:

Even a dog has a higher status if he has money.

toni nalgae [돈이 날개]: Money gives you wings to fly. (With wealth, a person can change status, appearance, etc.)

While these proverbs underscore the power and desirability of wealth, they may also be used to criticize the greedy person or another's wealth. In the right situation, some of these maxims could be used to be the equivalent of the English proverb "money is the root of all evil." However, there is no direct proverb that equals "to live within one's means."

Another proverb emphasizes that even though a Korean may lose face while acquiring wealth, he is dignified by the possession and use of it:

kaekach'i bŏrŏ, jŏngsŭngkach'i ssŭnda [개같이 벌어 정승같이 쓴다]: Work like a dog to earn money, but spend it like a Deputy Minister.

Some other proverbs emphasize the allure of quick and easy wealth, such as

ilhwakch'ŏngŭmŭi kkum [일확천금의 꿈]: To dream of sudden wealth.

Another maxim reflects the collective nature of Korean society:

jumŏni toni ssamjiton [주머니 돈이 쌈지돈]: Money in the (tobacco) pouch is money in the pocket. (This proverb means, for example, that a husband's money is the wife's money, and so it does not matter who pays or where it comes from.)

AMERICAN / KOREAN CONTRAST

Americans value fairness and frugality even with guests because they want to avoid obligation. Koreans value shows of generosity and look on obligation as a way of forging relationships.

What are debts and how are they paid?

American Ways

Debts are money owed, and many Americans have the dream of being "debt free." Debts are different from expenses. Expenses are regular daily costs, such as food or clothing. Debts are also different from bills. A bill is the statement that one receives for expenses, while a debt can include that bill and other, larger amounts that are not paid all at once. A debt also can be for things that a person is not billed for, as in the expression, "I owe you a debt of gratitude."

In general, Americans respect people who pay their debts. But, once again, the ideal is not always the reality. Common, monthly bills for Americans would be rent or mortgage, utilities, credit card statements, and a car payment. When people owe a lot of money, they are said to be "in debt."

A common way to pay bills is by receiving a **statement** in the mail and then returning that statement with the payment, either in the form of a check or a money order. **Automatic deposit** is possible for paychecks, and for some bills automatic payment is also popular. If you are working in the U.S., your employer may ask you if you would like automatic deposit. Some companies will offer that option for payment of bills as well.

> **NOTE:** Rent can be paid on apartments or houses. An apartment that one owns is called a "condominium." When one rents a house or apartment, the renter usually pays one month rent in advance as a deposit and receives a year's contract, called a "lease". If the renter breaks the lease, the deposit will not be returned. Any damage to the apartment that the landlord must pay to have repaired is also deducted from the rent. Otherwise at the end of one year, the deposit will be returned when the renter moves.

When Americans pay money, either by cash or check, they usually do so directly, from one hand to another. Because money and payment is separated from the personal relationship, it is common for money to **pass hands** or for people to discuss payments. The contradiction, however, is that it is considered rude to be confrontational about money, to argue over it, to discuss it, or to ask personal information about earnings. Koreans may say, "You must make a lot of money" or "You must be rich" in response to finding out a person's job. This is said in admiration and is meant as a compliment. However, Americans find these kinds of remarks rude, even when they are made by family members or close friends. Americans just do not normally talk about a person's income except as an abstract topic.

AMERICAN / KOREAN CONTRAST

Americans often pay bills by a check which they write and sign or by money order. Koreans often pay bills by paying at the bank. Korean generally do not actively use a checking service as is known in the U.S.

Korean Ways

In Korea, there has not been an established system of credit as there is in the U.S., and so many transactions are done in cash. This is changing as the economy continues to grow and change, but still cash is often the rule. As a result, house mortgages and car payments are not common. However, to allow more people to own apartments, a system of mortgages has developed in the past 20 years. Koreans, too, have the dream of being "debt free," and respect people who pay their debts.

Common monthly bills for Koreans would be utilities, telephone, and education costs. Bills are paid by receiving a statement in the mail, and then, most commonly, paying it at the bank. Automatic deposit is possible for paychecks, and automatic payments are becoming more common.

NOTE: The Korean rental system varies somewhat from that in the U.S. Most Koreans pay a large sum equal to at least 1 year's rent in advance (often referred to as "key money," *jŏnsekŭm* or *jŏnseton* [전세금, 전세돈]), and then pay only a small monthly rent or no rent at all. The "key money," is then returned in all or part at the end of the contract. The landlord has invested the "key money," so that its interest serves as the rent. In some cases, "key money" can be as much as 20,000 - 100,000 dollars, depending on the location.

Koreans in the business place will bargain and be confrontational about money. That is because there is no personal relationship established. On a personal level, however, and in general, Koreans prefer to pay debts discreetly. Whenever money is given directly to an individual, either as a gift or as a payment, the money is put in an envelope. A Korean will hand it over either with both hands and a degree of formality or simply lay the envelope near the person. The contradiction, however, is that Koreans can talk directly and ask questions about money in ways that Americans may find rude. Koreans find that financial interaction requires delicacy, but that the topic of money is not out of bounds. On the other hand, Americans find that the exchange is impersonal, but that the topic is personal.

NOTE: Both Americans and Koreans may withhold information about their salary or other sources of income in order to prevent others from borrowing money or taking advantage of them. People in both countries may not fully disclose the amount of money they have in order to have an advantage. This is considered reasonable behavior in both countries.

What are the different approaches to loaning and borrowing money?

American Ways

An important aspect of having debts in the U.S. is that Americans prefer not to have debts with friends or family. They may especially hesitate to loan money to a friend. Because Americans separate the financial from the personal, they try to have debts with impersonal companies. There is a maxim:

*Neither a lender nor a borrower be. (Do not loan or borrow money.)

That maxim refers especially to private relationships. Americans prefer not to loan money to friends because they feel it will injure the friendship.

Korean Ways

Koreans, through obligation, can solidify a relationship and bring it closer. The financial is not separated from the personal, and Koreans would rather borrow from someone they know than from some impersonal institution. Yet, two proverbs show that Koreans are aware of the dangers of their common practice:

ton kkuŏ jumyŏn ton ilkko ch'inkudo ilnŭnda [돈 꾸어 주면 돈 잃고 친구도 잃는다]: If you lend money you lose both the money and the friend.

anjasŏ juko suhsuh batnŭnda [앉아서 주고 서서 받는다]: Lend money in a sitting position, but beg to receive money in a standing position.

bitjugo bbyam matnŭnda [빚주고 뺨 맞는다]: Lend money and take a slap on the face.

AMERICAN / KOREAN CONTRAST
Americans are likely to borrow from an institution. Koreans are likely to borrow from an individual.

What is the relationship between employer and employee?

American Ways

Some common expressions that relate to how Americans see employees are:

You get what you pay for.
You get a full day's work for a full day's wages.

*Time is money.
*It is what I am paid to do.

In the U.S., when people move up the hierarchy in their jobs, they are usually paid more. By the general American understanding, people are paid more to carry more responsibility, which means to do more work. They also often consider the amount of pay equal to the amount of effort they should put into a job. However, a professional will work very hard as a professional responsibility, not as a reflection of pay.

Working in the U.S. is considered business. It is in return for a salary, and financial reward is often given as a motivator for hard work. A contradiction, however, is the fact that Americans also have a concept known as the **work ethic**. This work ethic places value on the hard work itself rather than on the compensation for work. It implies pride in a job well done. The work ethic ensures "a full day's work for a full day's wages." On the other hand, employment is not personal. For that reason, Americans refer to a "work relationship" as opposed to a personal relationship. It is why employers may say, "This is business, not personal." What this means, however, is that a personal relationship can continue (based on mutual attraction)[3], after the business relationship is over, or it can be established separately from the business relationship.

> **NOTE:** Americans have laws against **nepotism**. Nepotism is the hiring of individuals based on a personal relationship, especially relatives. This does not mean that nepotism does not occur, but the general attitude is that it SHOULD not occur.
>
> The law and attitude against nepotism are related to equal opportunity. In the U.S., it is against the law to discriminate by gender, age, or race. Hiring a relative can discriminate against others by not considering them.

Korean Ways

Working in Korea is considered business, but the individuals are expected to have a degree of loyalty and ownership to the group or company that they work for. Futhermore, the employees share any pride or any shame that would be attached to their employing company.

There are contradictions, however. Before negotiating and entering into a business deal, Korean businessmen socialize a great deal with potential partners and clients in order to establish a trusting relationship. They also socialize a great deal with colleagues. They may learn a lot about one another and spend a lot of time together. This socializing is considered part of the "work relationship," although no actual "work" as it is understood in the West may be completed. However, this is work related. After two people are no longer colleagues or no longer engaged in business together, the personal aspect of the relationship — the socializing — normally stops as well.

Until the economic crisis of the mid-1990s, employees were expected to have strong loyalty to their employers, and so traditionally it had not been common to switch jobs often. Koreans have always taken a more personal approach to employment than Americans generally do, and the Korean work ethic places value on hard work combined with loyalty and duty (for example, the employees cannot leave for home until their superiors have left the office). Until the mid-1990s the work ethic had also focused on the work more than on the compensation for work, although the Korean work ethic also ensures "a full day's work for a full day's wages." In the mid-1990s, however, many Koreans summarily lost their jobs, and so for the first time "job security" was not ensured with employment and loyalty to the employer. The long-term effects this economic change will have on Korean employers and employee remain to be seen.

AMERICAN / KOREAN CONTRAST

American work ethic has emphasized the intrinsic value of the work, but also doing the work that one is paid for. Korean work ethic has emphasized working hard and being loyal to one's employers.

What is a job and what is a profession?

American Ways

Generally speaking, a job is employment that does not necessarily require previous education or training and that does not necessarily require commitment, e.g. employment as an assembly worker in a factory or as a secretary. A profession is employment that requires previous training or education. The main professions in the U.S. are medicine, education, business, and law. However, there are many other professions.

Regardless of whether one has a job or a profession, Americans expect the worker to take individual pride in his or her work. Each profession has an ideal ethic of behavior according to that specific profession. This is known as "professionalism." To say someone is "professional" is a compliment, and it usually means that the person is trustworthy and very competent.

Professionalism: Americans speak a lot about being professional looking professional, acting professional, performing in a professional manner, yet professionalism is hard to define. Every job or profession has standards of behavior. One standard involves personal attitudes and behavior; another standard involves ethics. These standards both involve depersonalization and emotional control. The definition of professionalism can be subjective; it often depends on how an individual personally defines it. Still we offer as a guideline some general expectations of professional behavior and ethics in the U.S.

Professional attitudes and behavior: Americans may say that a professional

    *meets deadlines.
    *is fair and treats everyone equally.
    *is consistent.
    *is dependable.
    *does not let his/her personal life interfere with business/job/etc.
    *exercises emotional control (does not let personal temper or

feelings interfere with tasks)
*is objective.
*does not dress casually (Although Americans may put more focus on how one behaves than how one looks, dress is still important. That is, for men, a suit and tie is considered professional. For women, a conservative dress or suit is considered professional especially in business.)
*does not use foul language or make sexual comments or innuendoes.
*is trustworthy.
*is responsible.
*honors contracts.
*does not criticize employer in public.
*does not obligate clients or colleagues financially or emotionally.

Some examples of unprofessional behavior would be:

*A professor routinely yelling at students or staff.
*A businessman making sexual jokes with a client or an employee.
*A person being drunk in the office.
*A person not showing up for a meeting without first notifying others present.
*A person taking an argument outside of the realm of the profession, i.e. a professor writing a letter to the newspaper about something he is unhappy about in his department.

Ethics: Ethics refers generally to objective rules and standards of behavior in a profession. These rules and standards of behavior — called "codes of ethics" — are guidelines for all people working within a specific field. In many fields, if professionals break these codes of ethics, then they can be forced out of the profession. This can be done by losing a license to practice a profession (which had been given by a governing body), or by losing a job and being unable to get another because of that conduct. Some common ethical codes or standards for a professional are :

*does not become emotionally involved with clients.

*does not exploit others or his/her position or office for personal gain.
*fulfills contracts/obligations.
*respects confidentiality.
*performs duties regardless of amount of pay.
*respects the guidelines of the profession.
*does not accept money or products in exchange for influence.

Americans talk generally about professional ethics, but also specifically about legal ethics, medical ethics, etc. Americans expect ethics to exist and respect ethical behavior. Nevertheless, ethics are sometimes hard to define.

NOTE: Sexual harassment is against the law in the U.S. But what is sexual harassment? According to the law, there are two types of sexual harassment. One type is requiring sexual favors in exchange for employment, grades, etc. Another type of sexual harassment is making sexual comments or other discriminatory behavior to someone of another gender, especially in an effort to undermine that person's work performance.

When male colleagues — especially superiors — comment on a woman's physical appearance, sex life, or tell sexual jokes when they must socialize professionally, then that can be interpreted as sexual harassment. If a student understands that he or she must have sexual relations with a professor or perform other tasks related to gender (such as cooking or cleaning) in order to pass a class, then that is sexual harassment. Some women even claim sexual harassment when there is no sexual intent, but feel that their work is limited or defined by their gender. For example, a woman executive who is always told to get coffee for the men may claim sexual harassment. A woman worker who is always being asked why she does not stay home and take care of her children may claim sexual harassment. This is not to say that women are the only victims of sexual harassment. Men also may be sexually harassed by female colleagues or employers.

Korean Ways

Korea originally was primarily a land of farmers, merchants and the ruling classes. Since the 1960s, the country has become increasingly industrialized which has created many jobs in factories or in service industries. However, the professions of medicine, education, business, and law are the most respected, and the ideal of most Koreans.

Regardless of whether one has a job or a profession, Koreans expect the worker to consider the pride of the whole company and his part in it. Rather than seeing pride in the company as an abstract concept, pride is more situation dependent and related to *ch'emyŏn*. Thus, professional ethics in Korea are hard to define. While many of the behaviors that are expected of American professionals are expected of Koreans, these behaviors are less abstract, more personalized, and relate more to issues of loyalty and situational needs. That is, they reflect more a subjective ideal of the role than an individual, social based, immediate, and personal sense of pride. That pride may come more with the title than with the high standards of one's own performance in the profession.

Thus, there are subtle differences in ethics and standards from those in the U.S. which reflect the less objective, more personalized, more situation dependent nature of Korean society. Below we summarize some Korean standards of professional behavior. One standard involves personal attitudes and behavior. The other standard involves ethics.

Professionalism: For Koreans, professionalism is two-fold, but both aspects are related to social expectations. One side is related to status or class. It involves a standard of interpersonal relationships and obligations which are associated with the person's status rather than with the abstract, impersonal norms of a profession. Another aspect is related to performing and behaving according to the expectations of others of individuals holding jobs on a professional level. While Koreans do place emphasis on looking professional, professional behavior is also connected to interpersonal relationships that are related to status and personal expectations.

However, as Korea has changed as a result of Western influence since the 1960s, Koreans have continually begun to try to establish a standard of ethics and behavior within the professions.

The Korean concept of *ch'emyŏn* ('face') and how it varies from situation to situation and individual to individual greatly influences the appropriate behavior in professional and work life. We give below as a guideline some general expectations of professional behavior as related to status and to ethics in Korean business, but please keep in mind as you read them the situationally dependent concept of *ch'emyŏn*.

Professional attitudes and behavior: Many Korean attitudes toward professionalism are similar to those of Americans, but are more personalized. A Korean professional ···

*understands when deadlines cannot be met and will try to use gentle persuasion and negotiation over direct confrontation.
*is willing to work extra and long hours to complete a task that he is responsible for.
*is in charge of others, and so requires a certain amount of special consideration.
*dresses in a dark suit and conservative tie (men) or a conservative dress or suit (women); a good haircut is considered important.
*is allowed to exercise the authority of his position.
*can be called on by a superior night and day, and will respond
*is responsible.
*does not criticize the employer in public or question the employer's demands.
*may engage in a complicated system of mutual obligation.

Some examples of professionally unacceptable behavior for a Korean would be:

*for an employee to argue over the stipulations of a contract.
*for an employee to demand a contract in advance of work completed.
*to insist on individual rights and privileges from a superior.

Some examples of professionally acceptable behavior for a Korean would be:

*drinking together after hours and spending social time together during the day with colleagues.
*a superior exercising his authority with students or staff.
*a colleague not showing up for a meeting without first notifying others present.

Ethics: Ethics refers generally to objective rules and standards of behavior in a profession. These rules and standards of behavior — called "codes of ethics" — are guidelines for all people working within a specific field. In Korea, these ethics are more situational and less permanent in terms of their impact on continuing a profession than in the U.S. The codes of ethics involve behavior — often unclearly defined — that instill trust in others. Often, it is only when that trust is broken that the issue of ethics (or the lack of them) come forward. At that time, the ethical standards are defined by the broken trust in the situation. In Korea, when this trust is broken, someone may be forced out of a profession when the ethical conduct affects everyone. That is, when the ethical standard and trust have been broken, it involves a loss of *ch'emyŏn* for all involved.

However, there is the possibility for that trust to be re-established. The offender may be out of the profession for a short time only, and then return to the profession when political tides turn or when he has been repentant enough. The person has regained *ch'emyŏn* in some way, and the loss of *ch'emyŏn* may have been considered the punishment itself. Some common codes of ethics in Korea are that a professional:

*does not engage in extramarital relationships.
*does not use position to personal advantage.
*does not accept money or products in exchange for influence.

However, giving gifts is a common incentive and a means of ensuring attention to a situation. Thus, these behaviors are ideals that the professional must either not engage in or be very discreet about.

In the U.S., it is inappropriate and against the law to delegate responsibilities or inhibit job advancement in the workplace according to gender, to make sexual references, or to inquire about an employee's personal life. However, in Korea the workplace is still separated by gender, and open delegation of responsibilities (such as a woman getting coffee for the men) according to gender exists.

How is business conducted?

American Ways

In the U.S., there are three ways of thinking about business. One is as a customer. The other is as the business owner or businessman dealing with the customer. The third is as a businessman dealing with another businessman. We look at business from these three perspectives.

Customers

American customers believe in fair treatment. They also believe in honest merchants, but contradictorily believe that most businessmen are dishonest. American customers believe the customer is king. Americans also like to get a bargain, but generally do not like to bargain as part of shopping. They also believe that business is separated from the personal. A common maxim is "Don't mix business with pleasure."

Business is separated into small business and big business. Small businesses are usually privately owned businesses and abound in both small towns and large cities. For example, coffee shops, privately owned clothing stores, small manufacturing companies, restaurants, and bookstores, etc. are all small businesses. Large department stores and **chain** restaurants or stores are considered big business. Most industry is big business.

Regardless of whether the business is small or big, there are certain expectations that American customers have of the owners or managers:

Expectations of the customer when shopping:

*They will get what they pay for. (This means that customers expect quality for the amount of money that they pay.)

*They will get their money's worth. (This means they expect that what they have required to receive is equal in value to what they have spent.)

*The seller will "stand behind his product." (This means that the seller will take responsibility for the quality of the product.)

*Sellers will have a return policy. (That is, if you buy a product and it is faulty, then you can usually return it within a specified number of days and exchange the product or get a refund. Also, if you buy something and do not like it, you can return it and get your money back. Often, a product or company will state, "Money back guaranteed.")

*Stores will be competitive in pricing.

*Smaller stores may be more expensive than larger stores.

*A buyer can compare prices at different stores.

*The shopper will be fairly treated.

*The shopper will receive kind, courteous, and speedy service.

NOTE: Most merchandise is guaranteed or has a warranty. A warranty is given by the manufacturer and states that the product will function for a certain period of time (for example, one year). During that time, if the product breaks, the buyer can return the product to the manufacturer for a new one.

Expectaions at restaurants / coffee shops:

*The owners will take pride in their establishment.

*There will be kind, courteous, and efficient service.

*The servers will wait on customers in the order in which they were seated.

*The customers can complain about food being cold and it will be returned and made warm. If there is something foreign in the food, such as a bug, the owner/management will take the food away. The management will then replace the food with good food, or even not accept payment for the meal. The customer expects not to have to complain or argue about this.

The Businessman

The American businessman or business owner has a reputation of doing anything for a profit. Most business owners or businessmen, however, have a set of ethics for dealing with the customer and for dealing with other businesses. They have the following set of expectations of the American customer:

Expectations of the businessman, manager or owner:

*To have to please the customer.
*To have to compete with prices of competitors.
*To have to take precautions against **shoplifting**.
*To separate the business from the personal.
*For customers to want the best prices.
*For customers to be informed or to ask a lot of questions.

There is an expression, "(Someone) is very businesslike." That means that the person is impersonal and efficient and talks only about the matter at hand. The person may be courteous, but will not spend time on anything but the matter to be taken care of. American businesses expect to be friendly and courteous, but not to spend time getting acquainted with a customer. Instead, they generally expect the customer not to waste their time. They expect the customer to be just as conscious of time as the businessman is.

Doing Business with Another Business

The reason for being businesslike is because American businessmen believe both "**Time is money**" and that they should not mix business with pleasure." That is, whenever they are discussing business, they are working, which means they are making money. It also means that American businessmen believe that any use of time is money they can be making. In short, American businessmen believe that the shortest amount of time used to conduct business is the best because it will free the businessmen up to do other business.

Therefore, American businessmen generally discuss business first when together, but still may engage in small talk and otherwise be friendly. While they may have dinner with a colleague, client, or associate, business will still be the topic. Futhermore, American businessmen generally like completion. Their two primary business ethics center around respect for the contract: 1) don't promise what you cannot deliver; and 2) deliver what you have promised (contracted). They believe these two ethics are the foundation of trust. A third expectation, which is not exactly an ethic, is to receive something in return for an investment.

In doing business, negotiations about contracts, finances, and business details are taken care of and agreed upon as soon as possible. The contracts, finances, and business details are the foundation for the rest of the business relationship. The American businessman will no longer expect to have to negotiate once the contract has been agreed upon. As stated, American businessmen like to separate business and pleasure. After business arrangements in the form of a contract are arranged, then the pleasure part of the relationship can begin.

The American businessman will expect the contract to be respected or honored. He will expect deadlines to be adhered to regardless of situations. He will expect communications to revolve around and be in accordance with the contract.

AMERICAN / KOREAN CONTRAST

"Time is money." This is a common attitude in the U.S. Americans also talk about investing time, spending time, and wasting time. Americans think of time as a commodity. Thus, American businesses do not expect to wait. They measure efficiency by how well a company can meet deadlines and interpret punctuality as respect for the other person. On the other hand, they interpret lateness as a lack of respect for the other person. Americans think of time as something they can control and measure, and as something to honor and use. Their objective, depersonalized attitude toward business is related to this objective, depersonalized attitude toward time. If someone does not keep an appointment, rather than infer the other person's intentions Americans may follow up to find the reason and to schedule another appointment. Americans place themselves outside of the time frame and manipulate it. Thus, they talk about meeting schedules, meeting deadlines, etc. which they have created in order to ensure efficiency. They expect themselves and others to give up personal needs in order to meet the demands of these deadlines and schedules.

Koreans, on the other hand, may speak of there being time or not being time (*sigani it'da* / *sigani ŏp'da* [시간이 있다 / 시간이 없다]), but do not talk about saving or investing time. The Korean language does not have idioms or expressions for saving time, wasting time, or spending time. While Koreans respect punctuality, and often see punctuality as a sign of respect for the individual, they also have a respect for the vagaries of transportation in large and small cities. They also understand personal situations which inhibit the meeting of deadlines.

Koreans have a personal, subjective approach to business and business relationships. If something personal occurs that prevents the company or individual from meeting a contract or a schedule, then the Korean will expect the associate to appreciate the business's reasons for not meeting deadlines. Koreans may ask, "Please understand my situation," while the American attitude would be, "Regardless of my situation I have made a commitment that I must honor." The American sees his personal needs as outside of the business world. The Korean will see himself intertwined with it. Futhermore, Koreans may interpret someone's not keeping an appointment as a subtle way to indicate a lack of interest. Thus, Korean businessmen are not likely to follow up or pursue a client if an appointment has not been met. Conversely Korean businessmen would prefer to agree to a meeting and not show up than to have a confrontation or directly say "no."

Korean Ways

There are three ways of thinking about business. One is as a customer. The other is as the business owner or businessman dealing with the customer. The third is as a businessman dealing with another businessman. We look at business from those three perspectives.

Customers

Korean customers believe in fair treatment, but in their actions show that the person who makes himself / herself known the loudest and most persistently will get the attention. They believe in establishing a relationship with the merchants — even a temporary one — in order to facilitate the business at hand, especially if it requires negotiating prices.

Korean customers believe the customer is king. They also like to get a bargain and regularly bargain and negotiate as part of shopping. They respect the shopkeeper as the owner of the shop and are usually respectful of the clerks and assistants.

In Korea, business is separated between small business and big business. The majority of businesses are small, family-owned ones, and the Korean economy is very entrepreneural. There are many coffee shops, privately-owned clothing stores, restaurants, and bookstores, as well as the many small businesses conducted in the market place still common both in large cities and small towns. Big business also exists in the form of chain department stores and restaurants and large manufacturing companies and industry.

NOTE: Koreans have several conglomerates called *chaebŏl* [재 벌] that control many large corporations. Some of these conglomerates include Samsung, Hyundai, and LG.

Regardless of whether the business is small or big, there are certain expectations that Korean customers have of store owners or managers:

Expectations of the customer when shopping:

*to be able to bargain. (But not in large prestigious department stores).

*to not be able to return a product. There is rarely a "Money back guaranteed" policy in Korea. That is, once a product is bought, it cannot be returned.

*a higher price to represent higher quality.

*stores and vendors will be competitive in pricing.

*larger stores may be more expensive than smaller stores.

*to use comparison shopping as a bargaining technique.

*to be treated courteously.

*to be defensive, but aggressive shoppers.

*to get what they pay for. This means that they expect quality for the amount that they pay.

*the seller not to "stand behind his product." Therefore, the Korean customer may check the product out well before leaving a store.

NOTE: Most merchandise is guaranteed or has a warranty.

Expectations at restaurants/coffee shops:

*that the owner will take pride in the establishment.

*quick and efficient service, but not always kind or courteous service.

*to be able to complain about the food and make requests for service. However, there may need to be aggression, argument, or negotiation if the food is too cold or if there is some other problem with it. There may not be an automatic and understood agreement that if there is something foreign in the food such as a bug, the owner/management will take the food away and either replace the food with good food, or not even accept payment for the meal. The Korean customer may need to complain loudly or argue about this, especially if it involves a loss of *ch'emyŏn* for the owner.

*special treatment if the situation and position of the individuals warrant it.

The Businessman

Korean business owners — like business owners the world over — want to make a profit and have a reputation for being shrewd. They, too, have a set of expectations for dealing with the customer and with other businesses.

Expectations of the businessman, manager, and owner:

*to have to please the customer.
*to have to compete with prices of competitors.
*to have to bargain or negotiate with customers.
*to receive a certain respect from the customer.
*to not expect a lot of questions about a product.
*for the customers to want the best prices.

AMERICAN / KOREAN CONTRAST

Americans can bargain when purchasing real estate or when buying a car. They also bargain when buying used items. Otherwise bargaining is not a general practice when shopping. Koreans, on the other hand, may bargain when buying new merchandise in all aspects of shopping.

Korean business owners and businessmen will be courteous and aggressive when doing business with an associate or with customers. They will spend time on making small talk and discussing things other than business. That is, Korean businessmen expect to be friendly and courteous, but also to spend time getting acquainted with an associate or a customer. They may focus more on the value of the interaction at hand than on the use of each other's time.

Furthermore, there are two sides to Korean businessmen, managers, owners, or service personnel. On one hand, they may not be solicitous, but instead may wait for the customer to get the owner or clerk's attention. On the other hand, they may be aggressively helpful and contentious about prices and quality. That is, Korean businessmen, managers, owners, or service personnel may chat and ask personal questions along with trying to sell the product. They may engage in what is called a "hard sell." On the other hand, depending on the situation, some may seem relaxed and not attentive to the matter of selling.

Doing Business with Another Business

"Businesslike" for the Korean businessman is to take time to get acquainted. It means to take time to develop personal trust. Korean businessmen put more value on this personal trust — and how it can be worked to their advantage — than on contracts. That is the opposite of the American attitude toward business, and especially toward business relationships.

Korean businessmen may spend a long time talking, entertaining, and getting to know each other. Only after this relationship is established might they commit to doing business with each other. Even then, the details of a contract may not be formally decided until after a commitment has been made between the two associates or companies. That is, in doing business, negotiations about contracts, finances, and business details are taken care of and agreed upon at a later date. They may not even be agreed upon until after the partnership has begun. Furthermore, Koreans may assume that they can still negotiate long after the contract has been agreed upon.

From an American perspective, Korean businessmen generally

avoid completion. Koreans focus on maintaining a good relationship in the moment, and so they may agree to something to please someone at the moment. This conflicts with one of the American business ethics of respect for the contract: 'Don't promise what you can't deliver.' That is, Koreans might promise just to maintain harmony in the immediate situation, but not necessarily be able to deliver on that promise. To avoid confrontation, the Korean may explain this inability at the time the delivery is expected and ask for understanding. In such a situation, the Korean businessman may also stop communication altogether. This lack of response or ability to deliver conflicts, then, with the second American business ethic: 'Deliver what you have promised (contracted).' Korean businessmen expect the contract to be secondary to changes that may have occurred since the contract has been signed. They will expect understanding of this change in circumstances if it affects the timeliness of delivery of the contract. They will not expect communications to revolve around and be in accordance with the contract.

A final important aspect of doing business in Korea is the fact that Koreans may not expect equal return for investment. That is, in order to establish a relationship, they may expect much more than they may give or vice versa. This is because Koreans need to establish a trustful relationship first, and this is done by giving gifts or favors based on the situation dependent expectations of the other's ability or obligations. Korean businessmen, thus, do not separate business and pleasure. Only after trust is built through personal interaction is a contract negotiated.

Finally, Korean businessmen may give a gift before the service or at the beginning of the relationship as a show of good intent. The gratitude is for the relationship to come.

AMERICAN / KOREAN CONTRAST

Americans value written contracts. Koreans value personal trust. Americans value fairness and equal treatment which is ensured through rules and regulations. Koreans value personal consideration, which may extend beyond rules and regulations, based on the trust established in a personal relationship.

automatic deposit The employer deposits the money into the bank for the employee.

balance an account An idiom which means to reconcile the check someone has written with the statement sent from the bank. It can also mean to pay all of one's bill, e.g. credit at a restaurant, etc.

bill Paper money, e.g. a one dollar bill; the statement of what one owes.

cash Bills and coins.

chain A restaurant or store which exists in many different cities and states. For example, McDonald's is a chain of fastfood restaurants.

change/small change Coins. Change can also mean the money one receives back after paying for an item. For example, the total is $17.50 and you pay with a $20.00 bill, then your change will be $2.50.

clients A term used for the people that certain professions such as lawyers, social workers, and businessmen serve.

currency A general term for money. The dollar is the currency used in the U.S. The won is the currency used in Korea. This term can also be used to refer to paper money (bills).

denomination The amount of money a coin or bill is worth.

dollars and cents One hundred cents equals one dollar; $1.57 can be read as "one dollar and fifty-seven cents."

equal opportunity A concept (and law) which guarantees employment based on ability. It is supposed to ensure that a person's ability has been the basis of that person being hired, as opposed to the color of that person's skin, gender, or age.

frugality Careful attention to spending money.

guarantee The manufacturer assures the quality of a product.

income The amount of money a person earns.

maxim A short philosophical saying.

meet deadlines A deadline is the latest date by which something is supposed to be finished or delivered. You meet a deadline by finishing by that date.

nepotism Hiring relatives or friends on the basis of the relationship rather than on their qualifications for the job.

pass hands If you give someone money, and that person takes it, then money has "passed hands."

purse A pocketbook carried by women; it can also refer to a small leather or plastic container for coins.

punctuality Arriving before or at a designated time.

shoplifting Taking items from a shop without paying for them. If people are caught shoplifting, they may be arrested.

statement A list of bank transactions issued every month by the bank; a bill from a company listing the amount owed.

time is money An idiom that means that you should not waste time because you could be making money.

warranty The manufacturer assures that if a product breaks, it will be replaced or repaired at the manufacturer's expense.

work ethic An attitude toward the importance of work. Every culture and society has its own work ethic.

Glossary of Korean Terms

chaebŏl [재벌] A large conglomerate.

tchari [짜리] A suffix attached to an amount to indicate the value of an item. For example, you might purchase a 10,000 won *tchari* sweater.

jang [장] The suffix used for counting. It denotes a piece of paper money.

janton [잔돈] Small change.

jŏnsekŭm, jŏnseton [전세금, 전세돈] The deposit on an apartment. It can often be as much as one year's rent or more in advance.

kye [계] A neighborhood group which pools money together for various purposes.

sigani it'da/ŏp'da [시간이 있다/없다] This means literally 'there is time/there is no time.'

sugohaseyo [수고하세요] A common, familiar expression used when parting from someone of equal or lower status. It is often said by shopkeepers when the customer is departing. The customer says it to the shopkeeper as well.

up'yŏnhwan [우편환] Money order.

won [원] Korean currency. This term is used for both bills and coins.

yangban [양반] The elite scholarly class of Korea, especially during the Yi Dynasty.

Notes

[1] See *Korean Works and Days* by Richard Rutt (Seoul: Royal Asiatic Society, 1964), pp. 85-88, for an entertaining discussion of *kye*.

[2] Most of these were adapted from *Maxims and Proverbs of Old Korea* by Tae-Hung Ha (Seoul: Yonsei University Press, 1970), which is a rich compilation of sayings, and from *Wisdom of the Far East: A Dictionary of Proverbs, Maxims, and Famous Classical Phrases of the Chinese, Japanese, and Korean* by Young H. Yoo (Washington DC: Far Eastern Research and Publications Center, 1972). Paul Crane also includes a list of proverbs that reflect similarity with American attitudes on family, money, spirituality and self in *Korean Patterns*, 4th Edition (Seoul: Kwangjin Publishing Co., 1978), pp.151-153.

[3] In the Notes section of Chapter 2 we discussed Saccone's (1994, p.27) contrast of American and Korean attitudes toward friendship and how they relate to business.

The Authors

Susan Oak holds an M.A. from New York University and an Ed.M. from Harvard University. She is currently working on her Ph.D. degree in Second Language Acquisition. She began her long association with Korea in 1987. She is currently teaching English at Ewha Woman's University in Seoul.

Virginia Martin holds a Ph.D. in Applied Linguistics from Indiana University. She began her long association with Korea in 1979. She is currently an Assistant Professor in the English Department at Bowling Green State University in Bowling Green, Ohio where she coordinates the English as a Second Language Program and teaches in the MA TESL Program.

References

Abernathy, M. G., *Civil liberties under the constitution* (Dodd, NY: Mead, 1968).

Alcohol. [On-line], http://www.bgsu.edu/welcome/standards2.html#ss.

The Analects of Confucius (Beijing, China: Sinolingua Publishers, 1994).

The Asia Society, "Asia in American textbooks," In Luce, L. F., & Smith, E. C. (Eds.), *Toward internationalism* (2nd ed.), (Cambridge, MA: Newbury House Publishers, 1987).

Barnlund, D. C., "Verbal self-disclosure: Topics, targets, depth," In Luce, L. F., & Smith, E. C. (Eds.), *Toward internationalism* (2nd ed.), (Cambridge, MA: Newbury House Publishers, 1987).

Bowling Green State University, *1998/1999 Student affairs handbook* (Bowling Green, Ohio: Division of Student Affairs, 1998).

Catholic Biblical Association of America, *The New American Bible* (Nashville, TN: Thomas Nelson Publishers, 1983).

Choi, Sang-Chin and Choi, Soo-Hyang, *We-ness: A Korean Discourse of Collectivism*, Unpublished.

Choi, S. C. & Choi, S. H., *The conceptualization of Korean tact, noon-chi*. Paper presented at the tenth International Association of Cross-Cultural Psychology Congress (Nara, Japan, 1990).

Choi, S. C. & Choi, S. H., *Noon-chi: An indigenous form of Koreans' politeness communication*. Paper presented at Department of Psychology (Hawaii: University of Hawaii, 1991).

Choi, S. H., *The nature of Koreans social face,* Dissertation at the Center for Korean Studies (Hawaii: University of Hawaii, 1991).

Ch'u, C. & Winberg, C. (Eds.), *The sacred books of Confucius and other Confucian classics* (New Hyde Park, NY: Bantam Books, 1965).

Chu, C. N., *The Asian mind game: Unlocking the hidden agenda of the Asian business culture: A westerner's survival manual* (New York: Rawson Associates, 1991).

Claire, E., *Dangerous English* (Rachelle Park, NJ: Eardley Publications, 1983).

Cohen, H. & Coffin, T. P. (Eds.), *The folklore of American holidays* (Detroit, MI: Gale Research Company, 1987).

Crane, P. S., *Korean Patterns* (Seoul, Korea: Kwangjin Publishing Company, 1978).

Current, M. E., *Looking at each other* (Seoul: International Publishing House, 1983).

Daniels, M. J., *Through a rain splattered window* (Seoul: Taewon Publishing Company, 1973).

————, *In the shadow of the mountains* (Seoul: Samsung Moonwha Printing Company, 1977).

The declaration of independence and the constitution of the United States (New York: Penguin Books, 1995).

De Mente, B. L., *Korean etiquette and ethics in business* (2nd ed.) (Lincolnwood, Illinois: NTC Publishing Group, 1994).

Doty, G. & Ross, J. *Language and life in the U.S.A.* (New York: Harper & Row Publishers, 1981).

Encyclopedia Americana Vol. 16., (Grolier Incorporated, 1994).

Feinberg, W., *Japan and the pursuit of a new American identity* (London: Routledge, 1993).

Ha, T. H., *Maxims and Proverbs of Old Korea* (Seoul, Korea: Yonsei University Press, 1970).

Hall, E.T., *The silent language* (New York: Doubleday Anchor Books, 1973).

Hawkinson, A., & Clark, R. C., *Living in the United States* (3rd ed.) (Brattleboro, VT: Pro Lingua Associates, 1995).

Hearing of the committee on labor and human resources United States senate: One hundred fourth Congress second session on S. 1085 (Washington D. C. : U. S. Government Printing Office, 1996).

Howe, R. W., *The Koreans: Passion and grace* (NY: Harcourt Brace Jovanovich, 1988).

Hur, S. J. V. & Hur, B. S., *Culture shock! Korea* (Singapore: Times Books International, 1988).

Jang, S. H., *The key to successful business in Korea* (Seoul: Yong Ahn Publishing Co., 1988).

Jason, K. & Posner, H., *Explorations in American culture* (Boston: Heinle and Heinle, 1995).

Jeon, K. T. (Ed.), *Korean insights: Light of the East* (Seoul: Sejong Corporation, 1974).

Kalton, M. C., *Korean ideas and views* (Elkins Park, PA: The Philip Jaisohn Memorial Foundation, Inc., 1979).

Kearny, E.N., Kearny, M.A., & Crandall, J., *The American way: An introduction to American culture* (New Jersey: Prentice Hall, Inc., 1984).

Kenna, P., & Lacy, S., *Business Korea: A practical guide to understanding South Korean business culture* (Lincolnwood, IL: Passport Books/NTC Publishing Group, 1995).

Kilmer, J., *Binge drinking,* B. Cooley (series ed.), *Santa Cruz,* (CA: ETR Associates).

Kim, E. H., & Yu, E. Y. (Eds.), *East to America: Korean American life stories* (New York: The New Press, 1996).

Kim, H., *The long season of rain* (New York: Henry Holt and Company, 1996).

Kim, U., Triandis, H. C., Kagitcibasi, C., Choi, S., & Yoon, G. (Eds.), *Individualism and collectivism: Theory, method, and applications* (Thousand Oaks, CA: Sage Publications, Inc., 1994).

Klebanow, B., & Fischer, S., *American holidays: Exploring traditions, customs, and backgrounds* (Brattleboro, Vermont: Pro Lingua Associates, 1986).

Leiter, R. (Ed.), "Drunk driving," In *National survey of state laws* (2nd ed.), (Detroit: Gale Research, 1997).

"Liquor," In *The Ohio revised code* (Banks Baldwin Law Publishing, 1995).

MADD Statistics: DUI/DWI arrests and convictions [On-line], http://www.

madd.org/stats/stat_dui.shtml (1998).

MADD Statistics: General statistics [On-line], http://www.madd.org/stats/stats_gen.shtml (1998).

Marriages and blood tests [On-line], http://www.nolo.com/ChunkSP/sp15_table.html (1998).

Martin Luther King Day [On-line], http://www.usia.gov/education/engteaching/intl/pubs/mlkbday. htm (1998).

Min, B. C., *Ugly Koreans, ugly Americans* (Seoul, Korea: BCM Publishers, Inc., 1995).

Park, M. S., *Communication styles in two different cultures:* Korean and American (Seoul: Han Shin Publishing Company, 1979).

Pares, S., *Cross currents* (Seoul: International Publishing House, 1985).

Procedures and ceremonies [On-line], http://www.nolo.com/ChunksSP/SP15.HTML (1998).

Reporters guide to the distilled spirits industry [On-line], http://www.fi.muni.c2/tems/psychedelia/alcohol.html.

Robinson, James and Karen Becker, "Playing things by eye with Korean students," Paper presented at the 46th NAFSA Annual Conference, Miami Beach, FLA, May 1994.

Robinson, James and Patrick J. Dunham, "Confucian orthodoxy meets ESL: Teaching across academic cultures," *MinneTESOL Journal*, Vol 11, 1997.

Robinson, J., "The Importance of a good *kibun* in the ESL classroom," *Minne TESOL Journal*, Vol. 10, 1992.

Robinson, J., "Teacher expectations of students in Korean classrooms," *Korea Journal*, winter 1993.

Robinson. J., "Turn-taking across cultures," Paper presented at the 32 Annual TESOL Convention, Seattle, Washington, March 1998.

Robinson, J., "Cultural translations of TESL/TEFL teachers: Korean example," Paper presented at the International Conference on Language Teacher Education: Voices from the Field, Minneapolis, MN, May 21, 1999.

Robinson, J., "Ch'emyŏn in the EFL classroom," Unpublished paper.

Rutt, R., *Korean works and days: Notes from the diary of a country priest* (Seoul: Korea Branch of the Royal Asiatic Society, 1964).

Saccone, R., *The business of Korean culture* (Seoul: Hollym Corporation; Publishers, 1994).

Sexual harassment: Fact v. myth [On-line], http://www.vix.com/pub/men/harass/myth.html (1994).

Statistical Abstract of the United States. *The National Data Book* (Austin, Texas: Hoover's Business Press, 1996).

Steenson, G.P., *Coping with Korea* (New York: Basil Blackwell, Inc., 1987).

Stewart, E. C., & Milton, B., *American culture patterns* (Rev. ed.), (Yarmouth, Maine: Intercultural Press, 1991).

Svendsen, R., & Griffin, T., *Alcohol use by college students: A guide for parents* (Anoka, Minnesota: Health Promotion Resources, 1994).

Szalay, L. B., & Fisher, G. H., "Communication overseas", In Luce, L. F., & Smith, E. C. (Eds.), *Toward Internationalism* (2nd ed.) (Cambridge, MA: Newbury House Publishers, 1987).

United States Equal Opportunity Commission, *Employer EEO responsibilities: Preventing discrimination in the workplace, the law and EEOC procedures*, Technical Assistance Program, 1996.

United States Equal Opportunity Commission, *Sex discrimination issues: Sexual harassment, pregnancy discrimination, parental leave, fetal protection policies and wage discrimination*, Technical Assistant Program, (1996).

Weigelt, K. F., *Culture bridge* (Seoul: Si-sa-Yong-o-sa Publishers, 1993).

Yang, S. M., *Korean customs and etiquette* (Seoul: Moon Yang Gak, 1990).

Yoo, Y. H., *Wisdom of the Far East: A Dictionary of Proverbs, Maxims, and Famous Classical Phrases of the Chinese, Japanese, and Korean* (Washington D.C.: Far Eastern Research and Publication Center, 1972).